In a piece Immanuel Kant wrote in 1784 for a journal of the time, he responded to the question "What is Enlightenment?" (*Was ist Aufklärung*?), establishing that this should be the state in which men would emerge from immaturity: a coming-of-age defined by the courage to use one's own understanding. But be careful, the freedom inherent to that power was conditioned. This emancipation was a path to a freedom of thought that would lead you also to manage a "candid criticism" and obedience: "But only the man who is himself enlightened, who is not afraid of shadows, and who commands at the same time a well disciplined and numerous army as guarantor of public peace—only he can say what [the sovereign of] a free state cannot dare to say: 'Argue as much as you like, and about what you like, but obey!'." He concluded establishing that a reduced level of civic freedom would equal an expansion of a free spirit to the limits of its capacity. In a way, he was proposing a system that would secure the modern social contract, finding justifications in a capitalized Nature. Kant would also point out that not all men were yet capable of managing this so-called vocation of free thought and self-governance that would result in a state treating him as more than a machine... Of course, according to his time he always referred only to men, not women, not people in general.

Now, embracing our playful*ness*, we want to declare that we, as a diverse collective, have arrived to a very complex middle-aged crisis!

And what comes with that? Another kind of freedom of thought and a lot of very thrilling possible transformations. Questions, questions, and more questions. And a mantra repeatedly sounding at the back of our heads asking us: what for?

This issue's research started by posing and redirecting some of those questions, to understand more of the way they affect our built environments and then, our everyday life.

Should we develop new types and abilities? What are the bases to rebuild our cultures?

Can our bodies change to adapt to new technologies? Our memories, fingers, and eyes are already becoming dystrophic. Can we really imagine life in another planet? Should we declare the great failure of all the systems we knew and start rethinking entirely everything again? Generating fictions should not be the only way to tolerate this change of state.

Here, we bring you some different attempts to present and represent this mad and uneasy to synthesize world. We invited designers, philosophers, theorists, and architects to share their production, to reflect and defy comfortable manifestos.

Our idealistic and grunge egos firmly believe that in difference resides richness, and that thinking together still has an invaluable transforming power.

Pablo Gerson & Florencia Rodriguez

Please, don't hesitate to share your thoughts with us by writing to hello@nessmagazine.com

HIGH LINE

WE SAVED THE SPUR

OPENS JUNE 5

INTRODUCING: THE SPUR

On the High Line at 30th Street & 10th Avenue in New York City

In 2008, we initiated an advocacy campaign ("Save the Spur") to save this last section of the original rail structure. Now, the reimagined Spur is open to the public.

Designed by James Corner Field Operations (Project Lead), Diller Scofidio + Renfro, and Planting Designer Piet Oudolf.

To read all about the Spur, visit **thehighline.org**

Simone Leigh, *Brick House*, 2019. A High Line Plinth commission.
On view June 2019 – September 2020. Photo by Timothy Schenck

Lots of Architecture
– publishers

We edit magazines
We edit books
We edit films
We edit websites
We edit brochures
We edit posters
We edit fanzines
We edit boogazines
We edit podcasts

CONTACT US TO TALK ABOUT YOUR PROJECT
HELLO@LOTSOFARCHITECTURE.COM

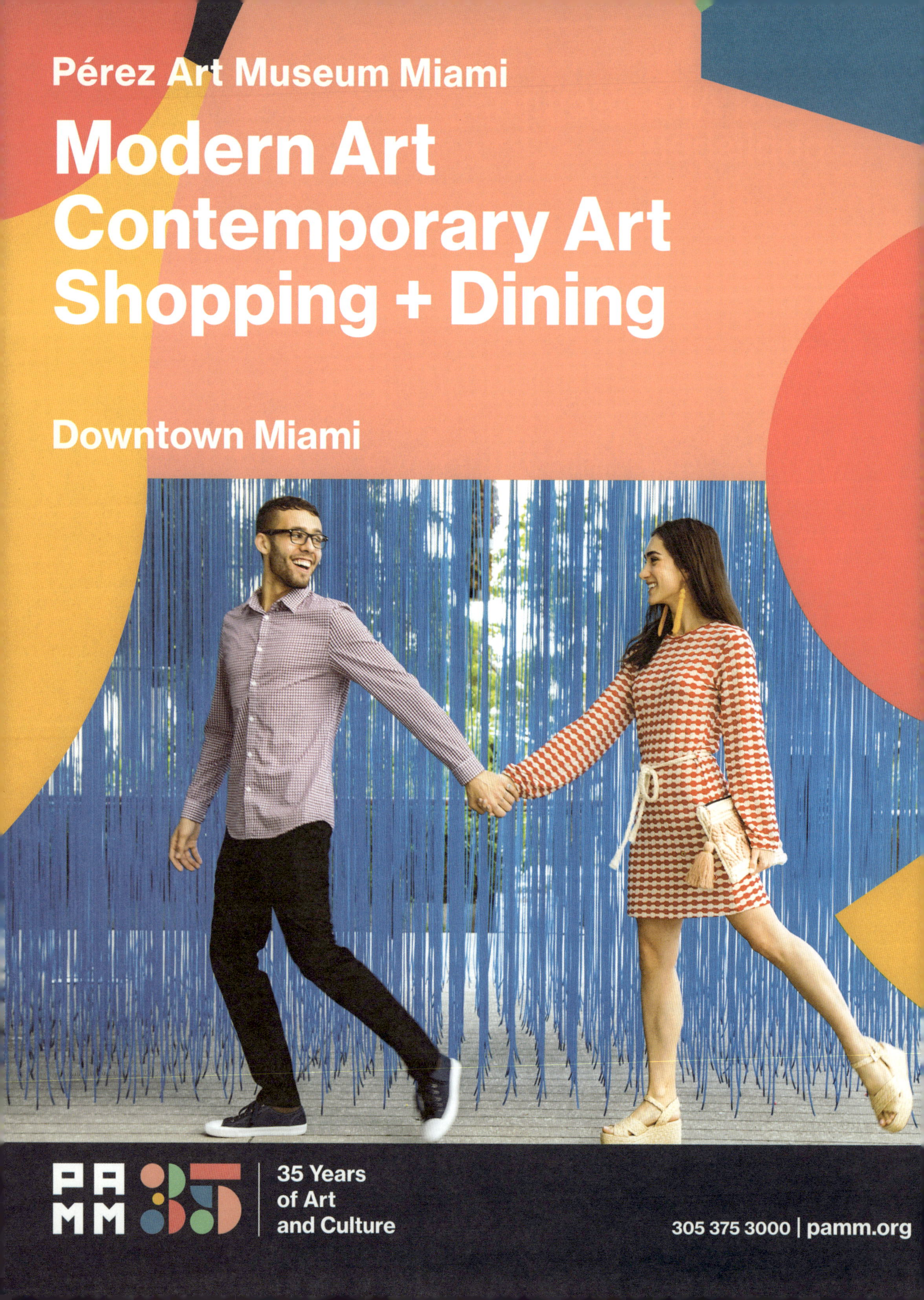

Pérez Art Museum Miami

Modern Art
Contemporary Art
Shopping + Dining

Downtown Miami

**35 Years
of Art
and Culture**

305 375 3000 | pamm.org

Our first issue of the monographic series –NESS.docs is dedicated to the work and thoughts of Hashim Sarkis, Dean of MIT School of Architecture and Planning, and Curator of the 2020 Architecture Exhibition La Biennale di Venezia.

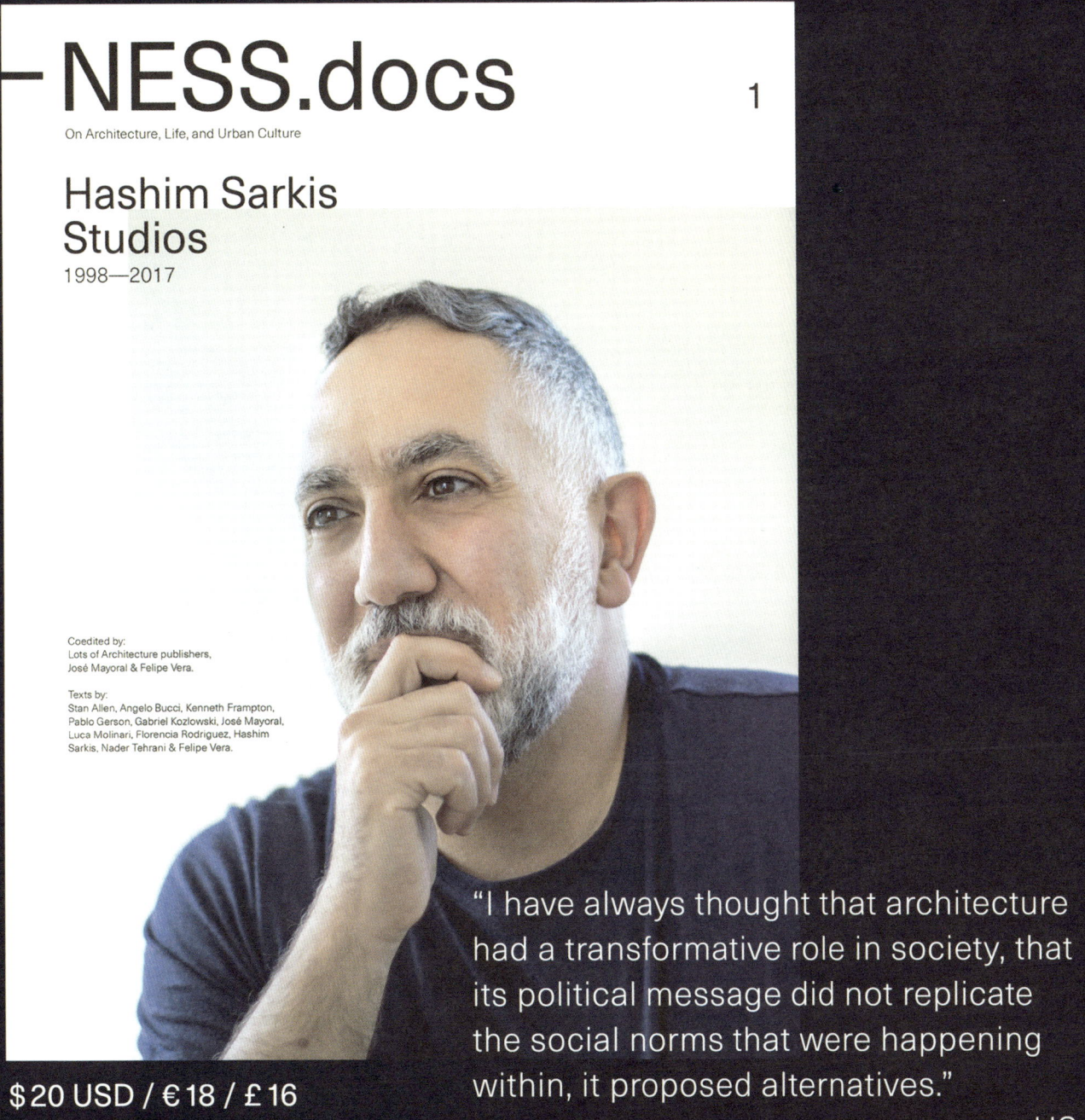

– NESS.docs

1

On Architecture, Life, and Urban Culture

Hashim Sarkis Studios

1998—2017

Coedited by:
Lots of Architecture publishers,
José Mayoral & Felipe Vera.

Texts by:
Stan Allen, Angelo Bucci, Kenneth Frampton,
Pablo Gerson, Gabriel Kozlowski, José Mayoral,
Luca Molinari, Florencia Rodriguez, Hashim
Sarkis, Nader Tehrani & Felipe Vera.

"I have always thought that architecture had a transformative role in society, that its political message did not replicate the social norms that were happening within, it proposed alternatives."

—HS

$ 20 USD / € 18 / £ 16

ORDER AT NESSMAGAZINE.COM OR
HELLO@LOTSOFARCHITECTURE.COM

Lots of Architecture
– publishers

Credits

CHAIR & EDITOR IN CHIEF

Florencia Rodriguez
flor@nessmagazine.com

CHAIR & CHIEF EXECUTIVE OFFICER

Pablo Gerson
pablo@nessmagazine.com

EXECUTIVE EDITOR

Isabella Moretti
imoretti@nessmagazine.com

EDITORS

Renee Carmichael
rcarmichael@nessmagazine.com

Daniela Freiberg
dfreiberg@nessmagazine.com

GRAPHIC DESIGNER & PHOTO EDITOR

Mariam Samur
msamur@nessmagazine.com

AUDIOVISUAL CREATOR

Natalia La Porta

PROOFREADER

Lisa Ubelaker Andrade

DRAWING EDITOR

Florencia Medina

CONTRIBUTORS

Sophia Al-Maria, Adriana Amante, Alexandra Arènes, Sol Camacho, Fake Industries (Urtzi Grau and Cristina Goberna Pesudo), Uriel Fogué, Laura González Fierro, Maria Jerez, Ben Fehrer, Bruno Latour, Jesse LeCavalier, Gabriel Kozlowski, F-arch (Virginia Black, Rosana Elkhatib, and Gabrielle Printz), Marcelo Maia Rosa, Parasite Lab (Stefano Colombo, Eugenio Cosentino, and Luca Marullo), Agustin Schang.

PHOTOGRAPHERS

Iwan Baan, Casey Carter, Ramiro Chavés, Ron Eshel, Peter Fabo, Marc Goodwin, Roland Halbe, Lucía Herrero, Imagen Subliminal (Miguel de Guzmán and Rocío Romero), Natalia La Porta, Matías Lix Klett, Gorka Postigo, Luciano Romano, Mariam Samur, Timothy Schenck, Jacqueline Young.

AKNOWLEDGEMENTS

Adriana Amante, Iwan Baan, Gonzalo Casals, Alecs Crespo, Ferdinand Porak, Argentinian National Weather Service (SMN)

To Felix and Bruno, our little partners.

Published in 2019 by
Lots of Architecture publishers

1680 Michigan Ave.
Floor 10, Suite 1000
Miami Beach, FL 33139
Tel: +1 (617) 674-2656
hello@lotsofarchitecture.com

ISSN 2574-8351
ISBN 978-1-7320106-2-8
Printed in the USA

ONLINE
nessmagazine.com
instagram.com/ness_magazine
facebook.com/nessmagazine
twitter.com/NESS_magazine

COVER CREDITS

1 Fragment of "The Encryption of Power: Disobedience and Exclusion in the City," Walls of Air. (full credits on p. 102)

2 Exhibition View of "Cosmo-Clinical Interiors of Beirut," feminist architecture collaborative.
Ph. Casey Carter

−NESS®

NESS is a product of Lots of Architecture publishers: an editorial platform dedicated to Architecture, Life, and Urban Culture founded by Pablo Gerson and Florencia Rodriguez in 2017.

Contributors

URIEL FOGUÉ holds a PhD from the *Universidad Politécnica de Madrid* (UPM), with honors. He was awarded the extraordinary prize for his doctoral degree. He was also awarded at the X Ibero American Biennial of Architecture and Urban Planning 2016. He currently teaches at the European University of Madrid and is co-founder of the architectural firm Elii (www.elii.es), which took part in the Spanish Pavilion at the XV Venice Architecture Biennale (awarded the Golden Lion in 2016). Elii's work has been selected twice for The European Union Prize for Contemporary Architecture – Mies van der Rohe Award, among others. Since 2012, he is the co-director of the Crisis Cabinet of Political Fictions. He co-authored the book "What is Home Without a Mother" (2015) and is co-editor of the publication UHF.

Fogué played spy in the Exquisite Corpse Game, in THE DOSSIER.

ADRIANA AMANTE is professor at the *Universidad de Buenos Aires*, where she teaches 20th century Argentinian literature. She holds a PhD in Literature from *Universidad de Buenos Aires*. She also holds a research post at the *Instituto de Literatura Hispanoamericana* and is Academic Director of the *Escuela Superior de Creativos Publicitarios*. She has been a Visiting Researcher at New York University, University of London, and *Universidade Nova de Lisboa*. Her essays have been published widely and she co-authored "Absurdo Brasil. Polémicas en la cultura brasileña," and translated from Portuguese to Spanish Fernando Pessoa's "El Banquero Anarquista" and Machado de Assis's "Memorias póstumas de Bras Cubas."

Amante interviewed Giuliana Bruno, in THE DOSSIER.

AGUSTIN SCHANG is an architect and independent cultural producer based in New York, where he manages and programs the GSAPP Incubator, a launchpad for new ideas and projects about architecture, culture, and the city, an initiative from Columbia University Graduate School of Architecture, Planning, and Preservation (GSAPP) in association with NEW INC, the New Museum's incubator. He studied architecture at the *Universidad de Buenos Aires* and graduated in 2015 from the Masters in Critical, Curatorial, and Conceptual Practices in Architecture at Columbia University GSAPP with a thesis on archives and architecture. Since 2003, he has collaborated in multiple art, architecture, and cultural projects with prestigious institutions such as the Chicago Architecture Biennial, Friends of the High Line, Emily Harvey Foundation, among others.

Schang interviewed Feminist Architecture Collaborative, in BROWSER.

RENEE CARMICHAEL is an artist, researcher, and writer whose work explores the relationships between dance, algorithms, and the body. She has written and produced work around themes such as choreography for hire as auction, masks, carrots and the web browser, The Dance Epidemic of 1518, the website's relationship to print, Obsessive Compulsive Disorder and technology, code poetry and singing IBM anthems and code. Her texts have been published internationally in both academic and artistic publications including #exstrange: a curatorial intervention on eBay (Michigan University Publishing), Perífrasis Journal, Unlikely Journal, Sync.io, among others. She graduated from Goldsmiths College in London with a Masters in Interactive Media: Critical Theory and Practice. She is currently an editor at NESS and is researching on dance and code for a PhD in Comparative Art Theory from the *Universidad Nacional de Tres de Febrero*, Argentina.

Carmichael wrote the report on Lafeliz, in BROWSER, and played spy in the Exquisite Corpse Game, in THE DOSSIER.

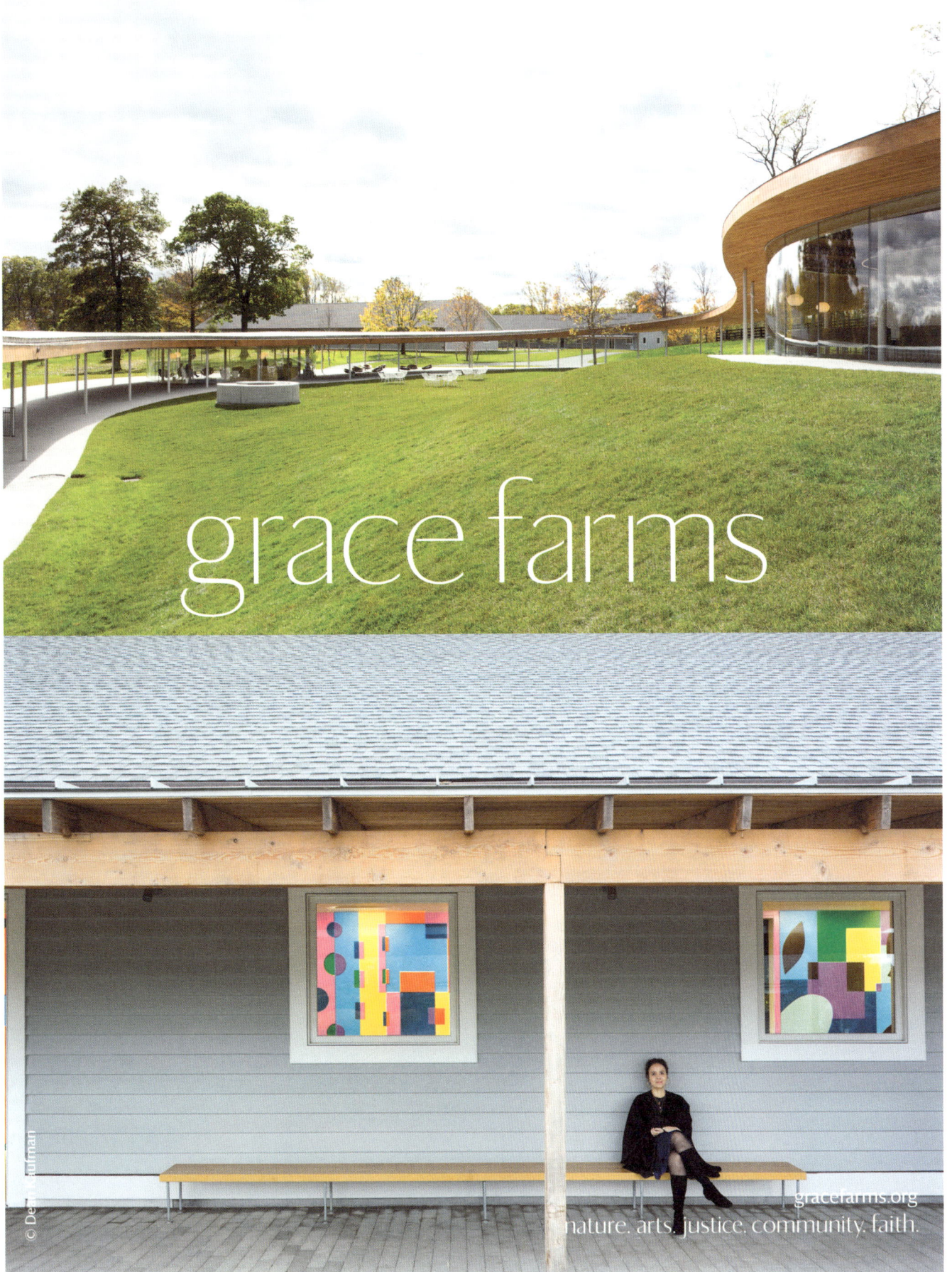

grace farms

gracefarms.org
nature. arts. justice. community. faith.

ACTAR

Actar Publishers
Books on Architecture
and Design

www.actar.com

urbanNext

Expanding architecture
to rethink cities

www.urbannext.net

Contents

64 The Dossier

MAD WORLD PICTURES

A contingent album of conversations and maps to place urgent matters. Architectural, environmental, political, and epistemological concerns projected onto that thing we call 'the world.'

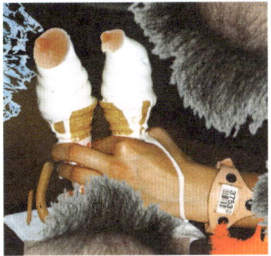

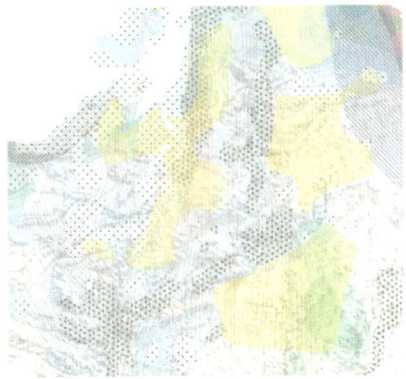

Ph. Iwan Baan

COLUMBIA BOOKS on ARCHITECTURE and the CITY

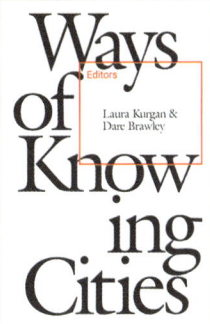

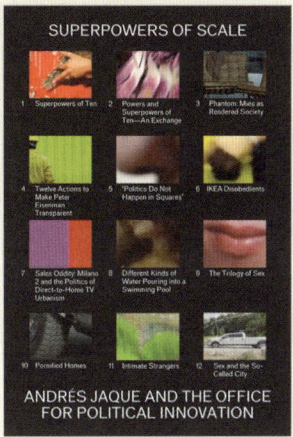

Forthcoming and recent books that expand the ground of architectural discourse, asking urgent questions about what architecture is and does.

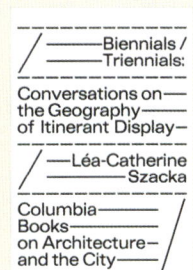

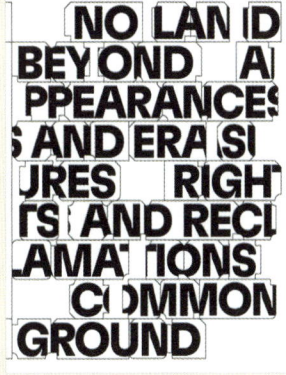

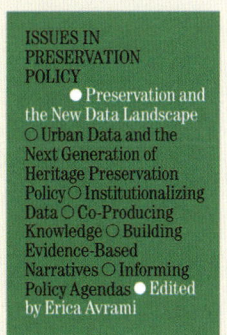

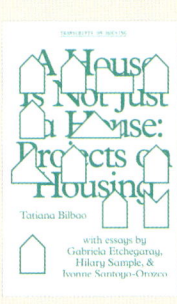

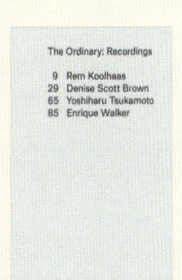

An imprint of the Graduate School of Architecture, Planning, and Preservation at Columbia University, arch.columbia.edu.
For more information and ordering, https://cup.columbia.edu/distributed-press/columbia-books-on-architecture-and-the-city.

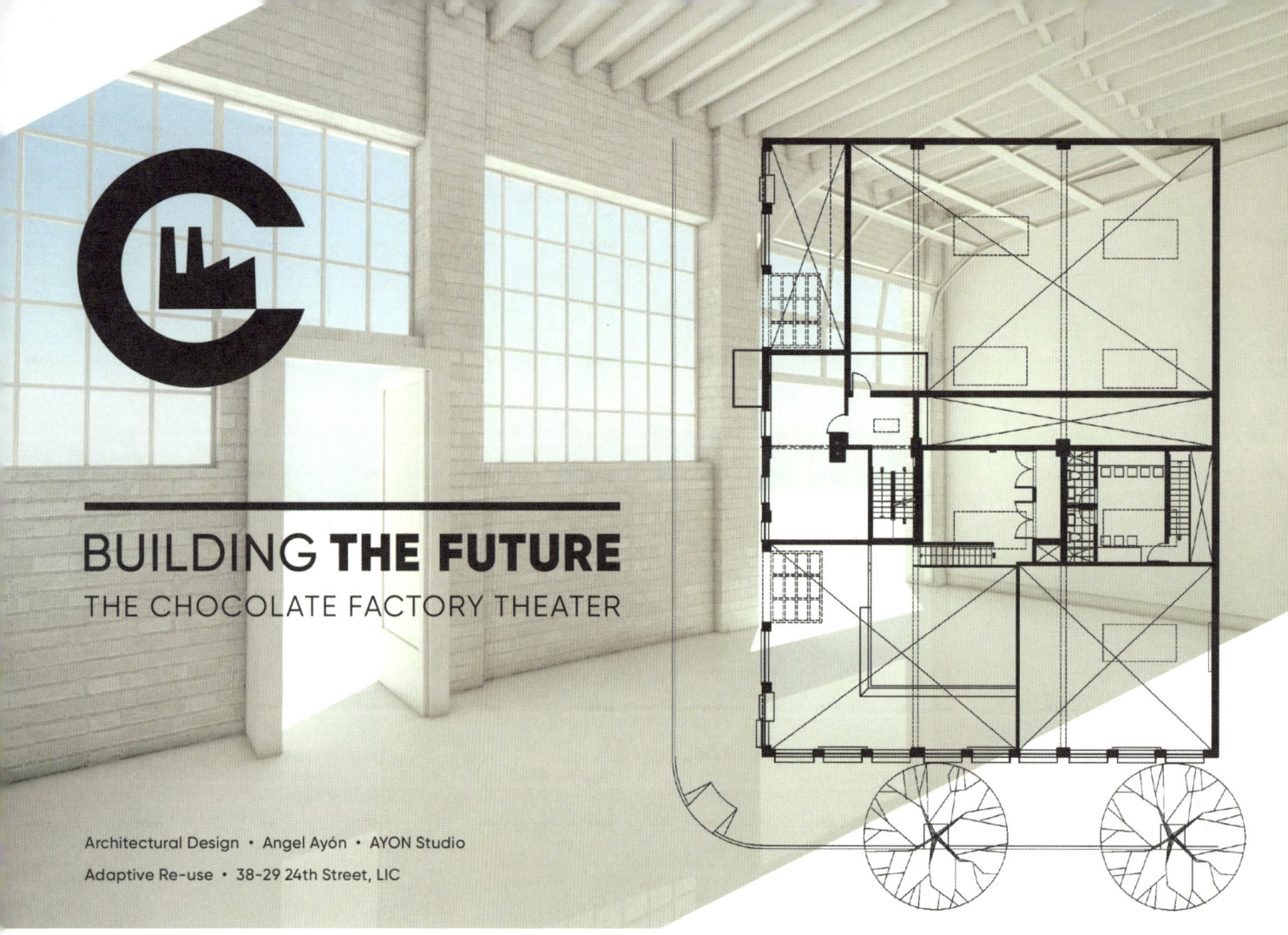

BUILDING **THE FUTURE**
THE CHOCOLATE FACTORY THEATER

Architectural Design • Angel Ayón • AYON Studio

Adaptive Re-use • 38-29 24th Street, LIC

Maria Bauman-Morales

(re)Source

[co-presented with the Bronx Academy of Arts and Dance]

September 2019

Antonio Ramos

El Pueblo de los Olvidados

[co-presented with Abrons Arts Center]

October 2019

Kristen Kosmas

The People's Republic of Valerie

October / November 2019

Tess Dworman

A Child Retires

November 2019

David Neumann + Marcella Murray

Distances Smaller Than This Are Not Confirmed

[co-presented with Abrons Arts Center]

January 2020

Stephanie Acosta

Good Day God Damn

March 2020

Jess Pretty

dream[e]scapes

April 2020

Ingri Fiksdal

Diorama

April 2020

Donna Uchizono

Iron Wings

[co-presented with Baryshnikov Arts Center]

May 2020

Creative Residency Artists

(curated by Blaze Ferrer)

Angie Pittman • Marion Spencer

ANTARCTICA 200
A CROSS-DISCIPLINARY RESEARCH PLATFORM

Human presence in Antarctica is an achievement that is approaching its 200th anniversary. The rapid transformation of the polar region under the effects of global warming and the unchartered nature of most of the continent urges the necessity to research and document the extreme southern territory.

Antarctica 200 is a cross-disciplinary project directed by Giulia Foscari and Francesco Bandarin, based out of the Architectural Association in London. The program relies on the close collaboration of a group of global experts in the fields of architecture, engineering, science, glaciology, international law, anthropology, literature, and art. The main research platform is the AA Polar Lab. In parallel, the Polar Lab AR is the Argentinian hub of the project Antarctica 200 directed by Florencia Rodriguez at NESS and Monte (team members: Renee Carmichael, Daniela Freiberg, Pablo Gerson, Rodrigo Kommers Wender, Natalia La Porta, Isabella Moretti, Victoria Nuviala, Violeta Nuviala, Mariam Samur.)

@antarctica200
@aapolarlab
@monte_buenosaires
@ness_magazine

POLAR LAB
THE ACADEMIC PLATFORM
OF ANTARCTICA 200

Printed Matter St Marks

38 St Marks Place
New York City
Located in the
Swiss Institute

Wed-Thu: 2-8 pm
Fri-Sat: 12-8 pm
Sun: 12-6 pm

printedmatter.org

BIOSUIT MIT
NASA INSTITUTE FOR ADVANCED CONCEPTS IN
COLLABORATION WITH TROTTI + ASSOCIATES

MIT scientists and engineers alongside Dava Newman and Guillermo Trotti worked on the development of a mechanical counter-pressure spacesuit to replace the present gas pressurized suits used in microgravity. This innovative design provides enhanced astronaut mobility during extra vehicular activities on the surface of the Moon or Mars. The suit acts as a second skin and is patterned from 3D laser scans that incorporate skin strain field maps for maximum mobility and natural movements, while requiring minimum energy expenditure for exploration tasks.

DESERT X

Iván Argote
Steve Badgett &
Chris Taylor
Nancy Baker Cahill
Cecilia Bengolea
Pia Camil
John Gerrard
Julian Hoeber
Iman Issa
Mary Kelly

Armando Lerma
Eric N. Mack
Cinthia Marcelle
Postcommodity
Cara Romero
Sterling Ruby
Kathleen Ryan
Gary Simmons
Superflex

The Desert X Board of Directors and team thank the above artists for their inspiring contributions to Desert X 2019, which welcomed an audience of 400,000. Desert X would not be possible without the generous support of our Major Benefactors, Desert X 100, Host Committee, and donors at every level. Coachella Valley cities, Desert X sponsors, partners, and volunteers welcomed people from around the world for Desert X 2019.

Desert X is funded by its board of directors, an extraordinary group of donors and municipalities, and by Canoo, formerly known as Project Evelozcity, its lead sponsor. Media Partners: Art in America, artnet, ARTnews, *frieze* magazine, Greater Palm Springs Convention & Visitors Bureau, Here TV, Palm Springs Life Magazine and The Desert Sun part of the USA Today Network.

canoo

WWW.DESERTX.ORG

@_desertx

ORCADAS STATION
THE ARGENTINIAN NATIONAL
WEATHER SERVICE IN ANTARCTICA

The Orcadas Station on Laurie Island is one of the oldest research settlements in Antarctica. The Argentinian base was founded in February 1904, and serves year-round as a meteorological station and a magnetic observatory, where the variation of the geomagnetic field is constantly recorded—the measurements are taken by hand regularly with a variometer.

The Argentinian National Weather Service (SMN) was invited to Polar Lab AR's second meeting. Their insight was vital to understand how meteorological analysis plays a fundamental role in the development of all types of research in Antarctica.

KENNEDY SPACE CENTER
NASA'S VISITOR COMPLEX

Each year, more than one million guests from around the world experience their very own space adventure by exploring the past, present, and future of America's space program at Kennedy Space Center Visitor Complex, built in 1967. Among other legendary objects from The Moon Missions, the Apollo 14 Capsule is showcased at the "Apollo Treasures Gallery."

#nesspicks_books

Ph. Natalia La Porta

Designs of Destruction: The Making of Monuments in the Twentieth Century

AUTHOR: Lucia Allais / PUBLISHER: The University of Chicago Press, 2018 / Available at press.uchicago.edu

More than the story of an emergent canon, "Designs of Destruction" emphasizes how the technical project of ensuring various buildings' longevity jolted preservation into establishing a transnational set of codes, values, and practices. It not only offers a fascinating narrative of cultural diplomacy, based on extensive archival findings; it also contributes an important new chapter in the intellectual history of modernity by showing the manifold ways architectural form is charged with concretizing abstract ideas and ideals, even in its destruction.

São Paulo: A Graphic Biography

AUTHOR: Felipe Correa / PUBLISHER: University of Texas Press, 2018 / DESIGN: Neil Donnelly, Ben Fehrman-Lee / Available at utpress.utexas.edu

Beyond presenting the first history of *paulista* urban form and carefully detailing the formative processes that gave shape to this manufacturing capital, "São Paulo" shows how the city can transform its post-industrial lands into a series of inner city mixed-use affordable housing districts. The volume offers a compelling vision of a much-needed urban restructuring that can help alleviate the extreme socioeconomic divide between city center and periphery. This 21st century urban blueprint thus constitutes an impressive work of research and presents a unique perspective on how cities can imagine their future.

Posthumous Life: Theorizing Beyond the Posthuman

EDITORS: Jami Weinstein and Claire Colebrook / PUBLISHER: Columbia University Press, 2017 / CONTRIBUTORS: Nicole Anderson, Frida Beckman, Susan Hekman, Myra J. Hird, Alastair Hunt, Akira Mizuta Lippit, Timothy Morton, Jeffrey T. Nealon, Luciana Parisi, John Protevi, Arun Saldanha, Isabelle Stengers, Eugene Thacker, Jami Weinstein & Claire Colebrook, Cary Wolfe / Available at actar.com

"Posthumous Life" launches critical life studies: a mode of inquiry that neither endorses nor dismisses a wave of recent 'turns' toward life, matter, vitality, inhumanity, animality, and the real. Questioning the nature and limits of life in the natural sciences, the essays in this volume examine the boundaries and significance of the human and the humanities in the wake of various redefinitions of what counts as life.

Projects and their Consequences

AUTHOR: Reiser + Umemoto (Jesse Reiser and Nanako Umemoto) / PUBLISHER: Princeton Architectural Press, 2019 / EDITOR: Sara Stemen / DESIGN CONCEPT: Liyan Zhao / DESIGN AND TYPESETTING: Reiser + Umemoto / Available at papress.com

Autobiographical, technical, prophetic, and meditative, this book is a genre-bending monograph presenting thirty years of work by RUR architecture, offering a unique view of the intersections of the visionary, the speculative, and the practical work of architecture and its relationship to art and culture. The book presents fifteen of the firm's key projects, alongside interviews and essays, and includes more than 400 original drawings, collages, and paintings.

The Berlage Affair

AUTHOR: Vedran Mimica / EDITOR: Vladimir Mattioni / DESIGN: Damir Gamulin / PUBLISHER: Actar Publishers, 2017 / CONTRIBUTORS: Wiel Arets, Kenneth Frampton / Available at actar.com

Kenneth Frampton once called Vedran Mimica, "the spiritual leader of the Berlage Institute." Through this multilayered book of diverse views, the essays, studies, reviews, and interviews investigate the educational legacy of that institution, and in the process, explore new ways to research and project new models of global urbanization. What sets the book apart from other architectural literature is its very subject. Rarely do we learn about innovative or alternative educational models that have produced and imparted applicable, real world knowledge in the field of architecture.

Geo Stories: Another Architecture for the Environment

AUTHOR: Design Earth (Rania Ghosn and El Hadi Jazairy) / PUBLISHER: Actar Publishers, New York, Barcelona, 2018 / DESIGN: Luke Bulman—Office / Available at actar.com

"Geostories" is a manifesto on the environmental imagination that renders sensible the issues of climate change, and through geographic fiction, invites readers to relate to the complexity of Earth systems in their vast scales of time and space. Through design research, it brings together spatial history, geographic representation, projective design, and material public assemblies to speculate on ways of living with such legacy technologies on the planet.

Architecture of Nature / Nature of Architecture

AUTHOR: Diana Agrest (with Yael Agmon) / PUBLISHER: Applied Research and Design Publishing, 2019 / DESIGN: Studio Lin, NYC / CONTRIBUTORS: D. Graham Burnett, Peter Louis Galison, Caroline A. Jones, and John McPhee / Available at appliedresearchanddesign.com

Based on documentation originating in the environmental sciences, history of science, philosophy, and art, "Architecture of Nature/ Nature of Architecture" explores the materiality and the effects of the forces at play in the history of the earth through the architect's modes of seeing and techniques of representation. The complex processes of generation and transformations of extreme natural phenomena such as glaciers, volcanoes, permafrost, and clouds are explored through unique drawings and models, confronting a scale of space and time that expands and transcends the established boundaries of the architectural discipline.

For six consecutive nights, one thousand singers from across New York City came together on the High Line for the performances of "The Mile-Long Opera: a biography of 7 o'clock," co-created by Diller Scofidio + Renfro and David Lang. Audience members were active participants in this ambitious, collective, free choral work. As they walked along the park, audiences moved in and out of groups of singers, immersing themselves in hundreds of stories about life in the rapidly changing city.

THE MILE —

At the heart of the work is an extensive community engagement initiative that activates non-profit cultural organizations across all five boroughs. The work focuses on the changing meaning of 7 o'clock, the time the performance began each evening, and a time that represents a transition from day to night, when people shift from one activity to the next. It is also a time traditionally associated with family, stability, and home. Yet today, those associations are less predictable. The diverse stories told in The Mile-Long Opera are inspired by first-hand interviews with New Yorkers from all walks of life. Their individual experiences reflect unique ways of coping with the contemporary condition—anxiety, humor, nostalgia, vulnerability, joy, and outrage—that together form a biography of 7 o'clock.

Acclaimed poets Anne Carson and Claudia Rankine wrote the text, inspired by real-life stories. These conversations reveal a vast spectrum of feelings and perspectives about life in our rapidly changing city and the misaligned rhythms of its inhabitants.

Ph. Iwan Baan

- LONG OPERA

"The park is a 30-block-long urban stage for an immersive performance in which the audience is mobile, the performers are distributed, and the city acts as both protagonist and backdrop for a collective experience celebrating our diversity."
—Elizabeth Diller

DATE: October 3-8, 2018 / LOCATION: New York, USA / CO-CREATED BY: Diller Scofidio + Renfro, David Lang / COMPOSER: David Lang / LIBRETTIST: Anne Carson / ESSAYIST: Claudia Rankine / DIRECTORS: Elizabeth Diller, Lynsey Peisinger / MUSIC DIRECTOR: Donald Nally / ASSISTANT DIRECTOR: Matthew Johnson / ASSISTANT MUSIC DIRECTOR: Kevin Vondrak / SOUND DESIGNER: Jody Elff / LIGHTING DESIGNER: John Torres / COSTUME DESIGNER: Carlos J. Soto / PARTNERSHIPS & PUBLIC ENGAGEMENT: Peoplmovr / COLLABORATOR: Robert Currie / CREATIVE ADVISOR: Ragnar Kjartansson / CO-PRODUCED BY: Diller Scofidio + Renfro, the High Line, and THE OFFICE performing arts + film / PRESENTING SPONSOR: Target / ANCHOR PARTNERS: Abrons Arts Center (Manhattan), ARTs East New York (Brooklyn), High Line (Manhattan), Jacob A. Riis Neighborhood Settlement (Queens), Greater Harlem Chamber of Commerce (Manhattan), Snug Harbor Cultural Center & Botanical Garden (Staten Island), THE POINT CDC (Bronx) / For more information and an interactive experience made possible by Target visit milelongopera.com.

Sarbalé Ke is a vibrant installation inspired by the *Burkinabè* baobab tree, created for the art program of the 2019 Coachella Valley Music and Arts Festival by Kéré Architecture, an architecture office based in Berlin, Germany. It consists of twelve towers with various heights that configure different gathering spaces and shaded grounds. The name means "The House of Celebration" in Moore, a language spoken in parts of Burkina Faso.

THE HOUSE OF

Kéré Architecture at Coachella

Ph. Courtesy of Coachella Valley Music and Arts Festival

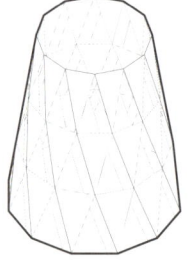

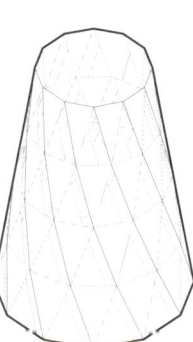

BROWSER

CELEBRATION

TITLE: Sarbalé Ke / LOCATION: Coachella, Indio, CA, USA / TYPE: Large-scale Art Installation / SIZE: 2152 ft² (200 m²) / STATUS: built / YEAR: 2018-2019 / ARCHITECT: Francis Kéré, Kéré Architecture, Berlin, Germany / DESIGN TEAM: Johanna Lehmann, Kinan Deeb, Andrea Zaia, Andrea Maretto / CONTRIBUTORS: N'Faly Ismaël Camara, Olani Ewunnet / PROJECT MANAGEMENT: Johanna Lehmann (Kéré Architecture), Raffi Lehrer (Goldenvoice) / CLIENT: Goldenvoice, Los Angeles, CA, USA / CONSTRUCTION: Goldenvoice, Los Angeles, California, USA / STRUCTURAL ENGINEER: Kyle Morris

Continuing Francis Kéré's exploration on the 'village' as a theme, the installation features twelve baobab towers that reflect on the material, texture, and spatial layout of the architecture in Gando, Burkina Faso. Likewise, *Sarbalé Ke* imagines the inner world of the *Burkinabè* baobab tree, which is deeply valued as a community landmark and for its medicinal and nutritional uses.

As the towers grow, their inside hollow; skylights develop throughout the central trunk. At the installation's center, the tallest baobab reaches a height of nineteen meters (62 feet); the tower, along with several adjoining structures, form the largest gathering space underneath. This conforms the heart of the 'village,' a light-filled space that is naturally ventilated and that also responds to the immediate need for shade in Coachella's sweltering spring climate.

Around the installation's periphery, another set of six smaller towers provide more intimate gathering spaces. During the day, their radial design allows rays of light to enter the structure. And, as the sun sets, the baobab towers are illuminated from within, functioning as a light source and landmark that brightens the festival grounds through the night.

The materials were selected considering affordability and local availability. Steel serves as the primary structural element for each baobab tower. Triangular wooden panels in blue, orange, red, and pink imitate the color palette of Coachella's sunrises and sunsets together with the nearby mountain range.

After the festival, *Sarbalé Ke* will be moved to its permanent location in the Eastern Coachella Valley, where it will serve as a public gathering pavilion.

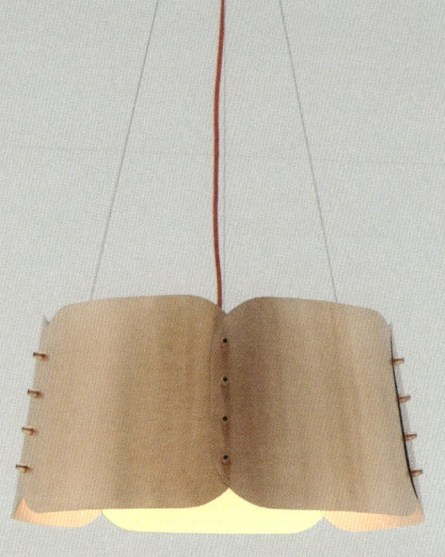

Patricio Lix Klett & Celeste Bernardini. Ph. Matías Lix Klett

Feliz, in English, is 'happy.' *La Feliz* (The Happy One) is understood as a concept, as a state of being: Lafeliz as happiness.

Lafeliz is an Argentina-based design studio run by designers Patricio Lix Klett and Celeste Bernardini and fueled by a poetic exploration of materials. Their story of working from the inside-out tells a tale of the Latin American design context and its search for a balance between a romantic approach to local creation and an outward-focused goal of commercialization.

RENEE CARMICHAEL

Like many design firms in Latin America, Lafeliz's Patricio Lix Klett and Celeste Bernardini began their careers looking to the outside. Design inspirations came from abroad, from Europe and the United States, rather than from local contexts. Latin American design objects themselves are hybrid and eclectic, using local materials with the aim of replicating a cosmopolitan object. Eventually, after a trip in 2002 to study abroad in Finland, Lix Klett realized that he wanted to turn inwards and understand what design meant for Argentinians. Lafeliz was founded by Lix Klett in 2005, and he joined forces with Bernardini in 2006. Like a reverse scientific method, they create by starting with an investigation into materials, then conducting practical tests of hypothesis, and finally, ending with intuition. Their methodology eventually led them from the introspective exploration of materials to collaborations with other design firms. Today, they are again looking outside to develop their studio as a brand, but perhaps this time with their feet more firmly planted on local soil. From the inside of the material looking out, Lafeliz's process says a lot about Latin American design.

Lix Klett and Bernardini define Lafeliz as a concept: it is 'happiness,' or the combination of two or more nouns into an abstract idea, rather than a simple meaning, 'happy.' For Lafeliz, the concept is the embryo from which design objects are born. It is not about creating new attributes or adjectives (smooth, beautiful, modern), but rather about exploring an idea or structure of the material itself—finding its concept—and then building from there. Lix Klett once asked himself how many materials could be used to make up a chair. He came up with a surprising estimation: eleven different materials to make five thousand versions. With this in mind, he began putting materials to the test, searching for their limits, and seeing what new conceptual possibilities could arise. Eventually, he was asked "But what is it made of?"—and there, in the question itself, a concept is realized. Lafeliz is a factory of nouns turned into concepts.

Massa Circular Table. Ph. Matías Lix Klett

Lafeliz's first exploration of material was a wicker-like plastic that came to represent a testing of Lix Klett's early experience in the textile industry. In 2003, Lix Klett began working under the direction of Martín Churba and the iconic textile design studio Tramando.[1] There, his process of experimentation was too slow for the fast-paced commercial world, which he realized when he only created one design in the same timeframe that others created forty. This learning from failure is a clear reference point for his position as a designer. When setting out on his own, Lix Klett took what he learned and began questioning how textile could transform from a garment to an object—a concept—in its own right. One day when visiting a hardware store, he was drawn to some rolls of PET plastic that could be stretched to different lengths. He bought 150 meters of the material and began testing it. Painstakingly weaving the plas-

tic like wicker, he realized that the memory of the material best lends itself to spherical forms. The first object he made was a wheel, something hard and yet soft that is symbolic of the material's limits. It was a form surging from the stretch of the material itself and not added on top. From there he made lamps, chairs, and benches as part of the collection Mimbre (wicker). Harkening back to the concept of found objects that arose in the 1920s, but this time with the material situating the object as design more than the designers themselves, Lafeliz's Mimbre collection can be seen as a local immigrating back into the local. The designs are at the same time familiar (in the style of wicker) and yet new (made from plastic).

Lix Klett's other main influence came from his time studying design at the University of Buenos Aires under the mentorship of Alejo Estebecorena, the co-founder of the industrial design studio Hermanos Estebecorena Design Studios (HEDS).[2] Estebecorena's interdisciplinary and explorative approach sent Lix Klett on a path of experimentation, which is notably in contrast to his commercial experience in Tramando. It is in this search for a balance between the commercial and the poetic that we can situate Lafeliz. Their lamp collection *Farola* (streetlight) illustrates this tension. *Farola*, like *Mimbre*, is made from a weaving technique, but this time from a nylon that allows for a faster, more industrialized mode of creation: literally weaving the poetic and the commercial. The *Piel* (skin) collection also illustrates this tension. The first samples from the series were made from leather, a ubiquitous material in Argentina, but the leather is coated in a laminate of wood veneer, which turns the leather away from the visible to the interior, making it appear as other. The different layers of the lamp illustrate the layers of Lafeliz as a design studio in Latin America: they manage to use local materials not to recreate an object resembling something from the outside, but to create a new concept of the possible from the inside.

Since 2012, Lafeliz has turned to developing their brand through collaborations with other design studios. One such collaboration is with The Andes House, a design studio based out of Santiago, Chile and run by architect Cristián Domínguez. Like Lafeliz, The Andes House works from an experimentation of materials—and has even created several projects out of wicker. In 2017, The Andes House designed a line of exterior furniture, Plaza, which was then edited in collaboration with the Lafeliz for the Argentinian market. This collaboration not only illustrates a desire to start to build a network of Latin American design studios that remain true to regional markets, it also illustrates an important element in the balance between the poetic and the commercial, the local and the global—the artisanal. Both design studios' different explorations of wicker come from a long history related to manual craft in Latin America. Their collaboration can thus be read as part of a larger movement to revalorize manual creation in Latin America. They look to build new ideas for the traditional through an exploration that begins with the possibilities of the material at hand. Perhaps the collaboration itself speaks to the beauty of manual creation always having an outside, a voice of the other, in conjunction with the internal.

With their *Colección Mayor* (Major Collection), launched in 2017, Lafeliz has once again turned to the outside, to sell their products internationally. They have also returned to the chair. Their *Silla #40* (chair #40) seems to be iconic of their brand, illustrating a design that could easily fit into a catalogue abroad and yet built using local techniques in new ways; the result: an object that has never before been seen in Argentina. *Silla #40* achieves a poetic yet functional balance of the inside-out that beckons the geometric metal shape towards the comfortable. Perhaps a similar gesture could be made from the conceptual deconstruction of the chair by Lix Klett in the beginning, to the Lafeliz as a concept today. Lafeliz could be divided into parts, chairs, lights, and collections, but these are only numbers. The beauty is in how the numbers come together through a process of creation that hinges on the commercial and yet folds together on the turn of the poetic.

Found in the last pages of their manifesto is a quote from "A Thousand Plateaus" by Deleuze and Guattari: "The territory is not primary in relation to the qualitative mark; it is the mark that makes the territory."[3] Lafeliz shows us that, in the end, design is not about going to the extreme edges of the local or the global, experimentation or commercialization, to build the territory. The real hurdle is to be able to look in and see the local layers beneath the cosmopolitan facade.

Piel Collection. *Grisín* (breadstick)
DATE: 2012
MATERIAL: shaped iron sheet, acrylic diffuser
Ph. Matías Lix Klett

Mimbre Collection. Cheta Lamp
DATE: 2012
MATERIAL: Plastic, woven like wicker
Ph. Lafeliz

1   See tramando.com
2   See hedsweb.com
3   Deleuze, Gilles and Guattari, Félix, "A Thousand Plateaus: Capitalism and Schizophrenia." Brain Massumi, trans., University of Minnesota Press, 1980. p. 314.

Major Collection

DATE: 2017-2018
PHOTOS: Matías Lix Klett

This is a collection that brought a new density to Lafeliz with a wide array of designs, including chairs, tables, lamps, and rugs. The collection is edited by material, texture, and color. It is a 'major' collection as it represents the maturity that comes with age, professional responsibility, and experience.

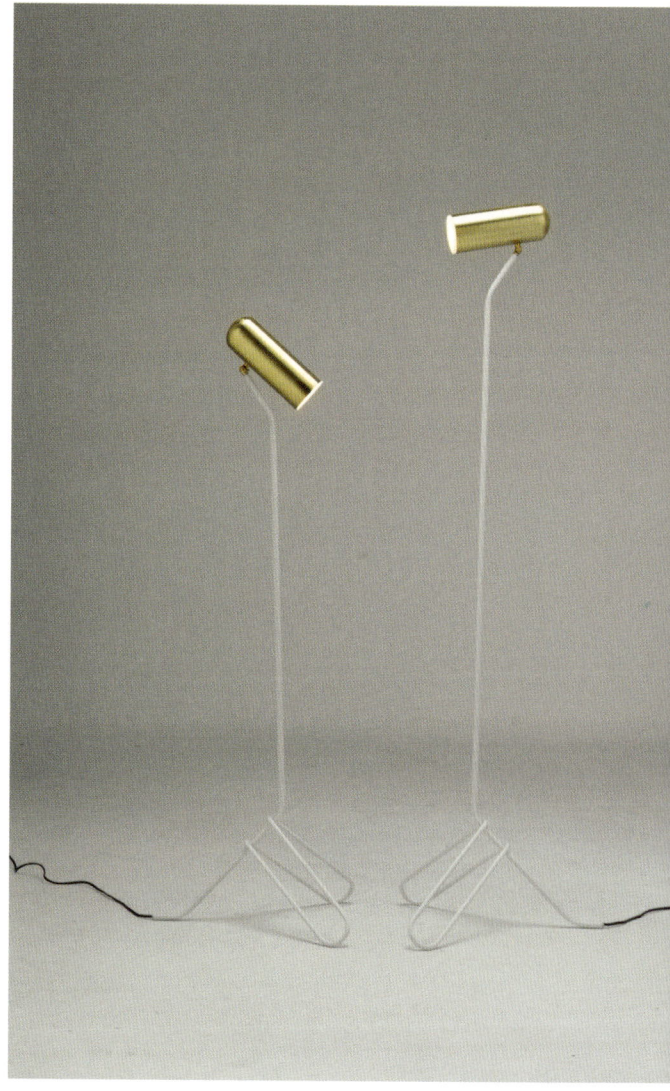

Studio Lamp
MATERIAL: Oven-painted iron

Massa Circular Table
MATERIAL: Marble, solid poplar, copper

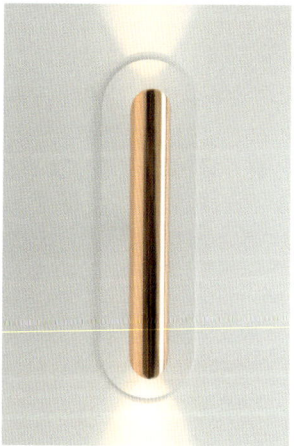

Le Chori Lamp
(*Chori* is a nickname for the classic Argentinian chorizo sausage)
MATERIAL: Metal tubing, LED

Chair #40
MATERIAL: Iron sheet metal, micro-textured metal, velour

Lafeliz could be divided into parts, chairs, lights, and collections, but these are only fragments. The beauty is in how they come together through a process of creation that hinges on the commercial and yet folds together on the turn of the poetic.

Plaza

DATE: 2018
DESIGNERS: The Andes House
PHOTOS: Matías Lix Klett

This collection was designed by Chilean designers The Andes House, directed by Cristián Domínguez, and edited in collaboration with Lafeliz for the Argentinian market. Reinterpreting the classic bench design, Plaza looks to create straightforward places of encounter. The designs are realized with a single material: iron. The collection represents Lafeliz's design process expanding to collaborations with other designers.

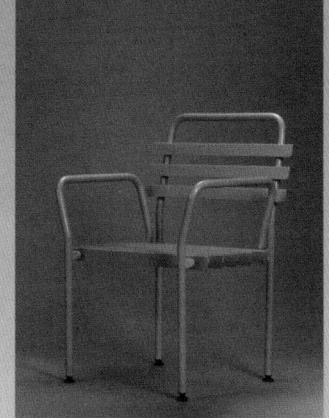

Consuelo Collection

DATE: 2017–2018
PHOTOS: Matías Lix Klett

Consuelo is a collection that is inspired by the use of inserts and pins. It attempts to move away from the standards that limit design.

Tanga Bookshelf
MATERIAL: Formica, metal tubing

Playboy Armchair
MATERIAL: Iron sheet metal, metal tubing, velour

Ruby Bench
MATERIAL: Formica, micro-textured iron

Despegar Bench
MATERIAL: Formica, micro-textured iron

Playboy Cabinet
MATERIAL: Formica, metal tubing, micro-textured iron

1

2

3

4

5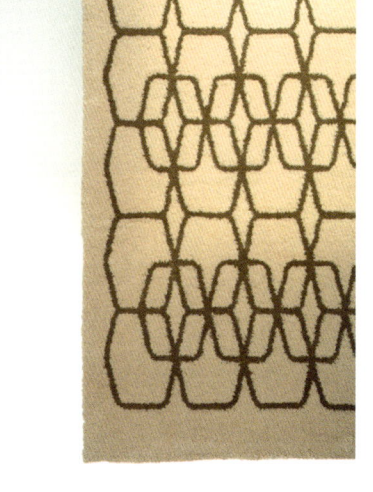

6

7

8

9

1. Chair #40. 2. Massa Circular Table. 3. Spot XL Lamp. 4. *Gajo* Lamp. 5. Chiloe Rug. 6. Ruby Bench.
7. *Despegar* Bench. 8. *Atacabo* Lamp. 9. *Le Chori* candle holder. 10. *De Rio a Sur* Collection, 2019.
Image: Andrés Reisinger

PERFORMATIVE ARCHAEOLOGIES

The Work of Luis Úrculo

Luis Úrculo is a peculiar storyteller who lives and works between Madrid and Mexico City. His work represents domestic or extravagant landscapes that travel through diverse media and allow ambiguous interpretations and fragile reconstructions. Leaning on his training as an architect, he suggests that "95% [of architecture] is not built, it stays on paper, the efforts go to imagining space through documents. These documents explain the possibility of a project, regardless if it is undertaken or not. What I do—although in a different manner—has to do with this way of imagining, of representing things through documents that require imagination."[1] In recent years, Úrculo presented three solo shows: "Perceived Landscapes Part I," "Perceived Landscapes Part II," and "A Green Chroma, Over Yoga Mats, Over Flashing Lights," where he let objects tune to and interpret the anthropological, archaeological, or ciminological 'songs' of our past.

1   Luis Úrculo in conversation with Amelie Aranguren (September, 2018). For the full version of the interview visit latamuda.com/luis-urculo-en-conversacion-con-amelie-aranguren.

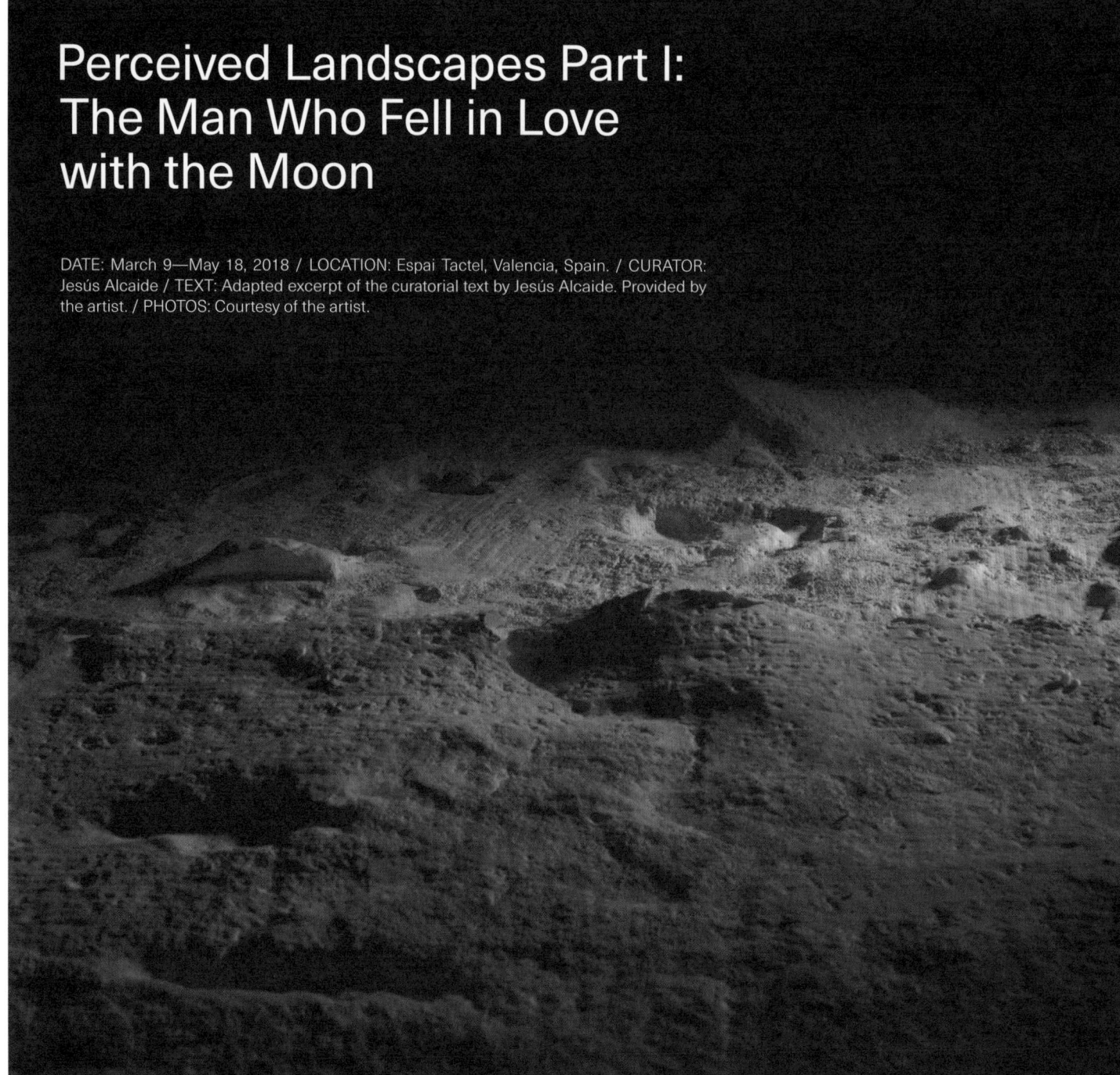

Perceived Landscapes Part I: The Man Who Fell in Love with the Moon

DATE: March 9—May 18, 2018 / LOCATION: Espai Tactel, Valencia, Spain. / CURATOR: Jesús Alcaide / TEXT: Adapted excerpt of the curatorial text by Jesús Alcaide. Provided by the artist. / PHOTOS: Courtesy of the artist.

Taking all the declassified material from the different Apollo mission programs as reference, the work that Luis Úrculo presented in "Perceived Landscapes Part I" not only discusses the moon as a place for a utopia, a dream of love as in the Sinatra song, but also the moonscape itself, or, at least, what we know of it from the photographic and video records that have been released by NASA. With that material in mind, he improvises models that become photographic objects,

printed images, drawings, and an *opera libretto*—conceived as a series of graphic symbols in which we may perceive the movements of two astronauts at the moment of landing. Úrculo's work may be thought of as 'space oddities' that explore the broad idea of archive, the double erosion of the image, and the relationships between fiction and performance in the construction of history: the moon is a white cube, a dance hall, a collection of abandoned

ready-mades, a carbon drawing, the *libretto* of a choreographed opera.

2   The song "Fly me to the Moon," originally written in 1954 by Bart Howard, became popular in 1964 by Frank Sinatra and was immediately associated with NASA's Apollo missions.

3   "Space Oddity" by David Bowie was released in 1969 and was supposedly launched to coincide with the moon landing of Apollo 11. It was used by the BBC in the moon mission coverage.

Fly me to the moon
Let me play among the stars
Let me see what spring is like
On Jupiter and Mars
In other words, hold my hand.[2]
                    —Frank Sinatra

Can you hear me, Major Tom?
Can you...
Here am I floating round my tin can
Far above the moon
Planet Earth is blue
and there's nothing I can do.[3]
                    —David Bowie

Perceived Landscapes Part II: The Double Erosion

DATE: September 13 - November 8, 2018 / LOCATION: Galería Max Estrella, Madrid, Spain / TEXT: Adapted excerpt of the curatorial text by Galería Max Estrella. Provided by the artist / PHOTOS: Courtesy of the artist.

In Madrid, Luis Úrculo presented "Perceived Landscapes Part II," an exhibition about what is hidden in archaeological remains and their integration in landscapes. After having visited numerous ruins in Mexico and soaking himself in archaeological literature, his findings reveal the idea of leaving things just as they are. How would a mural or a pyramid be if it would have been left to be? The artist rekindles the same material that makes up the ruins for his pieces, clay from Oaxaca, in order to carry out the 'anti-gesture' or the 'non-action' and put forward how these objects would look like if these spaces were not manipulated, excavated, removed; just as if the landscape would have been left to freely draw itself, sculpted only by time. Aside from these pieces of clay, he also presented videos that bury images of excavations, silencing this information under a veil of colored through spray paint, assimilating this gesture to the passing of time. The entire project has this idea of accumulation, of strata: layers of knowledge, matter, object, and memory coexist.

4   Luis Úrculo in conversation with Amelie Aranguren (September, 2018). For the full version of the interview visit latamuda. com/luis-urculo-en-conversacion-con-amelie-aranguren.

"In archaeology a lot is hidden, a lot is unknown. In fields in which pieces are missing, interpretation plays an important role. Since I moved to Mexico, I have started to travel more frequently to archaeological sites, and what really astonishes me is not what can be seen, but what cannot be seen: that which is covered. They consider it something natural, saying 'these mountains are pyramids, but the government is not interested in excavating them because of the huge economic costs of an archaeological recovery.' So, they let them become landscape. And this is precisely what seemed wonderful to me: leaving things as they are, watching time become landscape. This is where the idea of working on the archaeology book came from."[4]

—Luis Úrculo

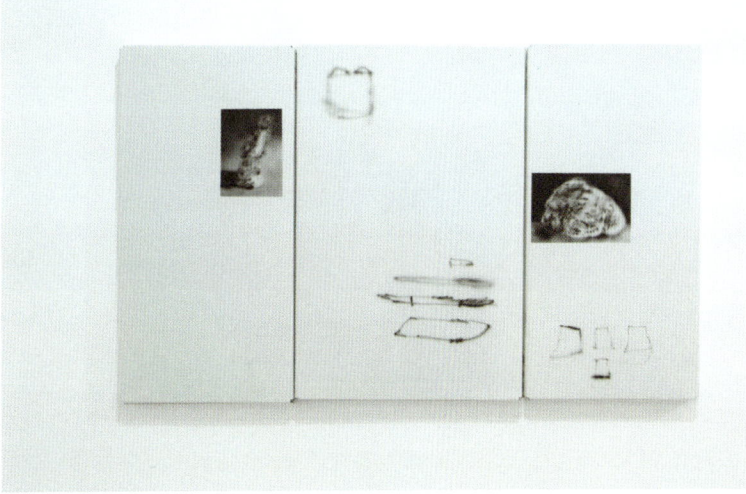

A Green Chroma, Over Yoga Mats, Over Flashing Lights

DATE: November 2018 / LOCATION: Arredondo \ Arozarena, Mexico City, Mexico / CURATOR: Bárbara Cuadriello / TEXT: Adapted excerpt of the curatorial text by Bárbara Cuadriello. Provided by the artist / PHOTOS: Ramiro Cháves, courtesy of the artist.

For this exhibition, Úrculo has altered twenty stratigraphic representations extracted from archaeology books. By using mud to cover images of ruins, he metaphorically advances the passage of time and questions the evocative power of those possible future landscapes. The work done seems to be the reverse of that of the archaeologist. While the field work of the latter happens between acts of unearthing, both physical and epistemological, Úrculo's work consists of accumulating and burying. The works shown in this exhibition highlight what comes after the ruin. In a conceptual flip of the image that results from the phrase *sous les pavés, la plage* (below the cobblestone, the beach) used as a slogan by the students during the French unrest in May 1968, Úrculo proposes: "on top of the ruin, the landscape grows." And that which is growing on top of the ruins of modern societies, is it still possible to call it progress?

"The accumulation of concepts that we have integrated and naturalized, and that are a part of our popular culture (...) provoke the sensation of pieces, objects, and ideas laying one on top of the other, like Tetris pieces: Bart Simpson 'over' Capitalism 'over'..."

—Luis Úrculo

FEMINIST ARCHITECTURE COLLABORATIVE

Proposal for "Cosmo-Clinical Interiors of Beirut." Courtesy of f-arch.

Gabrielle Printz, Virginia Black, and Rosana Elkhatib are feminist architecture collaborative, f-arch—a three-woman architectural research enterprise aimed at disentangling the contemporary spatial politics of bodies, intimately and globally. Their projects traverse theoretical and activist registers to locate new forms of architectural work through critical relationships with collaborators across continents and an expanding definition of what a designer is. Their exhibition, "Cosmo-Clinical Interiors of Beirut," is part of a far-reaching research effort into the designed cultures and economies of virginity which began during f-arch's tenure at the Columbia GSAPP Incubator at NEW INC.[1] Gabrielle, Virginia, and Rosana maintain their wily practice and their deep friendship in Brooklyn, New York.

1   An initiative of Columbia University Graduate School of Architecture, Planning, and Preservation (GSAPP) in association with the New Museum of Contemporary Art in New York. More information at arch.columbia.edu

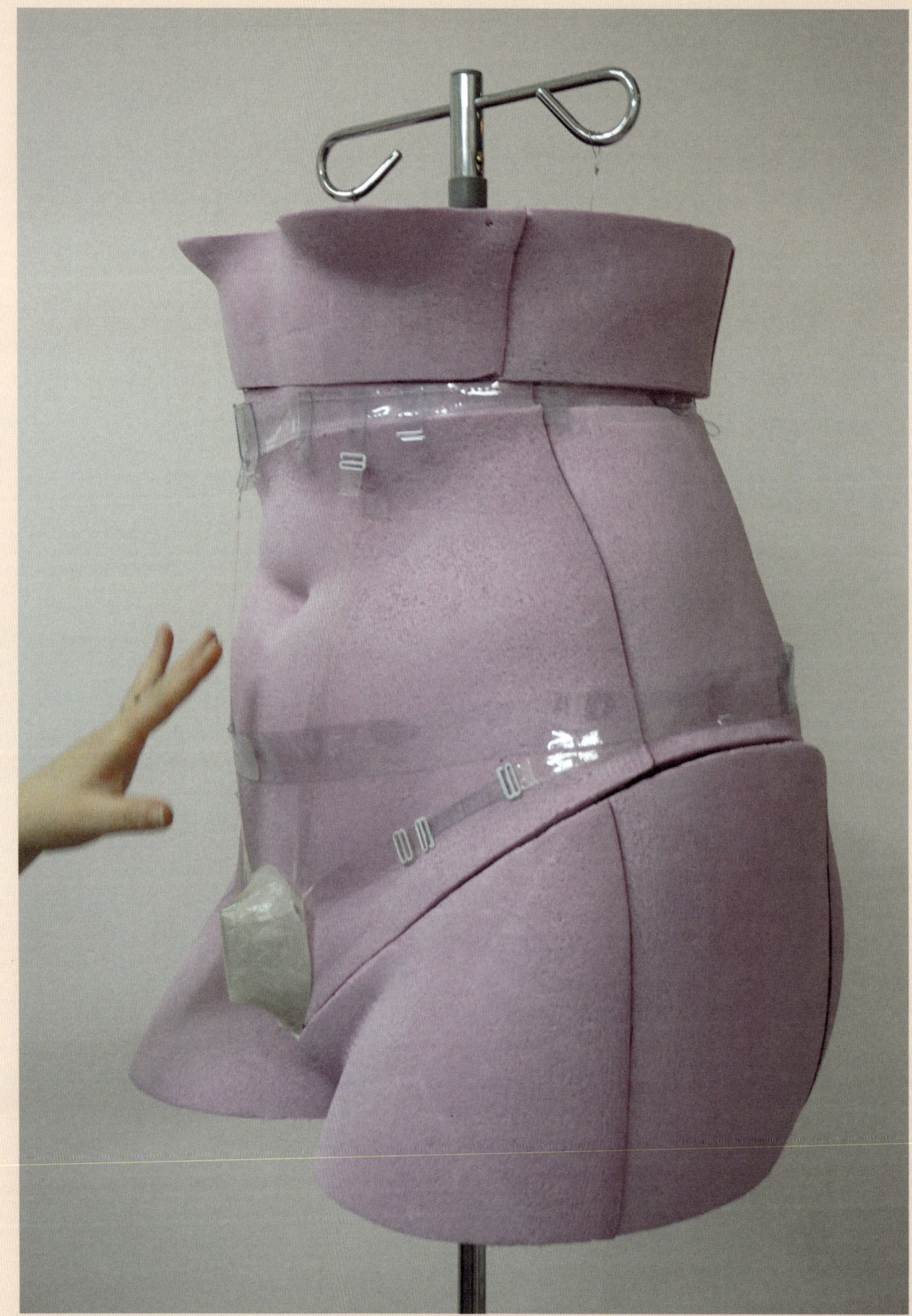

Installation view of "Cosmo-Clinical Interiors of Beirut." Ph. Casey Carter

NOTES ON PRACTICE + PROTEST

If the space of practice exceeds the frame of the office, where are the sites, fields, and territories in which spatial practice might be asserted as political practice? If these forms of work occur on otherwise estranged fronts, as Alejandro Aravena has previously nominated the arenas of social practice, how do we describe architectural work that is fundamentally and purposefully distributed, or itinerant, or best sited in instances of community engagement? Our own architectural actions and research take shape in the field, in site, and as such, are less recognizable as Architecture. This work tends toward advocacy, it involves cross-disciplinary collaboration and is formed out of relationships with organizations and communities whose issues are spatial and political, but are not typically engaged by spatial practitioners.

We are also interested in the more overtly political projects that can be taken on by way of architecture and spatial practice. Architectures of demonstration and the design of protest media have preoccupied us, especially post-election, post-inauguration, post-march. What are forms of political action that transpire beyond the ritual activity of voting? And what are the spaces—physical and mediatic—that accommodate or produce political discourse? How might we consider and amplify the concert of bodies assembling on the street? What infrastructures serve and delimit this kind of performative occupation, and how can we manipulate them? How do we as designers appropriate the spaces and aesthetics of power for use by those disenfranchised by that power?

These lofty questions beg others, namely: how is this labor supported? What are the economies and privilege systems that enable and delimit work that might be filed under 'alternative practice'? The tireless project of getting funded and getting paid makes necessary a host of practices which depart from conventional patronage models. We seek out projects to be resourced in ways that are conceptually consistent with the aims of the work—and where that is impossible, other entrepreneurial efforts, if not sheer will, have to sustain our less saleable (or more political or theoretical) work.

FEMINIST ARCHITECTURE COLLABORATIVE

HYMENS, MAMAS, WORDS, AND DRIVE
A CONVERSATION WITH AGUSTIN SCHANG

When I met Gabrielle Printz, Virginia Black, and Rosana Elkhatib, we were sharing the same shiny working space at NEW INC, Trump had been recently elected, and along with other graduates from Columbia University GSAPP, they were incubating the "Post-Fordist Hymen Factory" project and hosting political architectural conclaves surrounded by popcorn, light beer, sodas, and music. Since then, feminist architecture collaborative has multiplied their projects and collaborations around the world, tackling the relationship between bodies, spatial politics, intimacy, and intercontinental work structures. I met with them again to discuss further their current strategies and thoughts. Below is our conversation on disentangling dominant discourses, work privilege, and advocating for other ways of being.

Proposal for "Cosmo-Clinical Interiors of Beirut." Courtesy of f-arch.

AGUSTIN SCHANG

I am interested in knowing more about the beginning of your collaboration. I know you met at Columbia GSAPP doing the Critical, Curatorial, and Conceptual Practices in Architecture master's program. How did your friendship and that educational environment prompt the creation of your project? [They gazed into each other's eyes, back and forth, Virginia to Rosana, Rosana to Gabby, Gabby to Virginia. Lattes spilled around them. Drake played softly from a phone. The Google Drive organized autonomously into folders labelled: hymens, mamas, words, fun.] How did you decide to call your project feminist architecture collaborative? And besides your specific practice, how do you envision, and what are your thoughts on, the role of feminism in the current architectural field?

F-ARCH

Do you mean fuck-architecture? We wanted to name a thing that didn't appear to exist, the office we wanted to work for. feminist architecture collaborative isn't a project (because that would assume its separability from our lives, so entangled). It's a firm, a shared alias, an attitude, an aspiration to power, a way for us to be and work together under whatever circumstances. But ideally, we also design those circumstances.

AS

Collaboration has a significant presence in your work, from your own partnership to the association with other independent groups, enterprises, or institutions through different projects. How do you decide who to partner with? How do you navigate the most classical institutional world of architecture?

F-ARCH

Everyone wants to feminist-architecture with us, but proper collaboration takes time and resources. It's not just an 'x' between some upstart creative and some more resourced brand. We seek out alliances that result in a productive exchange of ideas and values, ones where we are not only advocating for someone

Ph. Casey Carter

or something, but producing something of some value, critical or practical.

AS

In a recent interview, you mentioned slow making and exploring process as a protest in itself. Could you elaborate more on this? How much of your practice is based on the reaction or the necessity of protesting against current political and social issues?

F-ARCH

I think we are interested in the logistics and tools of protest, which are often not

all that reactionary, but which take time and persistence and organizing. I assure you, we are not holed up in a studio carefully iterating plaster models. Rather, our work consists in laboring over a 'problem' that might not need a solution, but more information, study, critique, conversation, or representation, and forms of action in and between and from research.

Architecture is political. It works on people and their lives, and there is no separating political power and will from the space in which it's framed, or the processes by which the built world is financed, formed, and imposed upon its non/human occupants, and certainly not from the structural forms of oppression called patriarchy and white supremacy. So, a thread of resistance to those circumstances where architecture is made (not to build, to call bullshit, to make another claim) weaves through our process and in work that, generally, might fit under the banner 'intervention.'

AS
What is your approach to research as an activist spatial practice? What are the particularities of a feminist strategy to critical spatial practice? Who are your influencers in this field?

F-ARCH
The particularities of feminist practice rarely get to come to the fore, as one is constantly required to justify or qualify one's practice as feminist. We are getting tired, but embracing the term feminist requires constantly eschewing the stereotypes associated with the term, even in academia: "Will you ever collaborate with men?" is a question we've been asked on multiple occasions like, "do you imagine men are part of the audience for this project?" Which is to say that the content named 'women's issues' precludes them. We ain't gonna sit here and say we're not interested in content under the term 'woman' (I mean, we 3D-printed a hymen after all), but the way that work must proceed is a much stickier question, and like, who cares if we collaborate with men or not? Thank you, next.

Your question necessarily involves defending our position in the field, against its dominant discourses, the structures that privilege certain work over other 'theoretical,' 'speculative,' or purely 'political' work. The methodology is itself invested in disentangling structures of power, but we are always forced to address our own position in that web, in which we are not real architects, not real researchers, maybe artists or activists. But not advocates, some suppose, because the work is more slippery, more argumentative than true advocacy.

#feminism—one grounded in the pursuit of equity, in recognition of privilege, in a discursive framework that includes many voices, if we gotta define it for you—is at work in our writing,[2] the way we conduct our research, have conversations with collaborators, treat interns, care for each other, compensate labor, draw, specify finishes, sign emails, take up space, refuse to smile, perform for an audience, hiss at our detractors, embrace critique. Theory and practice, it's a swirl.

Here is a list of people you can @ on Twitter so they know we stand with them: @feministkilljoy, @AyeshaASiddiqi, @theorygurl

AS
Your research and exploration of public forms and contexts is connected with projects situated all around the world: from the Middle East to Latin America to New York. How do you adapt your discourse to these different locations and circumstances?

F-ARCH
The discourse emerges from a sensitivity to these sites, not western feminism made suitable for its touching down in Amman or Quito or wherever. It is informed by the specificity of an issue like virginity in the frame of honor culture, or like, the precise meaning of cultivating manioc in the *chagra*, or going to the capital to presence *parteras*. We have to engage directly with people at work in these places, in a way that negotiates between the urgency of a political situation and the desires, dreams, and ideals that might inform other ways of being.

AS
In November 2018 you opened an exhibition in Prague about clinics in Beirut as sites of bodily reinvention and production. How did this project come together from the research to the display itself?

F-ARCH
The exhibition was an opportunity to absorb and reproduce some of the strange object-forms we had encountered in our

research on the global virginity market and in the clinic environments we visited in Beirut—specifically those offering hymenoplastic procedures. The interior finishes, appealing to a hi-femme sensibility, and which hint at a luxury surgical experience, are remade into a curtained, clinic-like environment in the gallery, where we occasion other potential forms of bodily production or representation (via the critical hymen object) and listen to the voices of women who have had experiences with the procedure (via our soundscape in clinic VR). Here the pressure on the body and its proper form is deferred to the interior architecture of the clinic lobby, the recovery suite, the examination room.

AS
How do you envision feminist architecture collaborative in the next ten years? Do you think it could turn into a larger collaborative network of feminist practitioners?

F-ARCH
No. We have big dreams, but those are just for us to hold close to our hearts for now. We hope that a network of feminist practitioners comes into being, and that we are part of it, but we don't see it as our mandate to forge the structure for that coming together.

2   See "'Young Girls' and Their Real Worlds," in Harvard Design Magazine no. 44, Fall 2017. Available at f-architecture.com/publications

Post-Fordist Hymen Factory

A cosmology of virginity objects, patented and newly designed, surveys the extended field of artifacts that not only testify to virginity lost and kept, but are also configured to enhance the performance, appearance, and pleasure (whose pleasure?) of the vagina. Through the critical reevaluation and design of these objects f-arch asks how, by participating in the making of the hymen, even in service to an existing demand for virginity simulations, can they assert the means of production over our own bodies and their worth?

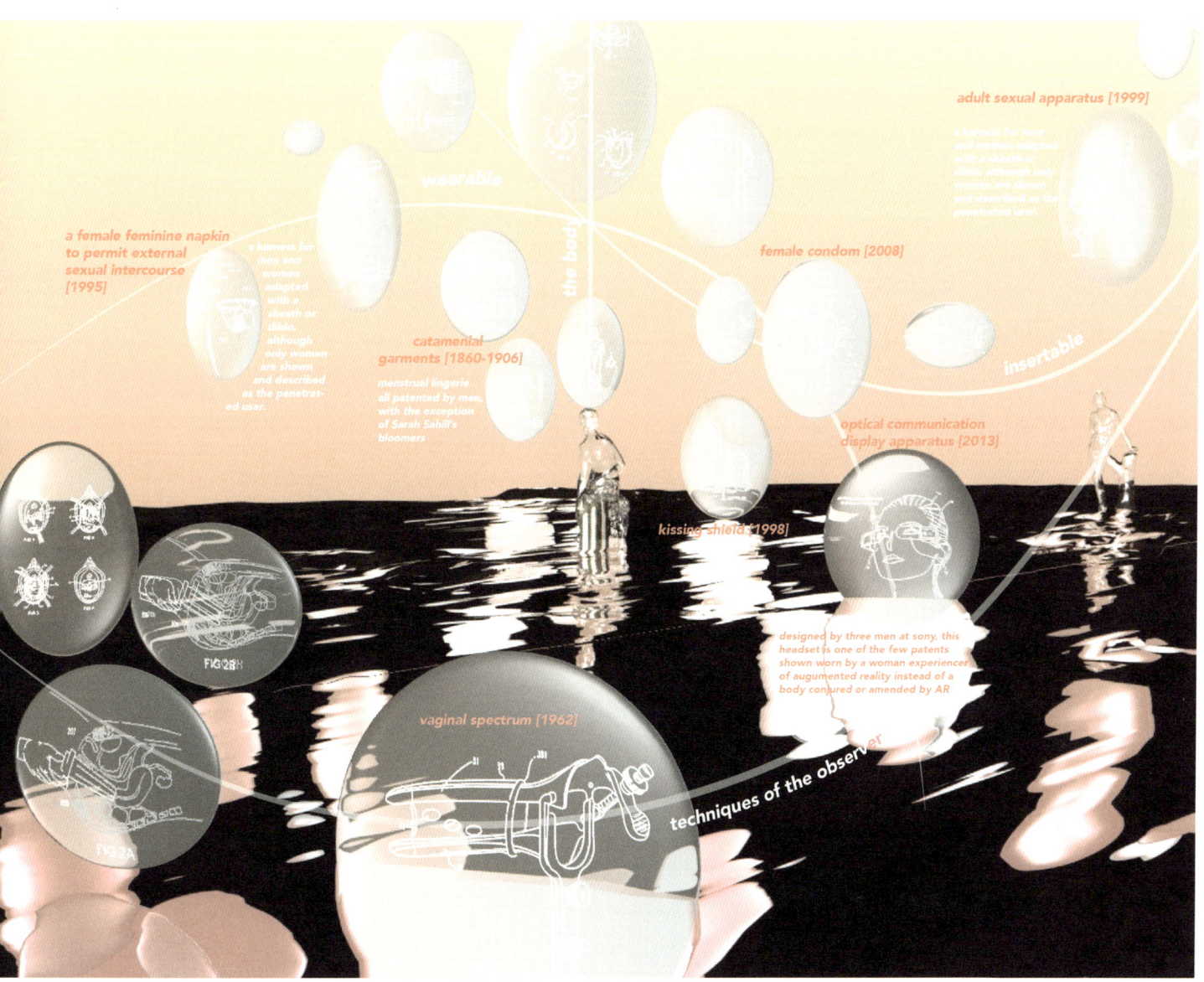

Conceptual map of "Post-Fordist Hymen Factory." Courtesy of f-arch.

"feminist architecture collaborative isn't a project (because that would assume its separability from our lives, so entangled).
It's a firm, a shared alias, an attitude, an aspiration to power, a way for us to be and work together under whatever circumstances. But ideally, we also design those circumstances."

—f-arch

Cosmo-Clinical Interiors of Beirut

DATE: November 23, 2018-January 19, 2019 / LOCATION: VI PER GALLERY, Prague, Czech Republic / PHOTOS: Peter Fabo

Cosmo-Clinical Interiors of Beirut examines the constructed space, interior finishes, and designed protocols of the plastic surgery clinic to make perceptible its role in shaping subjects, virginity culture, and an ideal body. Here, architecture is understood as the confluence of the technological, social, and economic—not a built fact, but an organizing force in a constellation of produced and productive objects.

Virginity remains consequential to the agency, empowerment, and self-possession of women around the world. The concept of virginity is constructed not just at the site of the body, but also in multiscale architectural operations, in the spaces that mediate between subjects and their desires. The clinic is a site of bodily reinvention and also production. Interior finishes, collateral objects, and aesthetic protocols aid in the spatial and cultural production of contemporary virginity and sexuality, available in new commodity forms. Beirut in particular—a Middle East capital for medical tourism, Arab soap-star beauty, and lingering gender and sexual norms—is a site where bodily indulgences and corrections converge in the plastic surgery clinic. This virtual and physical exhibition mines the interior spaces and urban appearances of hymenoplastic architecture observed in Beirut but broadly felt.

The landscape of commodified virginity is comprised of connected, masked interiors: a set of medi-cosmetic and vaginoplastic practices purposefully concealed by an assembly of innocuous, every-day building envelopes, secured VPNs, discrete packages, and informal networks of designers, manufacturers, distributors, clinicians, patients/consumers, and sometimes even the families of dis/honorable women. Visualizing the spaces of these exchanges—of social capital, self-preservation, and power—illustrates how bodily ideals are operationalized within otherwise abstract registers: among the economic, regulatory, social, and familial structures that govern proper relationships between bodies, often a relationship that serves men's desires at the expense of women's needs.

MAD
WORLD
PICTURES

A contingent album of maps and conversations to place urgent matters. Architectural, environmental, political, and epistemological concerns projected onto that thing we call 'the world.'

Picking up on the question "What are the limits to the possible?" posed by Jean-Luc Nancy 66, The Dossier places the issue of planetary representations at center: Richard Saul Wurman recounts maps as a tool for understanding 74; Alexandra Arènes and Bruno Latour develop new cartographies of The Earth 80; Giuliana Bruno defines 'tender mapping' 92; the exhibition Walls of Air drafts the immaterial barriers of Brazil's architecture and territory 102; and Fake Industries speculate on the sudden invention of the Indo-Pacific Region 110. Also, an Exquisite Corpse Game plays future guessing 118.

Mixed Languages

**AN E-MAIL EXCHANGE BETWEEN
JEAN-LUC NANCY AND FLORENCIA RODRIGUEZ**

It was Jean-Luc Nancy's idea to do this as a written interview via e-mail; it was our intention to reproduce it almost exactly as it happened—a proper epistolary exchange, even though one wrote in French and the other in English. Words, either constantly used or intentionally lost, are here rethought, their unstable meanings revealed: nature, global, politics. In this interview, Nancy argues that "Humanity today is both fetishistic and computational, it uses smartphones and sorcerers, it speaks with mixed languages stuffed with technical English, it drags along revolutionary Marxist tatters with trances of voodoo, democratic pretentions with cast or slavery systems, etc."

From: Florencia Rodriguez
To: Jean–Luc Nancy
August 14th

Dear Monsieur Jean-Luc Nancy,

It is a great honor to be in touch with you and to be able to carry out this digital conversation. Thank you very much for your kind participation.

As we told you in previous communications, our next issue is dedicated to the discussion and further understanding of what the idea of planet could be, or even what the 'world' might imply today. Many years ago, you were already writing about the concept of 'glomus' and this continuous, complex tissue that has wrapped and defined our planet. I would like to start our conversation by asking you about the contemporary pertinence of this idea.

A second part of my question is—to what do you think we are referring when we use the word 'nature' nowadays?

Please let me know what might be an approximate timeframe for your response.

Yours sincerely,
Florencia Rodriguez

From: Jean–Luc Nancy
To: Florencia Rodriguez
August 14th

Ok I will answer ASAP!

From: Jean–Luc Nancy
To: Florencia Rodriguez
August 15th

Dear Florencia Rodriguez,

Please find here my answers to your first two questions.
I did not copy your questions in this file, I just put the main word of each as a signal.
All the best on this 15th of August.

GLOMUS: I used long ago this biological and anatomical term to play with its sense of a game of 'boule' or 'pelote' with elements or entangled fibers in order to invoke, in contrast to 'globus,' a confused complexity, an indistinguishable melee. That which we call 'globalization,' coming from the 'global village' of McLuhan, has nothing to do with the beautiful sphericity of a globe: it is, rather, a skein, an interlacing, a labyrinth, and a brushy forest.

Such is, at least, the vision of the Occidental, which we still are even though the Occident is not only in Europe and the Americas, but also mixed in all cultures and all mores. Humanity today is both fetishistic and computational, it uses smartphones and sorcerers, it speaks with mixed languages stuffed with technical English, it drags along revolutionary Marxist tatters with trances of voodoo, democratic pretentions with cast or slavery systems, etc. etc.

But this grand melee is only a confusion for us who are perhaps old-fashioned, incapable of expressing ourselves other than according to certain organizations of rational thought, which we believe exclude any vicinity with the sacred, the naive, the magical. We ignore, in fact, how much of the humanity of the Occidental itself never ceased to be agitated by obscure passions, divinations, and irrational pulses. Newton alchemized and Einstein believed in god. Today, the rationalist fever is such that it produces its own superstitions, idolatries, and delusions (all these words are anyway marked by a value of criticism that is imprinted by that which is called 'reason'): for example, transhumanism, indefinitely prolonged life, cloning, etc. At the same time, for billions of human beings around the world, the middle class that has been covering Europe and the United States for a long time, and that is gradually gaining ground elsewhere, through urban and industrial cells, represents an ideal or at least an enviable condition. The automobile, running water, available electricity, the urban spectacle as well as a minimum of freedom and equality—even formal ones—form a desirable whole that deserves either that we work to produce it where we are, or that we migrate to find it.

If some religious fanaticisms display a condemnation of this style of life devoted to earthly satisfactions, it is nevertheless clear that entire sections of the technic and so-called pleasures of the Occident are adopted or desired by the same sworn enemies of this Occident who see themselves as more and more Oriental, or more precisely, omnidirectional. All of this 'glomal' phenomenon, or better said 'glomalic' (cluster of capillary vessels), develops with a power greater than that which accompanies it—by way of mixed causes and effects—with very large exponential growth numbers: population, speed, transmission, calculation, communication, and circuit-switching, information, deformation… everything happens on scales for which our mathematical habits are derisory. Billions of dollars are a subordinate unit, light years too, and the nanosecond or the micron are units of ordinary use.

The calculating civilization becomes itself incalculable, at the same that it continues to nourish the functioning of calculations, projections, and forecasts. But the paradox is that an increasing number of these calculations have to be employed to correct the inconvenient, or otherwise disastrous, effects of many technical interventions: depletion of fossil energy, depletion of soil, disappearances of living species and resources, etc. All of these 'repairs' require even more technical and economic means.

At the same time, however, it is not certain that the system of increasing production does put itself in difficulty.

None of this can be said to be a simple certainty. No era is ever able to appreciate itself; and to repeat again, it remains to be seen if, today, the judgment of the old, tired Occidental is better established than the decided, young non-Occidental youth. One thing is certain: we are no longer able to plan for a determined future. The idea itself of 'progress' is in a very serious regression. We are re-learning the unpredictable, the absolute obscurity of all to come—and this could likely change the spirit of this "world without hope," according to the word of Marx.

NATURE: When we speak of nature, we are still most often captives of the representation of an autonomous order characterized by an internal purpose, in which come together the mineral, plant, and animal 'kingdoms' themselves coordinated into a cosmic totality. The internal purpose is that of the life that it produces and that reproduces itself. At the same time, we see it as a sort of vis-à-vis with man, who forms both an environment in which he evolves and an ensemble of usable resources. We observe as well that the human technic has agitated this order and that it is necessary to correct these disturbances.

But with this representation we leave out two important questions. The first: what is the exact relation of man to nature? The second: how can the existence itself of this whole, especially as it contains man, be thought? To the first question it must be answered that man belongs first to nature. It is an animal in which life has access to a status or a particular function. The more our knowledge has progressed, the more it has shown to us our close belonging to a kingdom of the living, and in it, all its chemical, electrical, and mechanical characteristics. If man distinguishes himself by language and by technic, it must be recognized that this distinction belongs to a continuing thread. It must therefore be thought that the internal purpose of nature extends into a purpose of excess: man is himself "the being of ends," as Kant said. Language—that is to say the possibility of conceiving, representing, and projecting—has a corollary in the technic, in other words, in the possibility of adding to nature new devices with their own purposes.

The disturbance, indeed the degradation of nature, is therefore itself linked to a natural source.

We thus arrive at the second question: if the ensemble includes nature and technic, or nature and culture, if it includes its own overflow and the emergence of finalities that can no longer be explained by the operation of a complete order in itself, how thus can its existence be thought?

Religions have proposed to think the ensemble as ordered—or 'subordinated'—by the divine powers whose divine purpose would be the pure and simple existence of a world devoted to periodic destructions and rebirths, modelling a kind of vitality or infinite game—so be it the pure glorification of the immeasurable power of God. In a sense, religions are well thought in the projecting of excessive, absolute regimes on the world of our experiences. In a certain way, humanity does nothing but put these projections into practice and push nature, through man, towards the supernatural and towards a recreation of the world.

The fact remains that if it is so, man can no longer be situated in relation to the aims or superior forces of the gods. He must situate himself in relation to himself, and to the scope of this indefinite overriding of nature. He must take back that which seems to be reserved for gods: the secret, the enigma, or the mystery of existence of all that exists…

From: Florencia Rodriguez
To: Jean–Luc Nancy
August 16th

Dear Jean-Luc,

Thank you. I have never conducted an interview as an email conversation, and I must say that I'm enjoying this very much.

I will keep on sending the questions by email and you can work in the same word document. I don't want to abuse your generosity, so, if you agree, I will only send one more email with questions after receiving your answers to this one.

Here are my questions that are a mix of comments and spontaneous thoughts provoked by your answers:

I think the conceptualization of a rationalist fever (*la fièvre rationaliste*) is very appealing and appropriately represents an extremist faith in technics that has lately evolved into these ideas of the transhuman or even the 'posthumous.'

Can we interpret this blind belief as one of the causes of our own degradation as humans/nature? And is it possible to live fully immersed in the enigma, the mystery of existence, absolutely doing away with the—collapsed—fantasy of eternal progress?

So, in a kind of perverse way, may technology be emulating nature to desperately generate clumsy representations of that enigma that is in itself impossible to represent?

Feel free to avoid any of the questions if they are not clear, or let me know if you need me to rephrase them. I also feel that my English might not be enough to express these ideas in a more transparent and sensitive way.

All the best,
Florencia

From: Jean–Luc Nancy
To: Florencia Rodriguez
August 17th

Ok I will answer.
voici chère Florencia

The question is to what extent we can speak of a 'fever,' 'blind belief,' or 'perversity' as you have done—anyway, that is completely understandable because we are all forced to speak in this way since we must represent to ourselves a 'normality' or a 'naturalness,' or also a 'rationality' (without 'fever'), in human existence and in the world in which it appears. Yet we know as well that the human animal is an enigma to itself because it, precisely, has the ability to represent itself with a 'knowledge,' a 'truth,' a 'standard,' a 'norm,' etc. The very fact of speaking implies that I believe in what you have told me—and thus we can agree on certain meanings—and at the same time that I can think that you are mistaken or that you have concealed something from me. In other words, the 'truth' of what you say is not limited to the 'normal,' 'clear' meanings of your speech.

This is of course reciprocal, and it is also true of what you yourself perceive of what you are saying. You do not completely master the meaning, range, or resonance of your words. They can be insensibly (unconsciously) driven in directions that you ignore, and that I ignore as well.

For example, when you say that the enigma of existence is "impossible to represent": what makes you say that rather than "this enigma will eventually be explained" or "this mystery belongs to god"? You can assert that these two possibilities are excluded for you and have disappeared into the past. And yet some may still assert them…

Furthermore, what does 'impossible' mean? Why is there a limit to the possible? But if the possible is only thinkable from the already-given (as Bergson explains it), then the impossible could only be that which is not yet recognized as possible…

The word 'impossible' sometimes has (in Bataille, for example, from whom Lacan inherited it) designated that which does not belong to the register of 'possible/impossible'—which is that of the real/realizable—but more to that of the register in which it is not 'realizable,' but real in such a way that it is always already realized, or rather that it does not have to be realized because it already is. It has happened or it always happens (Wittgenstein: "The world is everything that is the case.")

Thus the "impossible to represent" could mean as well that which has not been represented because it is present in all representation: namely, that we exist, that the world exists.

In order to escape clumsy representations we must therefore learn to think this happening of the real given, poised, present in all presence. At least something is there that says "ergo sum," as Descartes says, and this proceeds any question of 'what' I 'am.' Kant says for his part: there is at least a real existence that interrogates existence, and that is enough to confirm that it exists.

We must now come to think 'that': not to the understanding of it scientifically nor mystically, but to think it—even as unthinkable. Here may be the direction for progress that needs to be made: a progress that can escape the progress of powers, of energies, of speeds, etc.

I will stop, because otherwise it will become too long…

From: Florencia Rodriguez
To: Jean–Luc Nancy
August 21st

Dear Jean-Luc,

I'm sorry for my delay in getting back to you. We had a holiday here in Argentina, and I had some family things during the weekend.
I will send my question later today.

Thank you for your patience.
Florencia

From: Jean–Luc Nancy
To: Florencia Rodriguez
August 21st

Absolutely not a problem!

From: Florencia Rodriguez
To: Jean–Luc Nancy
August 21st

Dear Jean-Luc,

I'm afraid I was trying to think of only one last question, but as I read and think, I feel the need to open the dialogue a little bit more...
You finished your last response with this comment:
"We must now come to think 'that': not the understanding of it scientifically nor mystically, but to think it—be it unthinkable.
Here may be the direction for progress that needs to be made: a progress that can escape the progress of powers, of energies, of speeds, etc."

My three last questions are:
How do the new technologies, their impact on our way of living, and the complex political scenarios that we are immersed in, take part in the direction of the progress you are suggesting?
There are some contemporary thinkers, such as Byung-chul Han or even Slavoj Zizek, that theorize our society as one that has become 'pornographic,' and has lost a valuable distance or space in between that—as I interpret it—might be relevant to feel or to sensitively understand something about that presentation of the real that you mentioned before. How do you feel about this?
My third and last question is in direct relation to the central matter of our issue: How would you imagine an appropriate method of mapping and representing our planet today?

Thank you again!
Florencia

From: Jean–Luc Nancy
To: Florencia Rodriguez
August 22ns

Here is my last answer—unless you want to ask a post-last question and so on: this is up to you!

> How do the new technologies, their impact on our way of living, and the complex political scenarios that we are immersed in, take part in the direction of the progress you are suggesting?

Our situation is very complex because technology and 'political scenarios' are not separable. That which you have called 'politics' is composed for the most part of techno-economic interests, including when it comes to interests of nations. In that respect, the United States today wants to protect itself from world deployment, and desires, among other things, to revive its production and use of coal. This accentuates its distance from the ecological standards that seem necessary to all experts. But above all, this could lead to technological and economic difficulties for the United States themselves: for example, in the competition between coal and natural gas, or in the production of electric cars. One starts from a political measure and immediately enters into an expert debate. Another well-known contemporary example: the lithium used in the production of smartphones requires an extraction of considerable amounts of water, which cannot continue without consequences in the regions or countries of exploitation. Yet smartphone producers are powerful companies, indifferent to the interests of these regions and capable of influencing the politics of the countries concerned.
One can continue indefinitely... At the same time, it is certain that our ways of life are already largely modified with regard to speed and the extent of movements, the capacities of information and calculation, and the general movement of book cultures and education from the invention of forms towards screen cultures, information, and the conception of performative forms rather than symbolic ones (I mean to say that an 800-meter high-rise building draws its meaning from per-

formance, whereas an Egyptian or Mayan pyramid, a gothic cathedral, a palace, or a Chinese pagoda draws its meaning from that which one calls symbolism.) One could venture to conclude this: we have entered in a sort of self-referentiality, the references, the guides, the resources of meaning find themselves with performative capacities. We can observe nano-organisms, send a probe to the sun, graft faces, etc., and that gives us our references. At an individual scale, this may be the use of Skype or the possibility of chemotherapy. Will this produce a general replacement of the symbolic? Of course, we are prepared to respond 'no.' But maybe we cannot know anything.

For millennia, humanity has lived by references to traditions, lineages, and totems—and that has already so profoundly shifted during the past ten centuries that today, without a doubt, for the majority of humans the reference of the technic accompanies, at least, or doubles, the symbolic reference. The smartphone and the wizard can very well coexist, like traveling by plane and believing in aliens or fearing the devil. By definition, one cannot foresee the future, and especially not in this register of the deep tendencies of the collective spirit. Think of Capitalism: who decided to start it? Who decided to invent the bank, the fiduciary money, the investment, the insurance? No one—it is society as a whole that pivoted slowly, that entered into a spiritual, symbolic mutation by transforming its practices, its codes, its interests…

> There are some contemporary thinkers, such as Byung-chul Han or even Slavoj Zizek, that theorize our society as one that has become 'pornographic,' and has lost a valuable distance or space in-between that—as I interpret it—might be relevant to feel or to sensitively understand something about that presentation of the real that you mentioned before. How do you feel about this?

'Pornography,' of which you speak, is the amplification of that which the Situationists have called 'spectacle,' which was itself the amplification of that which Marx has called 'commodity fetishism,' which was in turn the amplification of the condemnation of money by Greek philosophers and Jewish prophets. Yet if there is condemnation, it is because there is something to condemn. The Mediterranean world was very fertile in the development of commerce and all sorts of technics (for example maritime, but also financial) that prefigure capitalism. China has not been left out, especially in the period that follows, that of our 'Middle Ages,' but it had not yet embarked upon a mutation of its culture: it engaged with a prosperity that remained in reference to an altered symbolism, even transformed, but never to the point of becoming that what I have called the self-reference of the Occidental's Capitalism development (of course, I am not speaking about modern China).

Pornography is the demonstration of that which should not have been shown or even that which cannot be. Indeed, our world shows its appetite for performance, enrichment, unlimited production, and lack of recognizable purposes (Why there is more speed, more energy, more computation?). And it shows, at the same time, the physical and moral miseries to which ever more numerous populations are reduced. Yet all of that pornography does not create a revolutionary jolt. Some say that "the insurrection comes" (it is a phrase from the group calling itself in France Comité Invisible (Invisible committee)), but it is not easy to discern. Or instead it produces a reaction of rejection and withdrawal, which takes on nationalist and communitarian forms, and which would like to reanimate old symbols—but these pushes themselves continue to want to benefit from technical gains and therefore do nothing to move the levers of domination.

Demonstration. Indeed, self-reference is also a self-exhibition. But in order to understand that this display is obscene, it must be known how to think that which would be a new modesty, a new charm, and a new secret. A new intimacy. This is not invented. It can only come from the most profound movement of the real—from this real that is mankind.

My third and last question is in direct relation to the central matter of our issue: how would you imagine an appropriate method of mapping and representing our planet today?

The map and the representation are instruments intended for the mastering of movement, transportation, and a knowledge of themselves orientated towards intellectual mastery. However, we begin to figure out that all of these masteries encounter an unmasterable real. We can map the galaxies and the black holes just as well as the deforestations and the liquefactions of icebergs (which already shows that the map should be endlessly evolving), but it is rather to understand that the universe is not an object in front of us that we could master one day because it only exists in the movement of our knowledge production, and it obliges us, therefore, to think that all mastery operates against the backdrop of an unmasterable: of the enigma of existence. The enigma, or rather the dazzling clarity of this that is there without another reason for being, which is precisely an enigma itself.

This does not represent itself: it presents itself. A 'planet' means in Greek a wandering star. We are wandering, we have neither goals nor guides. No doubt, moreover, this truth was already there in all of the great religions and wisdoms (hidden, certainly, but not completely…); we have to invent a new symbolism, of new words, of new forms, for this unmasterable.

If, however, you really desire a map, I would propose to make an animated drawing in which the lands and the seas would change size, form, and color depending on the considerations of their territories, populations, and economic, strategic, and imaginary roles. It would reveal myriads of miniscule insects that would move in all directions and a shimmering bush of luminous or graphic signals. Finally, rains of question marks, exclamation marks, or ellipses, would arise stochastically in bursts. It would no longer be a sphere, but a flat two-sided expanse that would turn on itself like a Moebius ribbon.

From: Florencia Rodriguez
To: Jean–Luc Nancy
August 23rd

Thank you again, it has been a pleasure.
We will start translating and editing the exchange and will send you a draft for you to revise and approve.

Thanks again,
Florencia

JEAN-LUC NANCY is a French philosopher. He is the Georg Wilhelm Friedrich Hegel Chair and a professor of philosophy at The European Graduate School (EGS). He has been a guest professor at numerous universities, among them the Freie Universität Berlin, the University of California, Irvine, and the University of California, Berkeley. Nancy's research is very diverse and his work challenges the modern idea of systematicity. While he has written on numerous major European thinkers such as Descartes, Kant, Hegel, Heidegger, etc., he has also responded to many key 20th century French contemporaries, such as Jacques Lacan, Georges Bataille, Maurice Blanchot, and Jacques Derrida. The philosopher's most important topics include: the question of community, the nature of the political, German Romanticism, psychoanalysis, literature, technology, and hermeneutics.

Where am I?

**RICHARD SAUL WURMAN IN
CONVERSATION WITH NESS MAGAZINE**

Richard Saul Wurman, the founder of TED talks, coiner of the term 'Information Architecture,' cartographer of comparative maps, avid publisher of books, inquisitive mind, and all-around powerhouse takes understanding as his guide. His spirit of inquiry has led him to explore a diverse range of topics including cities, healthcare, The Olympics, guidebooks, finance… For Wurman, the list of possibilities to explore is endless, however, the journey always begins in the same way: with a question. Although his roots come from architecture, he has become a leading voice on information and design in today's media-saturated world. We spoke with him about his early maps from the 1960s, how to grasp the world around him, his relationship to Louis I. Kahn, and how he worked with the idea of the digital before it existed as we know it. One thing is clear: wherever he is, he brings with him a long history of mapping, exploring, and comparing a diverse range of curiosities.

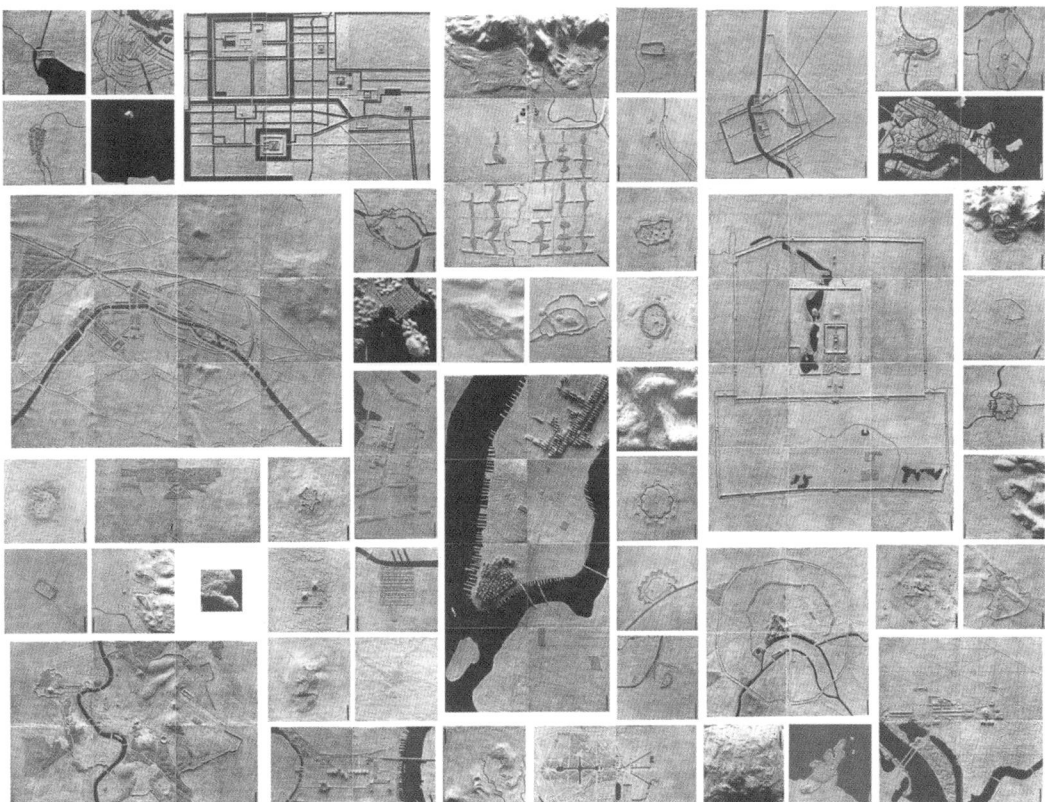

Composite of all 50 sheets and 108 plates from the book Wurman, Richard Saul. "The City, Form and Intent: Being a Collection of the Plans of Fifty Significant Towns and Cities all to the Scale of 1:14,400." School of Design, North Carolina State University, 1963.

"Good Morning, you are an hour early. It was supposed to be at 10 a.m. my time, but that is ok, we will talk" says Wurman as we begin the call. Indeed, from our different time zones, we had scheduled the call for the one hour time difference, however, we had forgotten about the fact that daylight savings had happened.

The mix-up was ironically fitting for a conversation with a man who lives his life always looking for new situations. Wurman graduated with honors in M. Arch and B. Arch from the University of Pennsylvania in 1959. Since then, he has written, designed, and published books on a wide variety of topics, including Louis I. Kahn, healthcare, finance, and design. He has received several awards, including the Lifetime Achievement Smithsonian Cooper Hewitt National Design Award in 2012 as well as the Boston Science Museum's 50th Annual Bradford Washburn Award in 2014. He founded and chaired TED Talks (from 1984 to 2003), the innovative series of talks that were designed to converge technology, entertainment, and design in a friendly setting—or as he has put it, the

dinner party he always wanted to have but could not.[1] One of his most recent projects is Urban Observatory, an online map application created in collaboration with RadicalMedia and Esri.[2] It is a first-of-its-kind system that allows for maps of different cities to be compared and contrasted on the same scale, digitally. He has also recently published a book, "UnderstandingUnderstanding," a journey through the different ways his various mentors comprehend the world around them.[3] There is no doubt that Wurman has been able to unravel a lot in his life, always ignited from his own spark. When we asked him about the personal scale in his maps, he responded:

I have parallel interests. The keywords are interest and interesting. I am 84 years old. I do all these things, because I feel like it. I have been enormously fortunate to explore topics that interest and allow their patterns to inform me. Conferences, forty or fifty, and ninety books—I just get a lot of stuff done. I do not know why I get so much done. Except that maybe I do not have people

working for me. I do not have committees; I do not have to wait for approval. So, all I get done are the ideas that are in my head. My father made cigars, my mother was a housekeeper, and her parents were butchers. I am not a fancy guy. I did well in architecture school. I graduated first in what was the best school in the world at that time, the University of Pennsylvania. And I studied with a brilliant genius—guru—named Louis Kahn. He allowed me to have a new kind of conscious about telling the truth. Telling the truth, not design, is what is important for me. In order to tell the truth, you have to understand something. So that has been my journey. It is not complicated. The word 'appropriate' is important to understanding. It is appropriate to understand something else relative to it so you can get in the front door. So that is why I do some things that are comparative analysis—not everything, but a lot of things are. It was years ago (1984), I was watching the Olympics, and there was not a book that allowed me to understand all of the sports. So, I did my own book. I just indulge the things that I sort

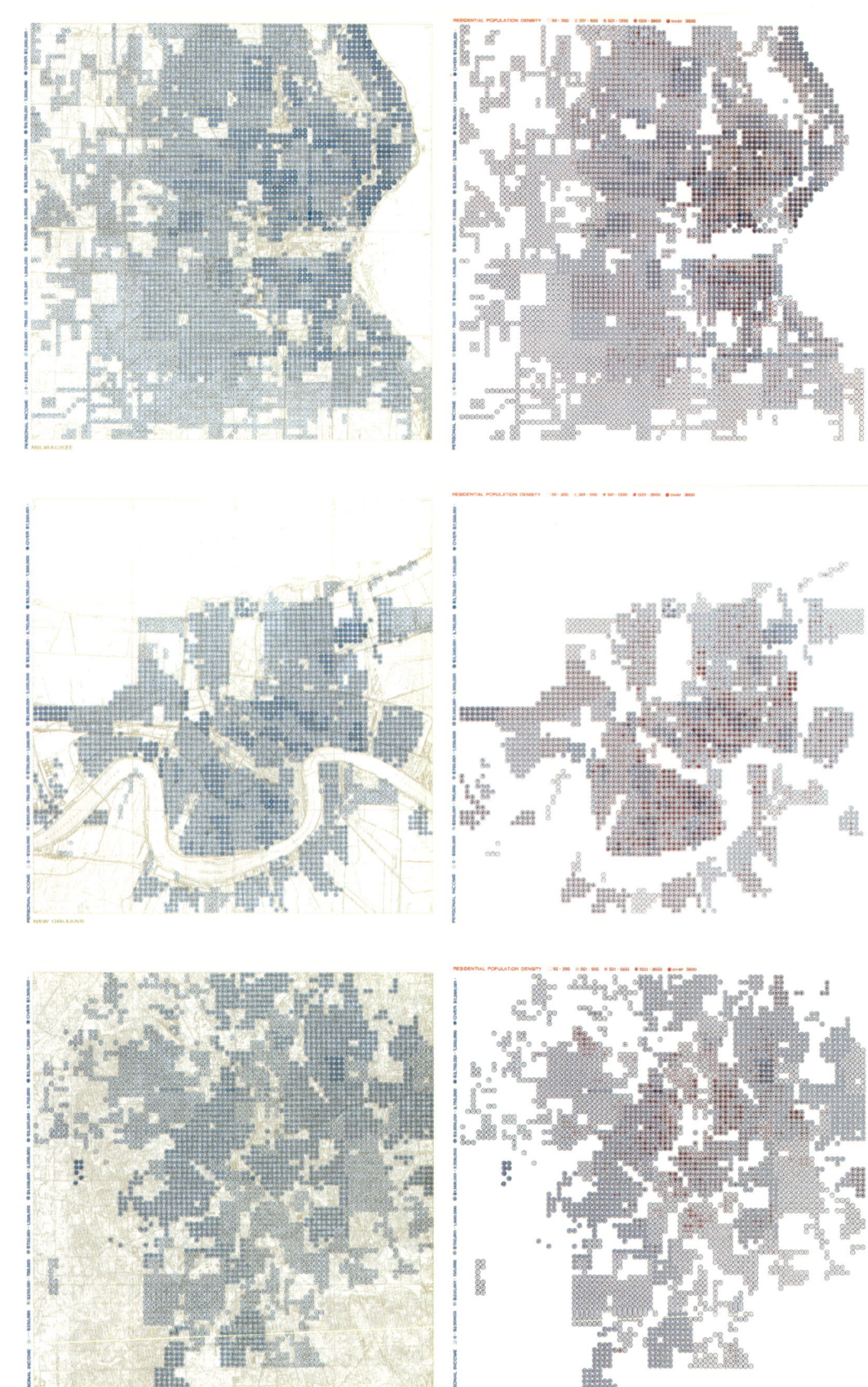

From top to bottom: Milwaukee. Personal Income; Residential Population Density / New Orleans. Personal Income; Residential Population Density / Atlanta. Personal Income; Residential Population Density. All from the book Wurman, Richard Saul and Passonneau, Joseph R. "Urban Atlas: 20 American Cities. A Communication Study Notating Select Urban Data at a Scale of 1:48,000." MIT Press, 1966.

of really feel that I want to understand. And I have been fortunate that many of them have gotten done. This pattern repeats itself in a road atlas, guidebooks, healthcare, children, and a current project focused on mortality.

Wurman's journey is marked by a decipherment of the world around him. As he mentioned, one of his main influences in his life was the architect Louis Kahn. In his famous "Order and Form," Kahn, wrote in 1955:

Design must closely follow that will
Therefore a stripe painted horse is not
a zebra.
Before a railroad station is a building
it wants to be a street
it grows out of the needs of street
out of the order of movement
A meeting of contours englazed.
Thru the nature-why
Thru the order-what
Thru design-how
A Form emerges from the structural elements inherent in the form.[4]

Wurman embodies this concept. It is not the street he is looking for but a 'true' street. It is through his own path that he eventually reaches the why, what, and how.

There is another quote from Louis Kahn: "I love beginnings. I marvel at beginnings. I think it is beginning that confirms continuation."[5] Wurman also starts with clean slates. He began mapping with two projects: "Urban Atlas" a book published in 1967 mapping twenty American cities, and the related project of mapping fifty cities all over the world in the same scale in collaboration with 61 students at the School of Design, North Carolina State University in 1963. We asked him about these starting points and how they impacted his career.

Raison d'être *in French, you know, the reason for being—there are several reasons that beginnings and maps coincide in my life. First of all, I am concerned about where I am. I know how perhaps dumb that sounds, but I am quite*

conscious when I go to a new place, a new city. When I land in an airplane in a city or its designated city—you really do not land in the city you land outside of a city someplace—I had no idea how far it was to get in, what I was passing through, what I was seeing, or how long it would take. That disorientation gave me some anxiety. Where I was and what was around me was the basis of doing all my access guides, those 22 guidebooks I did of cities around the world. And that was the whole formative idea. Nothing more esoteric. I moved to LA, there was not a good guidebook, I did my own. If somebody else had done a good guidebook, I would not have done one. I did not do a guidebook to do a guidebook. I did a guidebook to solve my immediate problem and discover the pattern language of a guidebook. The first thing I did when I did books were two books. One was on Louis Kahn the architect. And one was on a series of plates, a series of separate printed square plates of fifty cities around the world all to the same scale, and I had myself and students make models using that kindergarten clay, plasticine. It does not harden. And we made little models of these cities to the same scale. They were on units of pieces of wood—Masonite—and some of the cities took twelve pieces of Masonite and some of them took one. For the first time, I could understand, the size of something. And I realized at an early age, I was around 25, that I did not understand anything except relative to something I understood. Nothing has meaning, unless it has meaning and context. And every map I saw of a city was of a different scale, drawn in a different way, different colors in the legends, different subjects in the legends, there was no way for me to easily see how big Paris was relative to Rome. I was curious/interested. It was self-serving. I felt that many people must have done it before, but I could not find anything. It turns out it had not been done.

Recalling a comment made by the president of Xerox, Peter McColough, in 1970, that he wanted to make information more

habitable,[6] could it be that Wurman's lifelong project of using Information Architecture is exactly that? Whether he sees it this way or not, his inquisitiveness shows how information—and mapping—correlates with a viewpoint. He seems to move through life forever guided by his architectural information structures, his maps, his 'Where am I?'...

Wurman's definition of what a map is relates to what he later defined as Information Architecture. As he mentions:

[A map] is the most fundamental visual device for understanding our perception. So, if we take a company, a big company like Apple, and we show the amount that stock was worth since its inception, since its beginning, in a bar chart, you could call that a map of those numbers. So, I use the term map to mean bar charts, things over time—I use it in a very broad sense. If you cut my body in half, it would be a map of my body, a section of my body, it really shows you a map of my body. So, I use the word map in a very broad understanding and graphic sense. Its 'Mankind's Ability to Perceive,' and the clever part is that it spells MAP.

Information Architecture is like an acronym, it takes an idea and puts it into a structural design. Wurman's structure is that of comparison. It is not about finding the fact or form beneath something—the whole—but finding a way through it. For him, a pattern is a tool to be incorporated into a process of living. Perhaps, this is where the beauty of his pixelated aesthetic in his maps also arises: in the idea that we—nor Wurman for that matter—can see it all so perfectly clear from above. All we have is what lies directly below our feet.

One of his favorite maps was one he did of the Tokyo subway system in 1984. The map takes the routes and puts them into the shape of a *ying-yang*, a type of ordered beauty. Louis Khan explains this beauty:

Order is intangible
It is a level of creative consciousness

forever becoming higher in level
The higher the order the more diversity
in design
Order supports integration
From what the space wants to be the un-
familiar may be revealed to the architect.
From order he will derive creative force
and power of self-criticism
to give form to this unfamiliar.
Beauty will evolve

The intangibility of the map is the point where Information Architecture reaches its limits, but it is also where the charm of comparison comes in.

Combining Information Architecture with comparison, Wurman's maps from the 1960s seem to be iconic of the digital before the digital even existed. This is represented not only in their pixelated aesthetic, but also in their do-it-yourself or open source methodology. He mentions that these maps went viral: "This was 1962, or 1961, and I printed one thousand of them, that was all. And people viewed them virally, really, this is well before computers obviously. I was in North Carolina and there was not a publisher, we just did it ourselves at the school." For him, this 'digitalization'—or the standardization in a single form—was clearly the only way: "It was logical. I mean there is nothing technical about it. Or there is nothing that takes brains. It is a logical way of comparing information and making information the same, as it was not collected or described in a similar way before that. I have no training, no training in statistics, I had to learn statistics, I have no training in cartography, I had to learn that." He just does it, whatever 'it' may be.

Wurman's approach to mapping is contrary to the norm: he starts fresh, rather than improving what already exists. Through this process, a compelling tension between analog and digital emerges. Paper is an important—analog—aspect of architecture. Marco Frascari describes the analog of paper as "the future in front of the past." He goes on to tell the story of Vincenzo Scamozzi and how he folded

paper in four to create a square and thus changed the material in such a way that "paper is no longer the support; it becomes an active part of the game."[7] Based on Wurman's comments, we can start to see how mapping is in fact a part of his game and not solely an end to a means. The important thing is to reach an appreciation, regardless of the resulting format.

For him the digital and the analog are thus the same: they both allow for the ability to scale and compare. When we asked him about the ubiquitous use of maps today through smartphones his response was:

But those are different kinds of maps. Those are totally different kinds. I use my iPhone for maps of certain things. How to get from one place and another in Europe. And how long it takes and what roads I can take. But that is a different kind of map. That is comparative mapping of Geographic Information Systems, GIS mapping. Google maps do not come from landsat, it is not a comparative analysis, you cannot put two or three maps on your screen and compare anything, you cannot look at real information, it is a completely different beginning point for how the cartography is made. You cannot get from there, to where I am, and I cannot, and do not want to, get where I am to there.

Like a paper folded in four or left blank to be filled with ink, the value is in the context of its use. But if we return to the story of paper, Frascari also mentions that the *lucido* of paper—or the drawing on top with tracing paper—is the analogic. However, with the process of transferring from one medium to another—or of saving from one format to another, which is hidden in the realm of the computer—we start to lose the analogic and are left with separato, discrete objects. Frascari explains that a drawing of Kahn is the opposite; he puts the yellow tracing paper directly on top, which allows us to go to the source to see all the layers, to be able to compare.[8] The beauty of Wurman's maps from 1962 until Urban Observatory can be likened to

these drawings: they leave room for their stories to unfold. First-hand experience is at the root of it all.

Our conversation attempted to reach this point, but in the end what it showed us was that mapping was only the beginning. When we asked if this conversation could also be a map he replied:

You can verbally map something. But when I say learning and education, I am not mapping it I am just talking. I am not that rigorous. I am not trying to start a movement. I am not saying everything is a map, but it is quite pervasive in the communication system. Everything is not a word. Everything is not a number. I use everything that is appropriate. Appropriate is a word that spans and corrects them all.

The most appropriate way to understand Wurman is to read his life as an ever-evolving map that is filled with points that are relative to where he is at any given moment.

He ends the conversation with a note, "You might ask people what their questions are. It is the quality of the question, where the learning goes, where the learning comes from. It is the understanding of failure, where one understands what to do next." Perhaps we should have started with the questions of 'where am I?' and 'where are you?'— at least we would have learned from our failure to calculate daylight savings time. But that failure still helped us learn something about ourselves. If anything, we now know that the map emerges from the point where we begin.

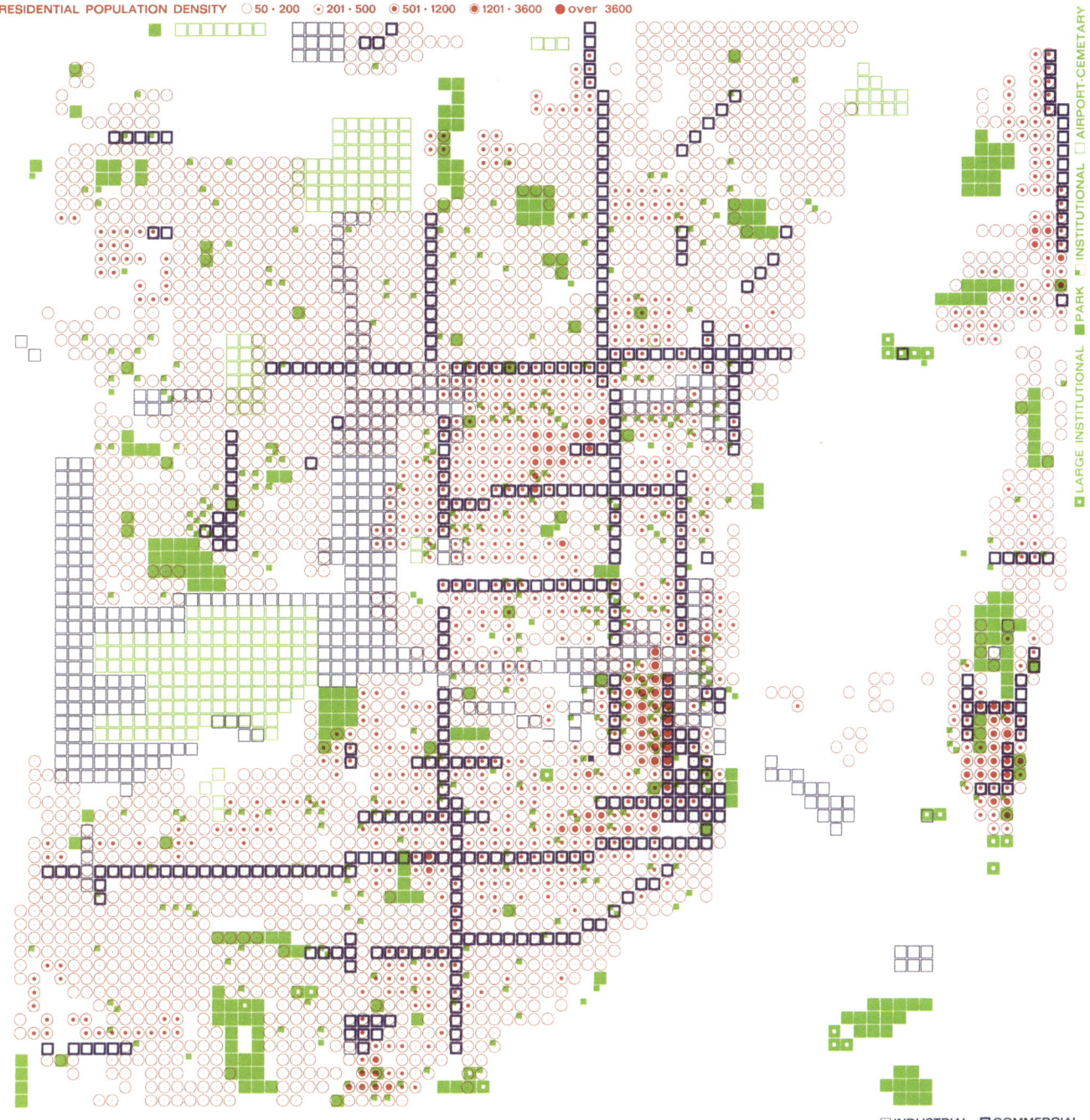

RESIDENTIAL POPULATION DENSITY ○ 50 · 200 ◎ 201 · 500 ◉ 501 · 1200 ◉ 1201 · 3600 ● over 3600

■ □□□□□ — LARGE INSTITUTIONAL ■ PARK INSTITUTIONAL □ AIRPORT-CEMETARY

□ INDUSTRIAL □ COMMERCIAL

Miami. Residential Population Density; Industrial, Commercial; Large Institutional, Park Institutional, Airport, Cemetery. From the book Wurman, Richard Saul and Passonneau, Joseph R. "Urban Atlas: 20 American Cities. A Communication Study Notating Select Urban Data at a Scale of 1:48,000." MIT Press, 1966.

1   Wurman mentions this in a video interview on his 80ᵗʰ birthday on March 26, 2015.
    The interview was organized by TNP Labs and Harbers Studios and was directed by Tom Scott
    and Daniel Honan. See youtube.com/watch?v=aHFNIoM7rmU
2   See urbanobservatory.org
3   Wurman, Richard Saul. "UnderstandingUnderstanding." Self-Published, 2017.
4   Kahn, Louis. Orden and Form, in "Perspecta," Vol. 3, 1955, pp. 46-63.
5   The Invisible City, International Design Conference, Aspen, Colorado, 19 June 1972. Wurman,
    Richard Saul. "What Will Be Has Always Been: The Words of Louis I. Kahn," Rizzoli International
    Publications, 1986, p. 150.
6   Steenson, Molly Wright. Information Archaeologies, in Goodhouse, Andrew. "When is the Digital
    in Architecture," Sternberg Press, 2017, p. 195.
7   Frascari, Marco. An Age of Paper, in Goodhouse, Andrew. "When is the Digital in Architecture?,"
    Sternberg Press, 2017, p. 30.
8   Frascari, p. 31.

If the Earth is not a Globe, How to Sketch it?

ALEXANDRA ARÈNES AND BRUNO LATOUR

The Gaia hypothesis was first developed by the chemist James Lovelock in collaboration with the microbiologist Lynn Margulis in the seventies. Named after the goddess who personified Earth in Greek mythology, the hypothesis proposes that the living interacts with its inorganic surroundings, forming a self-regulating complex system that sets the conditions for life on our planet. Philosopher Bruno Latour has been exploring Gaia for the past several years, giving this complex term a new and critical definition. For him, 'gaia,' as a prefix, focuses on the uniqueness of the situation at hand, something that 'geo' seems to downplay.[1] Joining forces with the landscape architect and founder of the *Société d'Objets Cartographiques*, Alexandra Arènes, the two have set out to create a new map of the globe moving towards representations of events rather than sites. This is a behind the scenes exploration of Arènes and Latour's first-hand experience.

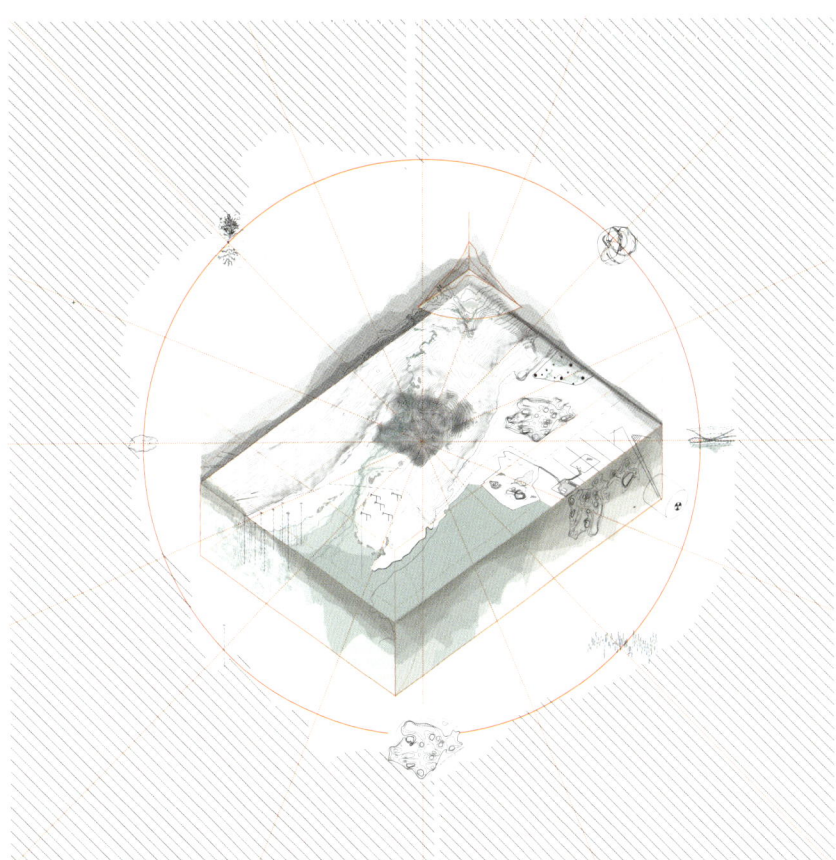

Watershed equipped with different instruments of each discipline (geochemistry, geomorphology, soils sciences, geophysics, ecology, hydrology)

We started from a simple question: visions of the planet that have been kidnapped by the 'Blue Marble.' Every time anyone tries to talk about an ecological question, the blue planet comes in. It would not be a problem if this global vision was not so dramatically wrong. We don't live on a globe. No one does. The 'Blue Planet' is actually a projection made on the older globes invented by cartographers from the 16th century onward to give an outside view, a God like view, of the Earth. But no one lives in this outer space. The view from nowhere, is exactly that, 'nowhere.' So, the paradox is that neither scientists nor citizens have a realistic view of how the Earth is actually spread, nor where humans fit in it. The global view is especially ill adjusted to any representation of Gaia.

Thus, we decided to come up with a better representation. For this, we contacted an emerging community of scientists working in Critical Zone Observatories (CZO) around the world. These observatories are well instrumented sites (most of the time watersheds) covering a vast diversity of geological,

ecological, and land use situations as well as monitoring the Critical Zone (CZ). The CZ is defined by scientists as the thin veneer at the surface of the planet. This is the zone between 'the rocks and the sky' on which all human activities concentrate. The CZ is not a scientific concept, but rather an appeal from many different, previously disparate, disciplines to concentrate their collective attention on the same zone 'in an interdisciplinary–holistic–way.' This zone is 'critical' in the many meanings of the word because it is one of the main interfaces of the planet, poorly known and fragile, given the impacts humans have had on it. To our great surprise, we discovered that no matter how many scientific papers they were writing about the dynamics of these CZs, they had no shared visualization to present their work to one another. They too were clamoring for a new representation of the zones that they were trying to describe. Thus, we decided to push them further and see what other visions of the

Earth could be offered. What follows is a description of some of the steps taken to shift away from the globe and toward the CZ and more specifically to CZOs.

ORGEVAL OBSERVATORY OF THE CRITICAL ZONE, ILE-DE-FRANCE, AGRICULTURAL PLATEAU, MONOTONOUS LANDSCAPE

With our feet in the mud (the most terrestrial sediment of all), we followed a Chinese delegation that came to visit the RiverLab technology. When we arrived, there was almost nothing. A green container was installed near a small stream. The interior housed a fully equipped mini-laboratory: computers, measuring tubes, refrigerator, etc. Of course, we did not understand what it is used for or how it works. Scientists presented the RiverLab in very technical terms. We gradually understood that they are measuring the chemical composition

1   Latour, Bruno and Lenton, Timothy. "Extending the Domain of Freedom, or Why Gaia is So Hard to Understand." 2018. Available at: criticalinquiry.uchicago.edu/extending_the_domain_of_freedom/

CAPTURE HIGH-FREQUENCY

High Frequency is a measurement with a high temporal recurrence and where measurements are made over a long period of time.

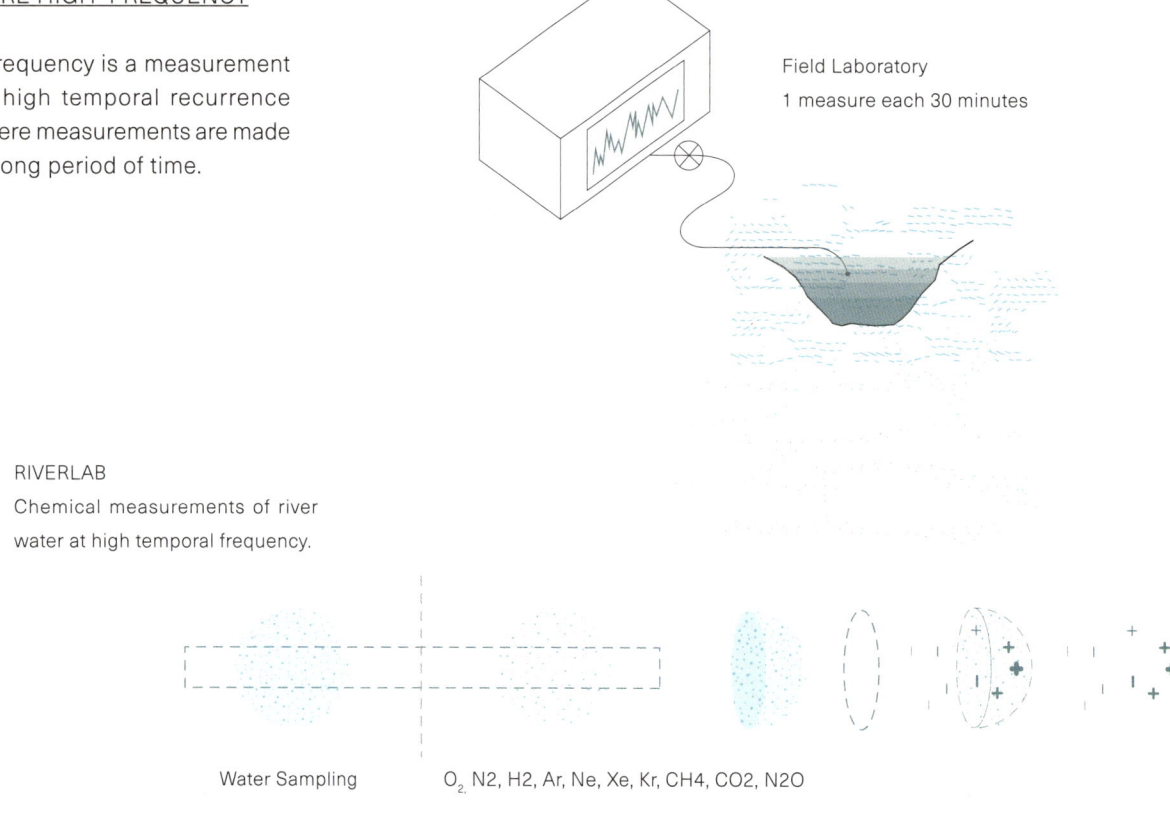

Field Laboratory
1 measure each 30 minutes

RIVERLAB
Chemical measurements of river water at high temporal frequency.

Water Sampling O_2, N2, H2, Ar, Ne, Xe, Kr, CH4, CO2, N2O

RiverLab operation (high-frequency multi-chemical analysis of stream water).

of the nearby small river every thirty minutes, which is a challenge and a major breakthrough for understanding chemical exchanges in the CZ. Indeed, these measurements allow them to understand, and consequently, forecast the hydraulic regime of the Seine (whose 100-years flood is approaching!). We begin to understand that the CZ is saturated with water, like a sponge that swells, charges, and discharges according to climatic variations. One of us is struck by the precision with which scientists present the behavior of the river. They do not use descriptive morphological terms, as in landscape architecture, but instead bring the river by using physiological terms.

First disorientation/change of scenery.
At night, the river does not have the same chemical composition as during the day: more ions, less cations (or vice versa). The same phenomenon occurs in the event of flooding or seasonal change. These events are reflected in the tiny particles that are transported by the river. They are then observed by scientists, who can discern them. The RiverLab is a kind of temporal microscope. Scientists capture the movement of a component, such as nitrate leached from the ground, through the ripples appearing on the screens. They can therefore, element by element, reconstruct the composition of the river. Scientists collect data, submit results to colleagues, try to decipher the pathway of the elements in the watershed and their temporalities, and develop the basic techniques to establish their observations. However, their work is not simply data gathering—they must constantly speculate on the composition of agents whose actions terraform the observatory's landscape in one way or another. The Orgeval is a typical multi-layered aquifer system managed by agricultural practices for centuries.

Recently, our contact at the CZO and the scientific mentor of our inquiry, Jérôme Gaillardet, sent us a quote from Alexander von Humboldt, the famous explorer-scientist-botanist-geologist: "every corner of the globe is a reflection of the whole Nature." This could be translated as: "every observatory of the CZ is a reflection of Gaia."

STRENGBACH OBSERVATORY OF THE CZ, ALSACE, EASTERN FRANCE

It is the beginning of March. We arrive late at night in the heart of the snow-covered Vosges forest. This time, we make up a small delegation: a philosopher, a journalist who follows him with two other photographers, an American scientist visiting France, Jérôme, and one of his postdoctoral students. We are greeted by the team of geochemists on site: Marie-Claire Pierret, her colleagues who are in charge of this CZO, the mayor, and a small group of residents. The observatory has been operational for thirty years, a time long enough to allow scientists to create close links with local residents. Everyone is worried about their forest. The next day, we put on boots, warm clothes, and backpacks to visit the mountain's instrumented watershed. We stopped at each surveillance point. In these woods, trees perish. The cause: acid rain that washes away the good nutrients from the soil. Without them, the roots can no longer feed. Anthropogenic forcing—the acidity comes from industrial pollutants released

WATER PULSATION IN THE CZ

Water is the preferred vector for
flow and energy transfers in the CZ.

GRAVIMETER
Flow path detection of water in the
soil by measurements of gravity.

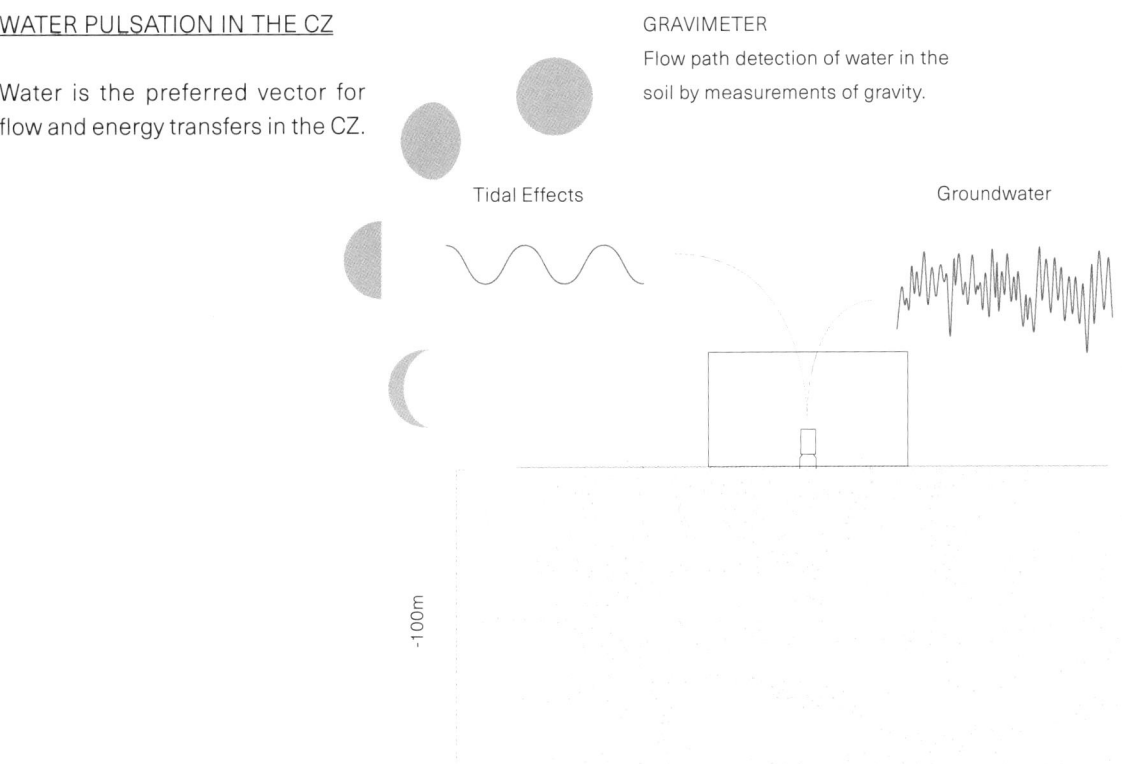

Tidal Effects

Groundwater

-100m

Gravimeter Operation

into the atmosphere—is recorded by geochemical traces measured in the river.

Second disorientation/change of scenery
Human actions appear as future geo-fossils that disrupt geochemical cycles across all layers of the CZ. The effects of the Anthropocene are materialized by particles barely visible to the naked eye. We finally arrived at the last instrument, on the upper part of the catchment area. The gravimeter measures the mass fluctuations of the ground. These variations are extremely small, and the measurement is alone a challenge. The variations of the mass, once corrected from a number of influences, is a measure of groundwater fluctuations, i.e. the water that occupies the pores of the CZ below our feet. Water is a vital resource. However, once again, scientists are not only focusing the conversation on resources; they also want to share with us some hidden dimensions of the Earth that are revealed to them through their instruments and meticulous observations, sometimes almost in an intimate way. Indeed, they are often alone in the middle

of the fieldwork, itself in the middle of nowhere! Through their instruments, they acquire an intimate relationship with the landscape—and might offer us a new understanding of nature. They care so much about their instruments for this reason: their tools allow them access to the world. This relationship is important, it has in a way guided the design of the model that we will describe below, a tension between microcosm and macrocosm. But let us go back to the field. Inside a very small shelter where we tried to warm up (we had been walking outside for several hours and some of us were not properly equipped for the cold), the screen connected to the gravimeter in the middle of the room displays new undulations, widening, then narrowing. Some of them reflect the water under our feet. Others—third disorientation/change of scenery—are the echoes of the tidal waves that break on the coast hundreds of kilometers from the Vosges forest. The gravimeter is so sensitive, and the tidal phenomenon so strong, that we are transported in an instant to the ocean shore.

Our eyes sparkled. The scien-

tists, despite being used to this given the time they have spent looking at these screens, also beamed. The next evening, we transported ourselves to the theater in Strasbourg where we replayed the CZ, in the performance-lecture "Inside." The scientists came to see and listen. Their eyes continued to sparkle.

The story that leads to what we call 'Gaiagraphy' is not a linear story. There are, of course, significant events on the ground, in observatories, which allow us to enter, sometimes literally, the instruments and the phenomena the scientists report. But discussions with a small group of scientists at the "Institut de Physique du Globe de Paris" (IPGP) where the CZ has its urban headquarters, are just as useful to propose a visualization of the CZ. Thus, at the IPGP: the fourth disorientation/change of scenery. Some scientists no longer study the planet 'as a globe' because it does not allow them to face the urgency of the surface situation (territories in ruins or ecologically damaged: pollution, chemical alteration, soil depletion, acidification, increase in CO_2)—a situation that leads to hybrid

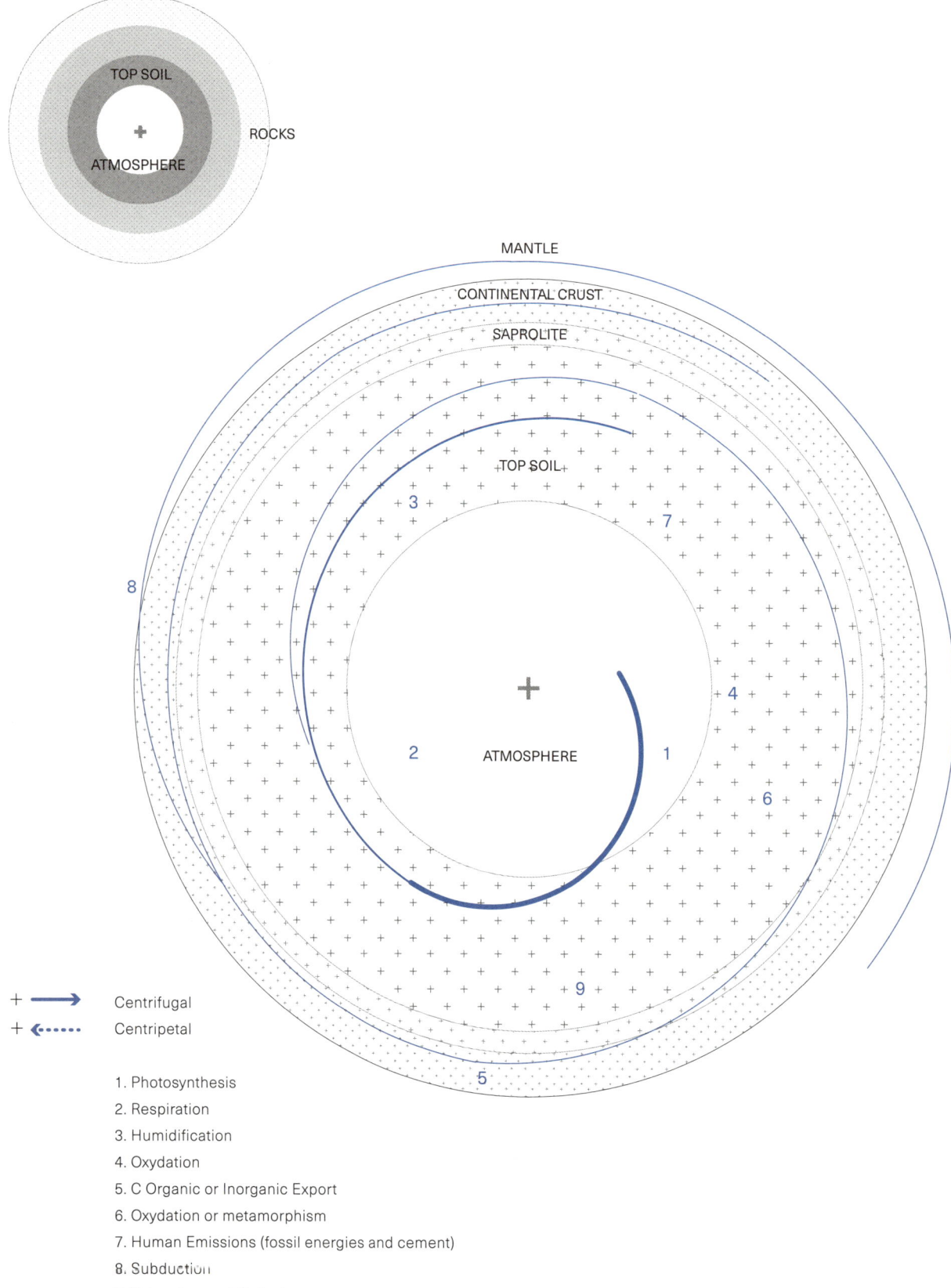

TOP SOIL

+

ROCKS

ATMOSPHERE

MANTLE

CONTINENTAL CRUST

SAPROLITE

TOP SOIL

ATMOSPHERE

+ → Centrifugal

+ ←····· Centripetal

1. Photosynthesis
2. Respiration
3. Humidification
4. Oxydation
5. C Organic or Inorganic Export
6. Oxydation or metamorphism
7. Human Emissions (fossil energies and cement)
8. Subduction
9. Volcanism and Plutonism

ALEXANDRA ARÈNES & BRUNO LATOUR

THE DOSSIER

The carbon cycle. The short-term carbon cycle created by photosynthesis and respiration processes is characterized by bigger fluxes than the subduction of carbon in the mantle. Note the importance of the anthropogenic flux associated with fossil fuels: from deep layers to the atmosphere, rapid injection, and big flux to the geological flux of carbon burial.

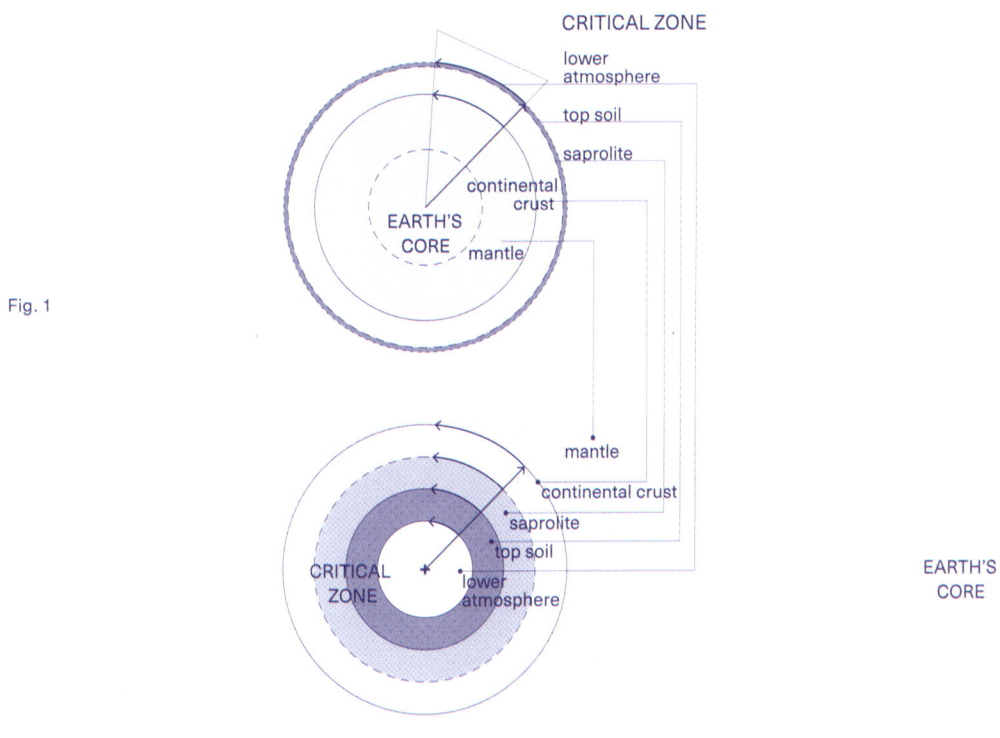

Fig. 1

Fig. 2

+ reference point (any observatory)

A new conceptual representation of the CZ. The different components of the CZ are deployed in nested circles around a reference point (of any CZO) in a circular plane. This operation is an anamorphosis that places the layers that are really critical for life on Earth in the center (Fig. 2) instead of being squashed as in the classical representation of Earth (Fig. 1).

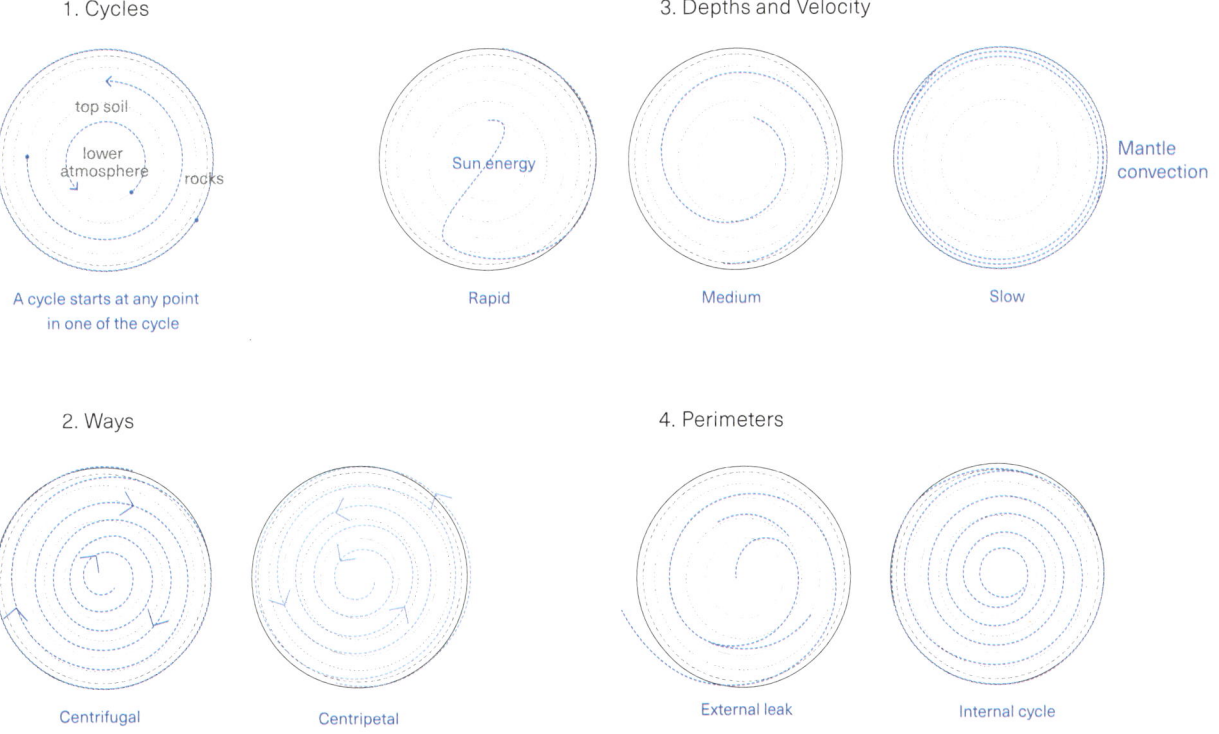

1. Cycles

A cycle starts at any point
in one of the cycle

3. Depths and Velocity

Rapid

Medium

Slow

2. Ways

Centrifugal

Centripetal

4. Perimeters

External leak

Internal cycle

Visual repertoire of mass and geochemical movements (processes) in the CZ in the new system of coordinates. The angle between the spiral's tangent and the radius of the nested circles indicates the velocity. A flat spiral indicates a slow movement and thus a long residence time in the reservoir. A centrifugal arrow means that the element's flux is directed from the atmosphere to the deepest CZ layers. A centripetal arrow means that the flux of the element is directed from the deep CZ to the atmosphere.

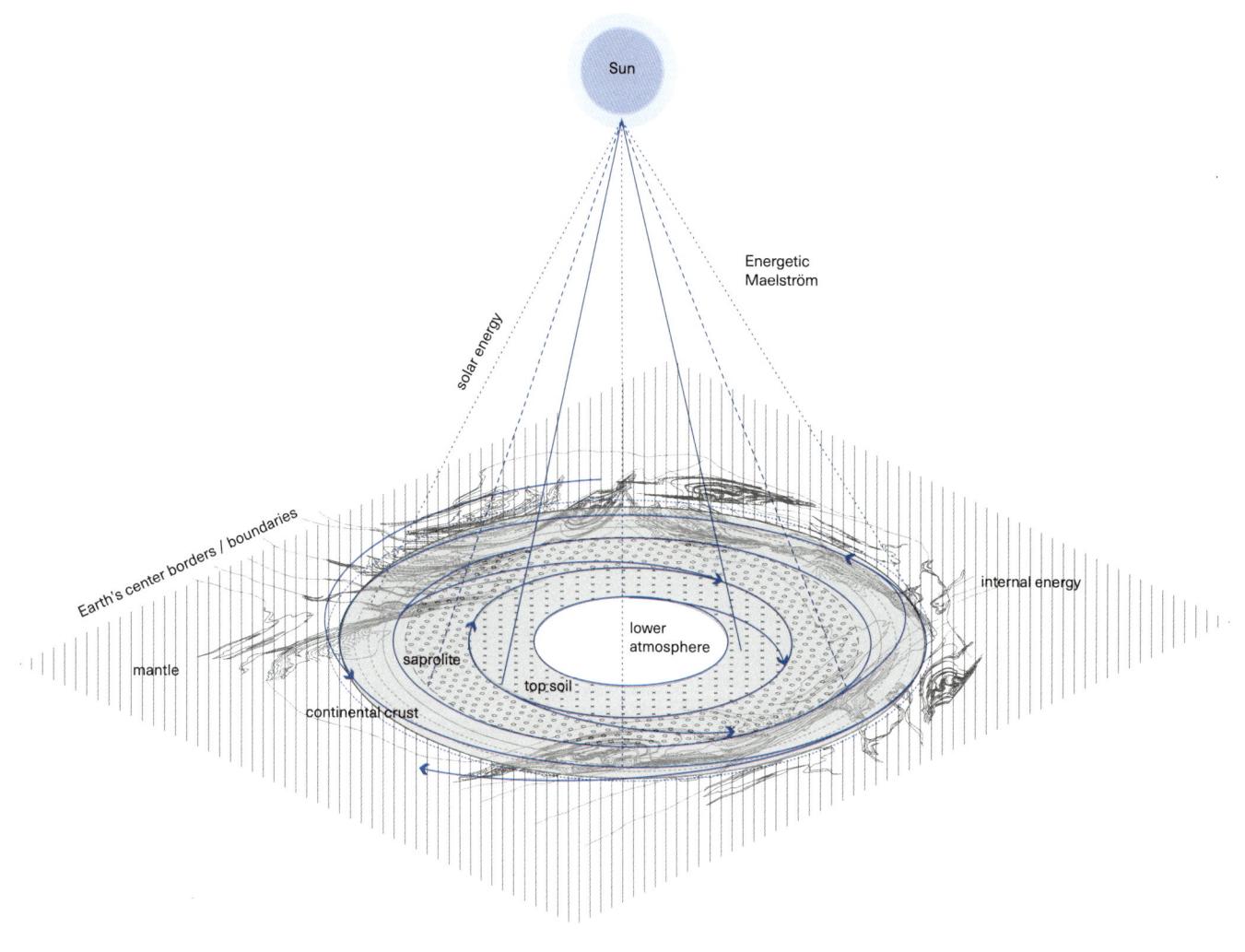

Axonometric view made to render visible not only the position of the sun in a cartographic view but also its role in a dynamic hydrological and geochemical perspective. This view shows that matter and elements are activated by a cosmo-tectonic circulation denoted here as the 'energetic maelström.' (Arènes, Latour, and Gaillardet. Giving Depth to the Surface: An Exercise in the Gaiagraphy of Critical Zones, in "The Anthropocene Review," Vol 5, Issue 2, 2018.)

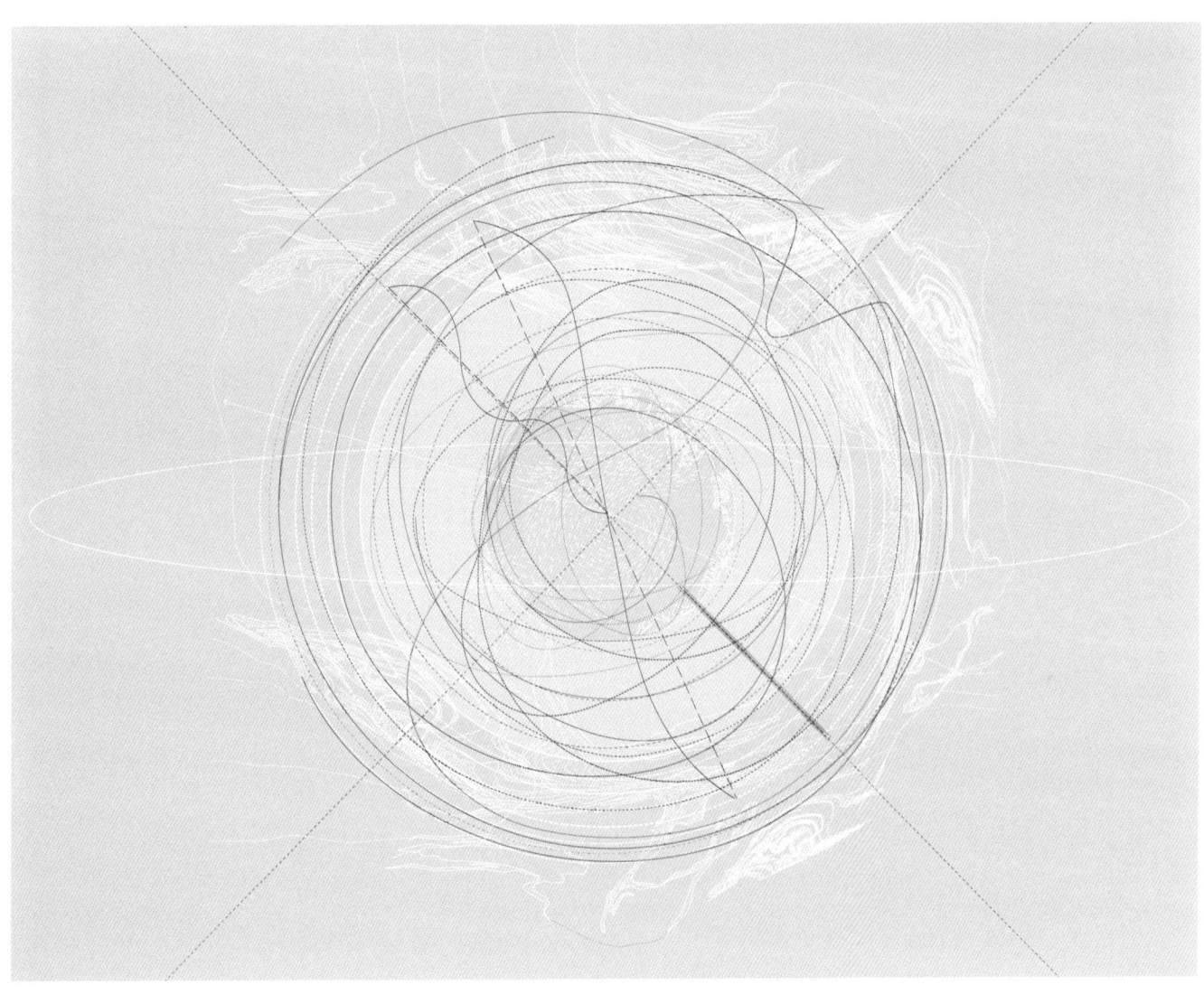

A new model of the Earth to visualize the dynamics of the CZ (biogeochemical cycles).

Layers of the soil, weathering process—CZO of the Strengbach in the Vosges forest.

Inside the RiverLab, a laboratory for fieldwork.

or wild landscapes that are sometimes uncontrollable. Paradoxically, these phenomena, at the surface, are much less explored and understood than galaxies or the Earth's nucleus. Therefore, these scientists are now studying the thin layer on the Earth's surface between rocks and canopy, the CZ where living beings interact and produce biogeochemical cycles. Geochemists do not consider life as an organism. They study it as traces among other abiotic agents in order to understand how the biogeochemical cycles that make the Earth turn—not around the sun, but around and in itself, under the combined action of the energetic sun and tectonic forces— are formed, regulated, or deregulated, balanced or unbalanced.

The scientists asked us apparently simple questions: how can we visualize the CZ? How can we experience it, feel it, estimate it, measure it, represent it? How can we move from the globe to the vision of the CZ, a planet full of life, more local, more complex, and more real? Our first intuition was to turn the seemingly infinite space of the globe upside down and

close it around us, to make our position in the CZ more realistic. The problem was also to give depth to the CZ, this thin layer in comparison to the immensity of the globe, an image that we all have in mind as the representation of planet Earth!

One of us solved this problem by making a fairly simple gesture, which scientists do not hesitate to sketch themselves. The gesture consists in turning the globe inside out like a glove to reverse the conventional order and size of the Earth's strata, by placing in the center of the diagram the atmosphere from which there is no escape and where cycles rotate rapidly. They then reconstitute the soils, the altered zones, and the earth's crust all around, in as many layers or envelopes, more or less porous, as there are geological times characterized by longer element cycles. The reconstructed interiority traps the atmosphere in its center (after all, the pollution clouds come back to us). The series of envelopes reconstitute the vertical strata of the CZ upside down: the soil, which has been thickened to better qualify and care for it; the altered

zone, where water and potentially life still circulate in deep fractures; and the crust, whose mass definitively encloses man's unlimited development potential.

The former space's infinity is nevertheless replaced by another kind of infinity: cycles, which constantly circulate between strata. The short timespan of chemical reactions are visible in the center, while the longer processes occur mainly in the periphery. This alternative topology of the terrestrial zone facilitates the visualization of these biogeochemical cycles that cross the Earth and determine its transformations; the map is thus 'cyclocentric.' The topology retains a 'false' circular geometry so that the second movement, the cycles, appears in the model. A new grammar for recording spiral cycles is proposed: direction, velocity, and angle in order to report on the circulation of the elements from one stratum to another. This grammar makes it possible to visualize the behaviour of the cycle to be studied, on a given site and at a given time, for example that of carbon.

Another location system is also suggested, abandoning the latitude-

"Inside"—lecture performance by Bruno Latour, staged by Frédérique Aït-Touati. Visuals & videos: Alexandra Arènes, Axelle Grégoire, and Sonia Levy. You can find the video on YouTube: INSIDE - Bruno Latour / Zone Critique (youtu.be/gzPROcd1MuE).

longitude system for a location in cycles: at what stage is this territory, in relation to its phosphorus cycle, at the moment when I am there? Which agents, identified by the chemical elements that they leave behind, disturb this cycle and thus shape this landscape in a particular way? It is this change in the cycle mapping system that is called "Gaiagraphy." The Gaia Hypothesis, elaborated by Lovelock and Margulis, argues that living beings generate or destroy their own living conditions and, ultimately, that it is their actions that terraform the Earth. It would therefore seem necessary to add to 'geography,' understood as an *a posteriori* reading of Earth's layers, 'Gaiagraphy,' understood as an interpretation of process-induced changes effective in real time.

It may be interesting to conclude our journey into the CZ and its specific earth science network with the scientists' varied reactions to this model as it was presented in conferences, discussed in workshops, or read in the Anthropocene Review. Some of them felt their work better represented ("we finally give importance to the surface layers on which I work

and push the deep layers towards the periphery"), others better oriented ("we know better where we are"), or reassured ("we no longer float in an infinite space as with the globe"). Others, on the other hand, felt claustrophobic ("but then we are locked in the CZ"), a feeling that was quickly mitigated by a proposal to visualize the infinite movement of cycles. Thus, for the first group, the important thing was to be able to define a new framework. For the second group, the most important aspect was to not lose the dynamics,

the 'cosmo-tectonic maelström,' i.e. the time scales and the speed of cycles, and especially the ruptures, introduced by human activities.

More work is required in order to escape the grip that the global vision of the Earth holds on our collective imagination. What this experience demonstrates is that it is productive for science as well as for the arts to have a geochemist, architect, and a philosopher joining forces to tackle the urgent question of representing the Earth.

We thank the OZCAR network for granting us access and warmly welcoming us to the CZO, particularly Jérôme Gaillardet and Marie-Claire Pierret.

BRUNO LATOUR is now an Emeritus Professor associated with the médialab and the program in political arts (SPEAP) of Sciences Po Paris. He has served as a two-year fellow at the *Zentrum für Kunst und Medien* (ZKM) since January 2018. He is also a professor at the *Hochschule für Gestaltung* (HfG) in Karlsruhe (Germany). He is a member of several academies and the recipient of six honorary doctorates. He received the Holberg Prize in 2013, written or edited more than twenty books, and published more than 150 articles. Bruno Latour is curating an exhibition on the CZ at the ZKM in Karlsruhe to open in 2020, with the participation of Alexandra Arènes.

ALEXANDRA ARÈNES is an architect and co-founder of SOC (*Société d'objets cartographiques*/s-o-c. fr), a research platform developing cartographic tools for arts and sciences. Since 2016, she has been collaborating with the IPGP (*Institut de Physique du Globe de Paris*) on the CZ project. She is now preparing a PhD at the University of Manchester on this subject. She co-authored the book "Terra Forma, manuel de cartographies potentielles" (B42, 2019).

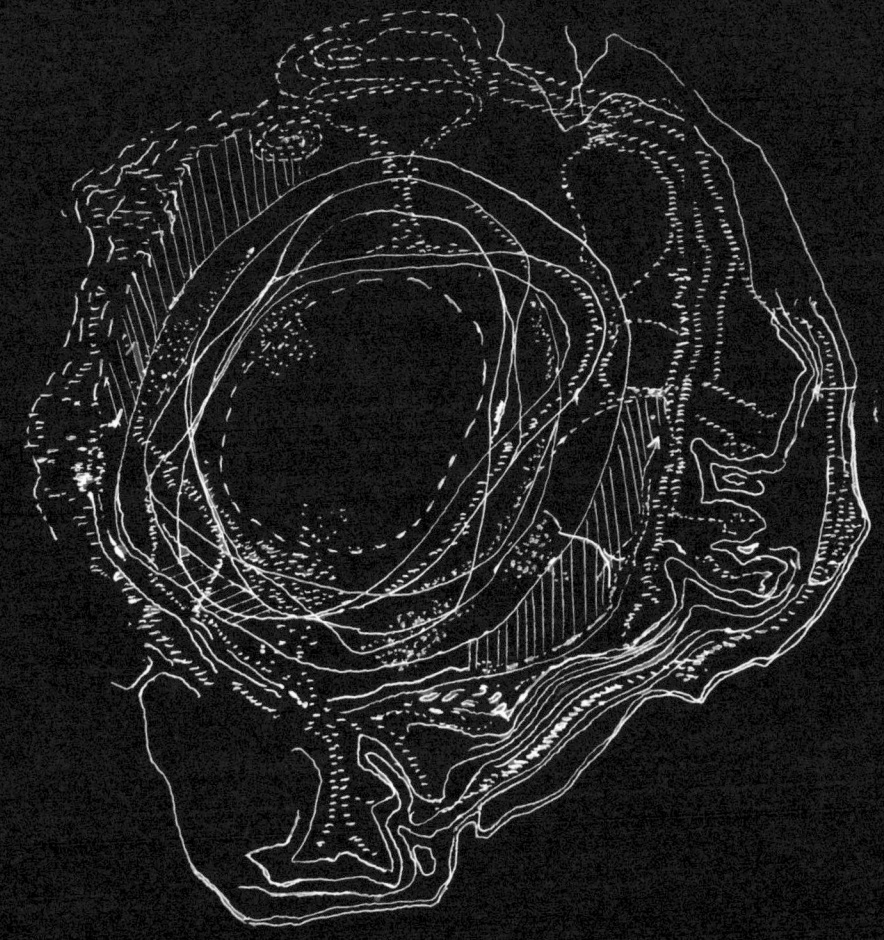

The terraformation of the Earth

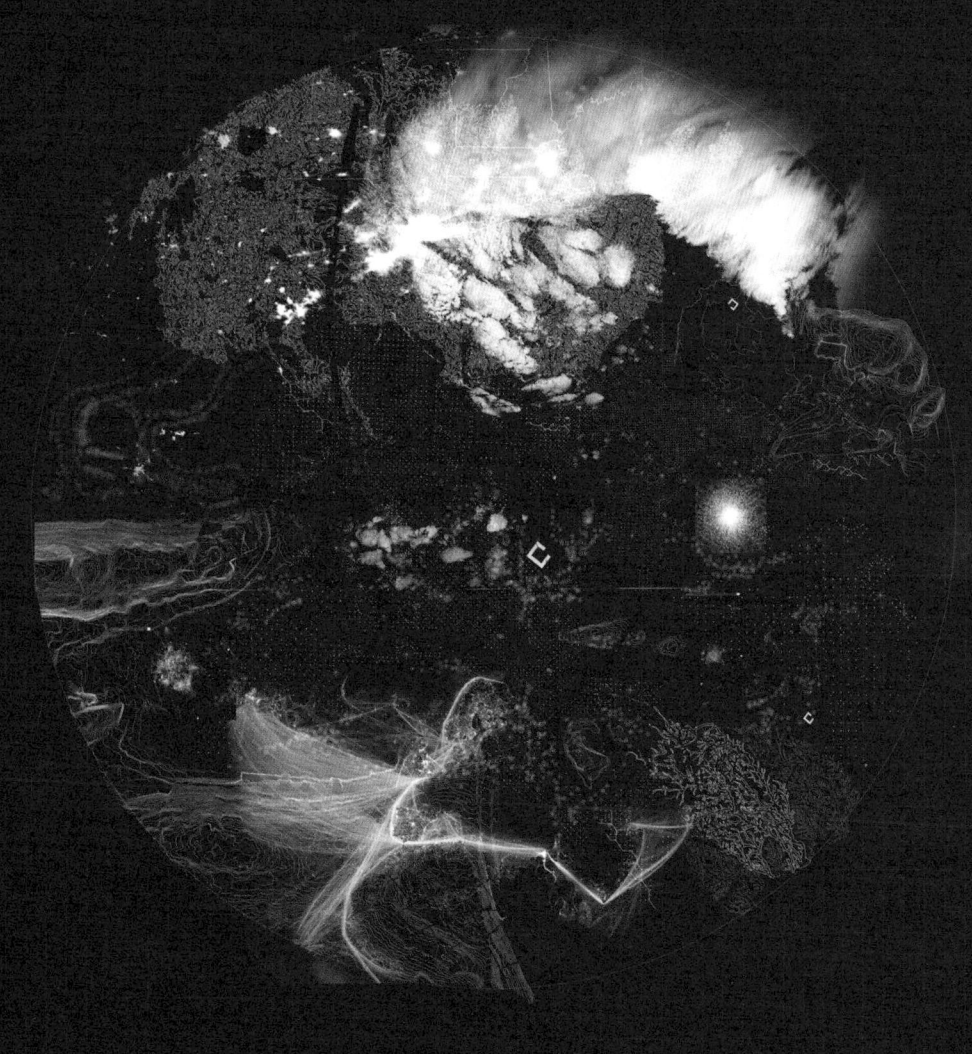

How can we have a better representation of Gaia from the inside of the Earth?

Wandering Through Affective Territories

**GIULIANA BRUNO IN CONVERSATION WITH
ADRIANA AMANTE AND ISABELLA MORETTI**

When Adriana Amante, a literary critic, translator, and academic, fleetingly met Giuliana Bruno in October 2018, she was eager to continue the conversation. We could not help but share in her excitement. In this interview, we interrogate Bruno's methods as we travel through her diverse fields of inquiry and narratives, focusing particularly on her way of resignifying cartography in a very singular manner. Her use of the concept 'tender' crosses such divergent territories as architecture, film, and art, allowing for a reading that transcends the conventional apprehension of the optic to become instead haptic and moving.

Wonder/Wander

ADRIANA AMANTE   In your research, different areas of knowledge converge into a very creative, personal, and playful, yet profound, approach. How do you construct your critical method, where architecture, film theory, cartography, visual studies, movement, and fashion meet?

GUILIANA BRUNO   My method is a process of movement: I move through different disciplines, diverse periods of time, and especially, across different artistic spaces. In the English language, there is a connection between the words 'wonder' and 'wander.' The relation between a sense of surprise, of pleasure, of wonder, and how that—in my mind—is connected to a sense of ambling about and wandering around territories is central to my approach. In particular, I have been interested in connecting the world of architecture to that of visual arts in relation to moving images. This is where I started an exploration of space intended in the largest possible sense. Architecture doesn't simply mean buildings; architecture means space, and the narrative of space is in some way a moving image as well. I am interested in connecting these terrains, wandering around and mapping their moving architectures.

Cartography has been an important part of my methods but from a new perspective, because cartography has often been seen as a disciplinary tool for ordering territories, a space of control. I wanted to change that view by looking at different kinds of performances of mapping, i.e. maps of pleasure, maps of desire, maps of love, maps of affects; a different kind of "cartographic imagination," let's say. This cartographic imagination does not function to regulate space, but rather provides guidance, in the same way a traveler would use a map to guide her in wandering through a city, and share the discoveries, the wonder, the surprise.

In "Atlas of Emotion,"[1] in particular, I used this method to create a cultural history of space that is not only physical but also mental, imaginative, and affective. When I wrote the book in 2002, it was the beginning of an exploration of this kind. In architecture school, where I have been teaching since 1990, the study of architecture was conventionally still focused on the analysis of buildings and structures that are static. Of course it's true that buildings do not move, but people do move through them. People appreciate architecture in motion, in encounters, in a montage of different spaces that are linked by the inhabitant of the space—the dweller as well as the visitor. I dislodge architecture from its static state and think of it in relation to movement and to the moving image. In order to mobilize the disciplinal territory, I had to move past interpretative models coming from semiotics and linguistics as well as narratives heavily based on the concept of the Lacanian gaze. This is an optical model that simply looks at moving images as visual configurations, products of the look, optical outcomes of culture. I wanted to change that. I wanted to put architecture in relation to film, not simply because film reproduces architecture—that's wonderful but somewhat literal—but also to go a step forward and claim that film itself creates a spatial language. And this language is not optic but haptic. It is an inhabited language of movement and montage; it's a language that does not produce optical fixation but haptical contact. Hapticity is a contact with the physical, yet through a virtual construct of a body moving through space.

Connecting architecture with visual arts through moving images has certainly allowed me to make a major shift from the optic to the haptic. The haptic is a navigation of space, a mapping of experience. People often think exclusively of the haptic as touch, which is certainly part of it because it comes through a sense of touch, but in Greek etymology, 'haptic' means "able to come into contact with."

Thus, it's part of a communicative experience in which a body is able to attract other bodies in space, and connect to them. My claim is that architectural space is such a form of contact: we don't just look at houses, we inhabit and experience them. To me, there is a fundamental relation between habit and habitation. One inhabits a space by way of habit. And habit is a tactile form of experience, it's being enveloped in space, and this is different from merely looking at it or contemplating it. Whilst looking at a film, the spectator is also inhabiting and being enveloped in the space of the moving image. Film enables you to constantly move across frames, through assemblages and montages, around atmospheres of tones and colors, and ultimately, through your imagination and frame of mind. Here, the movement is not only physical but also mental and emotional. In this sense, I emphasize that there is a relation between 'motion' and 'emotion.' In this transitive passage, we are 'moved.' An emotional 'transport' is a process that enacts a transformation.

Objects That Tell a Story

ADRIANA AMANTE You have a very particular way of entangling material things with their symbolical dimension and vice versa. I was thinking about your interest in travel literature, Louis Vuitton's devices for travelers, wallpapers in relation to travel, optical devices as dioramas, and the anatomical theater in regard to film; the conceptual span that goes from cartographic objects, such as the "Veduta di Venezia" by Jacopo de' Barbari, to the "Carte de Tendre" by Madeleine de Scudéry. You work amidst a literary dimension that feeds your critical approach. Or, to put it differently, you have a narrative drive that allows you to read objects, which are not narrative *per se*, in those terms. The way you entangle the objects of study with your writing makes me suspect that you are often left at the threshold of fiction or critical fiction. Have you ever thought about writing fiction?

GIULIANA BRUNO [Laughs] It is truly so. Thank you very much for this reading of my way of thinking. You're completely correct in deciphering my imaginative, even narrative desire to move creatively from the visual to the haptic by reconsidering objects of material culture in my analysis. I think of the images of these materials not just as optical but as having a body, a proper consistency, as in any space of materiality. Since "Atlas of Emotion," but especially in my latest book "Surface: Matters of Aesthetic, Materiality, and Media,"[2] I went in search of objects that could, in a sense, tell a story. I do believe that objects contain on their surfaces narrative layers that accrue in the voyage they take as they circulate. So, their stories are told in traveling through space. In "Atlas of Emotion," it was particularly objects of travel that fascinated me because I thought they could tell the history of the way space itself had been mobilized in modernity. As you mentioned, Louis Vuitton's devices were a fantastic discovery. I went to Paris to their archive to search for the way space had been 'fashioned'—I use fashion in the sense that, to me, space is a cultural 'fabric' that is fabricated, it is both dressed and addressed. I encountered fantastic objects that told the history of mobilization in modernity so well, for example, the traveling desk—what a great idea! Mostly women used them, and by looking at this object, I could not only tell the story of travel but also the story of the way in which women, who had been considered enclosed in domesticity, were in fact moving a lot through space and writing at the same time. These incredible accoutrements of travel allowed them to write their stories—I'd love to have a traveling desk! Now, we have the computer, of course, which performs as a traveling desk. The laptop and all these devices into which we tell our stories and exchange images travel with us as objects of dwelling, as movable furniture, and even as architecture in motion. Looking at portable objects such as luggage and their usage tells a history of travel that is most revealing. I discovered that Nellie Bly (Elizabeth Cochrane Seaman), for example, was the first female journalist to tour the world—only in 72 days!—and she only carried a little compact bag with everything in it.

The other object you mentioned, "Veduta di Venezia," is one of the first imaginative views. It takes on the entire scope of the city in just one picture. But it is actually not one view at all, it was made as a montage, as a series of images, of 'shots.' In a sense, this map is almost like one of the first films because, even though it was made in 1500, it anticipated a way of thinking of space that is sequential. It is in this sense that I see images as having a materiality, which can be read on their surfaces, because they are material forms of cultural transport. This is important, and it's further discussed in "Surface…" By the time I wrote about surfaces, thinking about materiality had become even more pressing because the digital had made tremendous changes in our culture. My desire to interrogate material objects gained relevancy for many people who were debating "the loss of materiality." To me, the thought of the virtual replacing materiality did not make sense—we've been living in a virtual-material world

"Cartography has been an important part of my methods but from a new perspective, because cartography has often been seen as a disciplinary tool for ordering territories, a space of control. I wanted to change that view by looking at different kinds of performances of mapping, i.e. maps of pleasure, maps of desire, maps of love, maps of affects; a different kind of 'cartographic imagination,' let's say."

ever since cinema was invented over a hundred years ago. Instead of looking nostalgically at materiality as the loss of physicality, I'd rather reimagine it as a form of resistance in which the way of relating to the material world is reinvented. As I looked around, I realized that many artists and architects, as well as other thinkers, were producing creative constructions along these lines—there was a sort of elective affinity around materiality that I saw especially as I walked in and out of art galleries. I've always been interested in the skin of things, of objects that retain their stories on the surface, and many artists share this concern. They seem to be really interested in the texture of the material, in the material condition of their mediums, like the canvas itself, and especially in the superficial imprint of different histories. Architects, as well, are reinventing the skin of the building, the face of the façade, and refiguring the interior walls as mobile partitions, as if they were screens. These new textures, or rather 'architextures,' are not just ornamental but structural—especially the surface of the screen, of course! We are surrounded by surfaces, by objects of material culture like screens that are now not only inhabiting our quotidian space but even structuring our daily lives. Screens have become the material condition of our existence.

This is why it seemed important to write a history of the screen: a surface that seems invisible but is very substantial. People often talk about the images projected on it, they talk about the film, they talk about what goes through it, but what about the screen *per se*? Interrogating it as a material object, in "Surface…," I discovered that the screen is in fact born early on in architecture. The term screen was used way before cinema or even pre-cinematic objects were invented. It appeared during the early Renaissance, and its Germanic root became part of many languages: screen in English, *écran* in French, or *schermo* in Italian. Interestingly, it designated an architectural object, consisting of a frame and, inside, a translucent material, it could be paper, tissue, or fabric. This framed surface was either put on windows to filter out the light or in the middle of the room to separate public from private space. Through this investigation of the screen, then, I was able to strengthen the link between architecture and moving images. This particular object creates an ambiance, an atmosphere, a filtering not simply of light but also of social space, of personal space. It can create a space of 'public intimacy.'

Last but not least, and in response to your question, yes, it is narrative theory in some way! I take pleasure in writing, in telling a story through the flow and the texture of the language. It's not something all academics do. The wonderful academics who write very studious books often use a language that is scientific and demonstrative. I go into wandering explorations instead, and I try to empathize with both the material of my study and with the reader through the narrative. Through the material experience of writing, of weaving a story, you can get a sense of how objects of study create a culture. Therefore, I don't try to collapse a theory onto the narrative, instead, I try to make it emerge out of this process of close contact and interweaving. It was not always easy for me, an Italian moving to the United States, not only because English is not my first language, but also because it's not something that the Anglo-American academia does naturally. People often expect to know precisely what you are going to talk about, and I attempt to lead the reader through the pleasure of the voyage, weaving into the narrative the subject of discovery.

Weaving a Narrative

ADRIANA AMANTE

The pleasure you take in writing is evident as you span from wonder to wander, and vice versa, in an exploration that is coherent with your research methods. Your books are a showcase of how academic writing can be informed by aesthetic value and beauty without losing its depth and rigor. Through the weave, a ludic and sometimes arbitrary, yet grounded, writing, you create original objects and resources—it was a novel approach when, in 2002, you decided to release architecture from its static condition. While overviewing your *oeuvre*, I have the feeling that every book leaves you at the steps of the next. Is that an expression of the narrative drive as well, the plot, or as we say in Spanish *trama*, between one book and the next?

GUILIANA BRUNO

There is indeed a narrative connection between the books as a kind of intersecting cultural voyage. Each one of them makes a distinct contribution, but they are linked in subtle ways. It's actually complicated because the exploration takes me to different places, and I have to go all over the map, so to speak, and navigate the connections—when the weave between the different objects works, I know that a book is happening. Then, there's a moment when the book ends, and something else happens and begins again. So, for me, all of these investigations have led me to the next narrative. When I finished "Atlas of Emotion" in 2002, I looked up and observed what was happening around the world, and my own internal desire pushed me to continue that exploration of hapticity in "Public Intimacy: Architecture and the Visual Arts."[3] It is like a drive; you can't stop it. In "Surface…," I continued to expand my horizon in light of what was taking place in contemporary visual culture and art, in their visual fabrics. There is a *trama*, like you're saying. There is no perfect English translation of such a beautiful word, you could say 'weave,' but *trama* in Spanish, as well as in Italian, means weave and narrative at the same time. It's an important term for me, and it's actually at the center of my work. My next book of theoretical interweaving will deal with questions about the texture of ambiance and will focus on the atmosphere of projection. The fiction or imaginative space of projection is very present in contemporary culture, just think of how artists are reinventing it today in the art gallery and the museum. But projection is a pre-cinematic concept that comes from

Ph. Mariam Samur

The "Carte de Tendre" was designed by Madeleine de Scudéry and first engraved by François Chauveau in 1654. Source: Giuliana Bruno, "Atlas of Emotion", p. 168. Ph. Ness Magazine.

very ancient studies of alchemy as well as from psychoanalysis, perspective, and architecture. At the moment, I'm in the middle of weaving together this history of 'the projective imagination' with an 'atmospheric thinking.' I often ask myself: how am I going to do this?

My first book[4] was already set to 'street-walk' through apparently disparate terrains, and already set to explore a 'public intimacy.' It was a book on the culture of modernity and on cinema as one of its public spaces and urban agents. It was especially devoted to the city that I'm from, Naples, in Italy, but seen through the eyes of a pioneer woman filmmaker, who had made over sixty feature films and over a hundred documentaries between 1906 and 1930. Elvira Notari has been completely exiled from history. Afterwards, many people assumed I'd stay in that territory, that I would always talk about woman or about modernity. I had also published an essay on "Blade Runner"[5]—at the time nobody cared about the film—and postmodernism. Many considered these distinct territories and thought I had to choose my turf. But it always seemed natural to me to go from one to the other because, in "Blade Runner," I was specifically thinking about the ruins of modernity. That film expressed something that was extraordinarily important for contemporary public culture, which is the accelerated decrepitude of our ever increasing technological worlds. Cultural history has always been important to me as an interwoven story.

To Claim the Space of Affect

ISABELLA MORETTI

As you've mentioned, you incorporate women or female activities in your way of history making and weaving things together. Weaving, at the same time, can also be thought of as something accounted as feminine. In that sense, going back to fiction and cartography, we are very interested in how you've constructed 'tender mapping' as a category in itself. How did feminist theory help construct your ideas on cartography, particularly the role of women in geography and geographical representations?

GUILIANA BRUNO

This is something that is important to me and constitutes another 'thread.' I grew up in an era when feminist theory in particular was changing the outlook on culture and politics. It's very much a part of my upbringing, and partly, the skeleton of my thinking. What's interesting to me is not so much the woman as an object of study but what you are saying—to create a method that speaks of the feminine as a form of exploration. It's more complex than just writing about women; it's about extracting from history concepts like 'tender mapping' or 'public intimacy,' or 'surface materiality,' or more specifically 'weave,' or 'thread,' in order to imagine worlds that represent a different outlook on it: a feminine outlook, and sometimes a polemic one. For example, I wanted to recover 'the picturesque,' which has always been considered a feminine aesthetic because it's about gardens and affects. I wanted to reclaim the space of affect in cartography in order to move past the cognitive interpretation. Tenderness and emotion are very much a part of the way we perceive, create, and know the world as well. Today, in neuroscience, Antonio Damasio talks about 'the feeling brain.'[6] It has taken this long to acknowledge something that women have known forever! Moreover, people usually discuss mapping as a form of discipline and domination or as a cognitive instrument, and a lot of writing has gone towards the fear of getting lost under the prompt "let's try to control this territory." All of our contemporary devices are used mainly to assure directions and orientations instead of explorations. I wanted to break that, and, in the face of technology, I believe even more strongly about affirming tender mapping.

It is an alternative history of cartography; I said to myself, there has to be another way that the world is being threaded together, mapped, and imagined. In fact, it was the discovery of a particular map by Madeleine de Scudéry that led me to write the whole book "Atlas of Emotion." I came across this fantastic map that was completely the opposite of the regimented maps. It is called "Carte de Tendre," the map of the Land of Tenderness, and it was drawn in 1654. Scudéry was a writer, who had her 'salon' in Paris, and in one of her novels, "Clélie, histoire romaine," a female character draws this map to describe the path to her heart. The map is an incredible act of imagination; how do you describe something invisible like affect? Most interestingly, she did it through the representation of architecture, landscape, and the body. This map of affect is 'tender' in philosophical ways, it's subtle and nimble. An important feature is that it has no frame. Usually maps are contained, but in this case, everything flows outside the corners—there's an off-screen space. A sea, a landscape, little villages, and little people contemplating compose this image that is truly intended to be a voyage, understood only through the motion from one place to the next. Each emotion is architecturally designed. For example, Pride is a village on top of a mountain you sit on—that is exactly how you feel when you're proud! As you travel from one emotion to the next, the map exhibits tender movement, meaning a cognitive and affective transformation. There is only, interesting enough, one enclosed space: The Lake of Indifference. The only place where you don't move because when you're indifferent nothing can ever change; you cannot change and the world cannot change. In 1654, this woman did something that I think is very profound. At the moment of taking an even closer look, I realized that the map actually looks like the interior of a woman's body, the fallopian tubes in the uterus. The map became the site of a methodological shift towards an alternative and feminine way of imagining the world. The architecture, the body, and the movements were inscribed in this very fascinating form of borderless cartographical thought.

In thinking about how space is mapped, I am also concerned with location, both physical and cultural. In my first book, when I wrote about the city of Naples through the eyes of this pioneer woman filmmaker, I emphasized that Elvira Notari shot on location early on. In the history of cinema, 'Neorealism' or Post-World War Cinema are regarded as the first genres that used the real city. Most films shot in Hollywood were done in a set—you think you're looking at New York, but actually you're inside a studio in Los Angeles. But, starting in 1906, this Italian filmmaker went into the streets and showed the reality of urban life, and made sixty films on-site. Recovering from this particular event was not just about filling the gaps of the history of cinema, but rather about discovering a different look on the city itself, a different representation of mapping a place.

"I look at different cultural or artistic objects and their surfaces as threads, as weaves, as imaginative forms of thought and touch. After all, the original surface is our skin. It's not through the eye that we encounter ourselves and the surrounding world. Even back in the eighteenth century the philosopher Condillac understood that space is apprehended through the sense of touch."

So there is a thread, almost a fictional thread, of tender mapping that connects "Streetwalking on a Ruined Map," "Atlas of Emotion," "Public Intimacy," and "Surface…" In the last book, the tender aspect is in fact in the exploration of surface. I am attracted to surface because this is the most tender of materials. It is even arguable that, in some way, the skin, the tactile, and the approach to surface, texture, and hapticity could be associated with a feminine aesthetics or mode of narration. If this is the case it is because I look at different cultural or artistic objects and their surfaces as threads, as weaves, as imaginative forms of thought and touch. After all, the original surface is our skin. It's not through the eye that we encounter ourselves and the surrounding world. Even back in the eighteenth century, the philosopher Condillac understood that space is apprehended through the sense of touch. The skin is an epidermic place of transit: it's a porous membrane and the permeable envelope that connects the interior of the body to the outside. From there, in the book, I move to the surface of fashion, the second warp. The clothes that envelop us, the weave, the textile threads that are the way we present ourselves to the world, configure a personal and social identity. Very often fashion is disregarded as an object of scholarly study or is categorically determined as exclusively a women's matter. Of course none of that is true. I, however, am interested in dressing the surface or clothing the image, on the one hand, and in reinterpreting the surface itself as a form of dress, on the other. In pursuing this 'superficial' methodology, I move from skin to fashion to the textural aspect of architectural spaces and, finally, to artistic surfaces. I want to show that there is nothing superficial about such surfaces. As I was saying, contemporary artists and architects are interested in rethinking the surface, the material forms of their mediums, threading and weaving together wall, canvas, and screen. This is a way to reimagine a new aesthetic that would not simply focus on the object but also reaffirm a tender method of 'surface materiality.'

ADRIANA AMANTE   It was definitely a pleasure to talk to you and to experience first-hand your passion and ability to connect and move vigorously through territories. In the closing comment you just made, you came back to something that is the basis of your methodical thinking: through third person narrative, you turn a fact, a biography, or an image, into a story that is as much a first person narrative as well. That incisive story, told in movement and thought geographically, takes your readers from the world around you to your internal world via the body. In the end, it is your passion and impulse that structure your critical theory. We are very grateful.

GUILIANA BRUNO   In "The Arcades Project," Walter Benjamin recovers this quote by a madman: "I travel in order to get to know my geography." That is very true. Very often the presumption of critical distance in academia is overrated; as if an objective way to detach yourself from the way you think or live really exists. I always believed that Michel Foucault was right: the best thing you can do is to announce the position from which you speak. Everyone speaks from a position, from a viewpoint, and our eyes are placed in our bodies. To me, this is important because the position from which I speak is an exploration, a geography of discovery that is very personal in many ways. It never ceases to be a discovery of the object, but I also learn a lot about myself and my own desires in the journey. It's wonderful when I feel that it comes through in the books. I thank you deeply for these wonderful comments.

From December 2017 to June 2018, "Carta Bianca Imaginaire" was on view at the Museo di Capodimonte in Naples. For this exhibition, Giuliana Bruno explored the dungeon of the museum in order to unveil lesser-known, forgotten, or crafted works and offer them to the public eye. As she mentions, "I scoured the museum's deposits as if they were geological strata, or strata of time, moving like an archaeologist, careful to find mysterious works, worn down by time, ruined, or even broken." These works conceive a *trama*—various narratives that recover the memories of the museum and the city, awaiting to be recollected by the visitor.
On this page: Installation view "Carta Bianca Imaginaire;" ruined painterly surfaces and empty frames, mounted on metal grids used in museum storage. Ph. Luciano Romano. On page 100: Installation view "Carta Bianca Imaginaire;" left: Gian Domenico Valentino, "Interno di cucina", ca. 1680, oil on canvas, 48 x 64,5 cm; back: Giovan Battista Recco, "Natura morta con testa di caprine", ca. 1640-50, oil on canvas, 132 x 183 cm; front: Royal Manufacture of Berlin, "Servito da tavola", ca. 1860-1870, painted porcelain with gold, and Royal Manufacture of Porcelain of Capodimonte, Fragments of Pottery, 1743-1759, porcelain. Ph. Luciano Romano.

1   Bruno, Giuliana. "Atlas of Emotion: Journeys in Art, Architecture, and Film". New York: Verso Books, 2002, reprint 2018.
2   Bruno, Giuliana. "Surface: Matters of Aesthetic, Materiality, and Media". Chicago/London: The University of Chicago Press, 2014.
3   Bruno, Giuliana, "Public Intimacy: Architecture and the Visual Arts." Cambridge, MA: MIT Press, 2007.
4   Bruno, Giuliana. "Streetwalking on a Ruined Map: Cultural Theory and the City Films of Elvira Notari." Princeton, N.J: Princeton University Press, 1993.
5   See Bruno, Giuliana. Ramble City: Postmodernism and Blade Runner. In "October," 41, 1987, pp. 61-74.
6   Antonio Damasio is a Portuguese-American neuroscientist. His books include "The Feeling of What Happens: Body and Emotion in the Making of Consciousness" (Harcourt Brace & Co., 1999), "Looking for Spinoza: Joy, Sorrow, and the Feeling Brain" (Harcourt Brace & Co., 2003), "Self Comes to Mind: Constructing the Conscious Brain" (Pantheon, 2010), and the recently published "The Strange Order of Things: Life, Feeling, and the Making of Cultures" (Pantheon, 2018).

GIULIANA BRUNO is the Emmet Blakeney Gleason Professor of Visual and Environmental Studies at Harvard University. She is internationally known for her research on the intersections of the visual arts, architecture, film, and media. Her books include "Surface: Matters of Aesthetics, Materiality, and Media" (University of Chicago Press, 2014), "Atlas of Emotion: Journeys in Art, Architecture, and Film" (Verso, 2002), which won the 2003 Kraszna-Krausz Book Award in Culture and History, "Public Intimacy: Architecture and the Visual Arts" (MIT Press, 2007), and "Streetwalking on a Ruined Map" (Princeton University Press, 1993). Her work has been translated into a dozen languages and she lectures at universities and museums internationally.

Walls of air. A Brazilian Pavilion

GABRIEL KOZLOWSKI, LAURA GONZÁLEZ FIERRO, MARCELO MAIA ROSA, AND SOL CAMACHO / CURATORS

The concept and title for the exhibition that represented Brazil at the 2018 Architecture Exhibition La Biennale di Venezia, was conceived as a response to the theme of "Freespace" proposed by curators Yvonne Farrell and Shelley McNamara in order to provoke questions about: 1. the different sorts of walls that construct, on multiple scales, the Brazilian territory; 2. the borders of architecture itself in relation to other disciplines. Therefore, a reflection began on how much Brazilian architecture and its urban developments are, in fact, free. Without the ambition of reaching an answer, but hoping to open the conversation to a large and diverse public, the curatorial team chose to shed light on processes that often go unnoticed due to their nature or scale. The immaterial barriers built between people or neighborhoods and the processes of urbanization in Brazil on a continental scale are examples of questions that were considered.

COMMISSIONER: João Carlos de Figueiredo Ferraz. *Fundação Bienal de São Paulo* / ORGANIZER: *Fundação Bienal de São Paulo* / With the support of Ministry of Foreign Affairs, Embassy of Brazil in Rome Ministry of Culture, Funarte / CARTOGRAPHIES TEAM: Gabriel Kozlowski, Laura González Fierro, Marcelo Maia Rosa, Sol Camacho / COLLABORATORS: Gabriel Duarte, Bárbara Graeff, Chiara Scotoni, Haydar Baydoun, Heloisa Escudeiro, Olivia Serra, Miguel Darcy, Manoela Pessoa, and Rafael Marengoni, MAPS 01-10. Marc Angélil, Rainer Hehl, Patricia Lucena Ventura, *Rede Cidade e Moradia*, and Cota 760, MAP 08. *Equipe Escola da Cidade:* Pedro Vada (coordinator), Newton Massafumi, Pedro M. R. Sales, Beatriz Dias, Bruna Marchiori, Giulia Ribeiro, Isabela Moraes, Karime Zaher, Marilia Serra, Mateus Loschi, Pedro H Norberto, MAPS 09-10. Quapá – FAU USP, MAP 09. Cripta Djan, MAP 10.

Walls of Air - *Fundação Bienal São Paulo* - Ph. Imagen Subliminal

To research each of these approaches—and achieve the goal of involving a larger and more diverse team in the process of constructing the exhibition—a multidisciplinary board was set and various outstanding agents and professionals from different fields were invited to participate: filmmakers, historians, real estate developers, activists, artists, businesspeople, geographers, anthropologists, physicians, public managers, mathematicians, lawyers, data scientists and *pixadores* (activists who use walls as spaces of controntation).

With one representative per theme, the multidisciplinary board was tasked with guiding the team throughout the research and pointing out sources and paths for the use of data and the development of ideas. In parallel with this, the curatorial team probed the national scene in search of researchers and professionals with works relevant to these ten approaches, and invited more than twenty specialists to write essays exploring each of them more in-depth. From Brazil's North to South, this group of people produced essays that reveal the countless ways of understanding the walls that shape the country, thus reflecting on the meaning of "Freespace." In addition to the consultation and exchange with these professionals, the project included organized work dynamics involving more than sixty immigrants, a workshop with master's students from the School of Architecture and Planning of Massachusetts Institute of Technology (MIT) and, above all, the rigorous data mining carried out by a team of young architects based in São Paulo, Rio de Janeiro, New York, and Boston, who dedicated themselves exclusively to lending consistency and precision to the research. The result of this complex constellation of people, who worked for six months, was presented at the Brazilian Pavilion in the form of ten large-scale cartographic drawings. Measuring three by three meters each, they were created specifically for the exhibition, and provided a detailed cartography of the ten approaches that seem relevant for the team in the practice of those responsible for constructing the physical environment, whether they are architects or not.

Ten scales; ten approaches; ten ways of understanding architecture and relating it with other disciplines.

The choice of a cartographic language to present this research was one of the most emphatic decisions of the exhibition design. It was made in part with the aim of escaping from traditional exhibition models, saturated by realistic images (photographs, renderings, etc.). On the other hand, it also aimed at combining the use of drawing—the architect's main tool to represent space—with advanced geo-referencing tools.

The large-scale format of the panels refers to the immeasurable extension of the Brazilian territory, the fifth largest country in the world, and sheds light on the hundreds of layers that the research reveals. They are narratives within narratives. At the same time that they offer new ways of understanding the information presented: the drawings also bear a carefully articulated aesthetic which, in a certain way, refers to the idea of painting and a relationship with the world of the visual arts, impossible to ignore in the context of La Biennale.

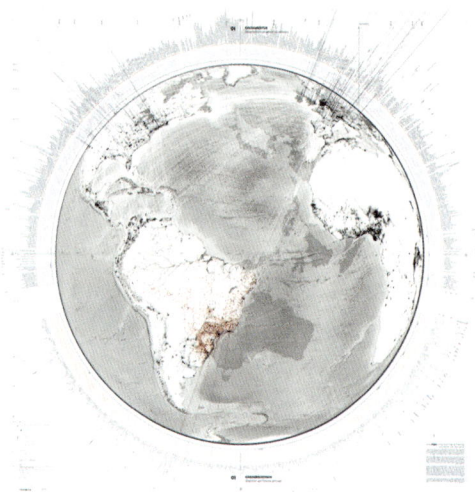

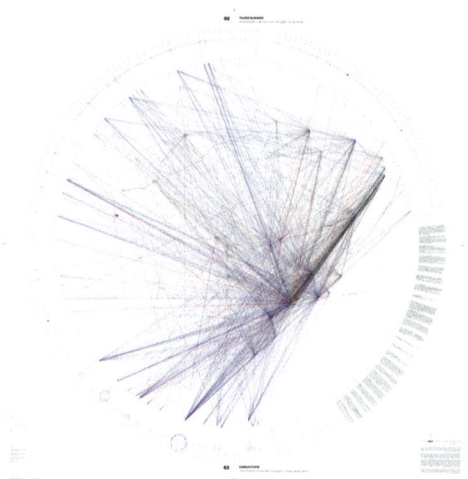

01 / Crossbreedings: Brazilian Architects Abroad

How frank is the exchange of Brazilian architects with the world?

Beginning at the global scale, data was gathered on Brazilian architects who study or work abroad to get a better look at this expanded territory of contemporary architectural practice; an understanding of the foreign influences and exchanges that are continuously modifying local practice was sought.

02 / Human Flows: the Dilution of Barriers through Cultural Assimilation

How open is Brazil to the reception of immigrants?

Contemporary movements of immigration, the search for refuge, and the internal migration in Brazil were mapped in order to spark a conversation about the country's permeability to these global dynamics.

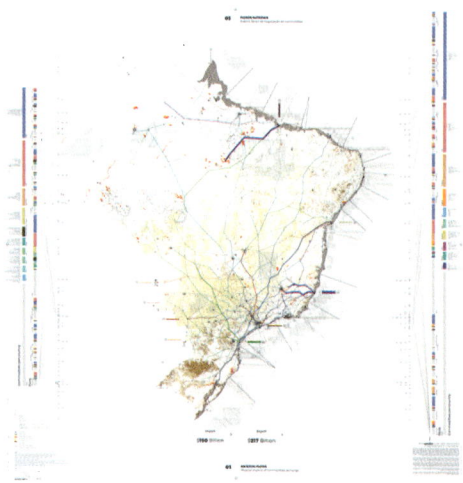

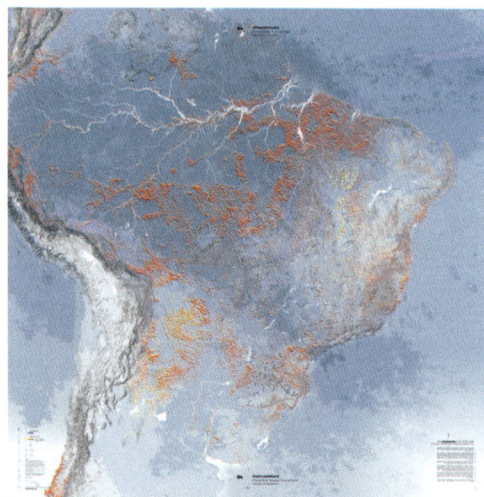

03 / Material Flows: Physical Imprint of Commodities Exchange

How sensitive is the urban environment to the movement of commodities?

Besides the flow of people, an understanding of the movement of commodities was sought, analyzing the link between the country's large infrastructures, the production and transportation of commodities, as well as the scars that these flows leave on the territory.

04 / Fluid Landscape: Encounter Between Human and Natural Ecosystems

How unregulated is the relationship between human and natural ecosystems?

To explore the relationship between the human and natural ecosystems, a parallel was traced between natural elements of the landscape—like the geographic conformation of Latin America, the humidity of the atmosphere, and the movement of the winds—and the impacts of the country's urbanization in order to encourage architects and urbanists to seek a holistic understanding of the place in which they operate.

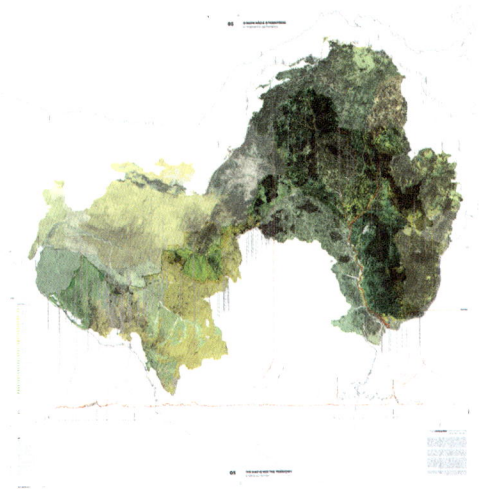

05 / The Map is not the Territory: a Retraced Border

How unimpeded is access to the Brazilian border?

Brazil's immense political borders were 'redrawn,' relating them to the possibilities of access and to the biomes that cut through them, in order to show the difficulty of reaching—or even understanding—them with precision.

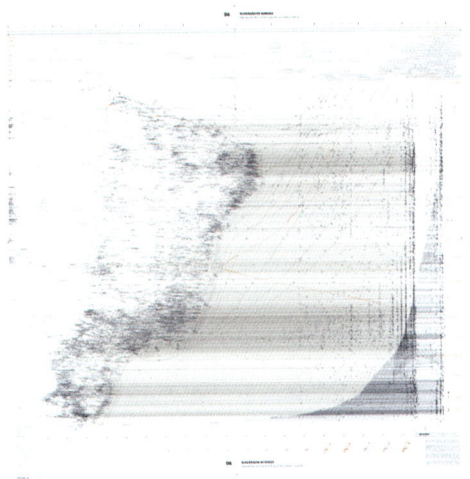

06 / Succession of Edges: Narratives on the Building of an Urban Country

How detached from a cohesive vision of Brazil has the urban formation of the country been?

The location and foundation dates of the 5,570 Brazilian cities were researched, underscoring the continuous process of the construction of an almost entirely urban country.

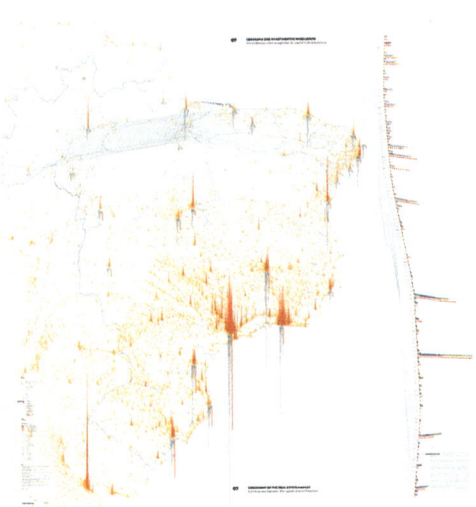

07 / Geography of the Real Estate Market: Controversies between the Agenda of Capital and that of Architecture

How unobstructed is the agenda of the real estate market against that of architecture?

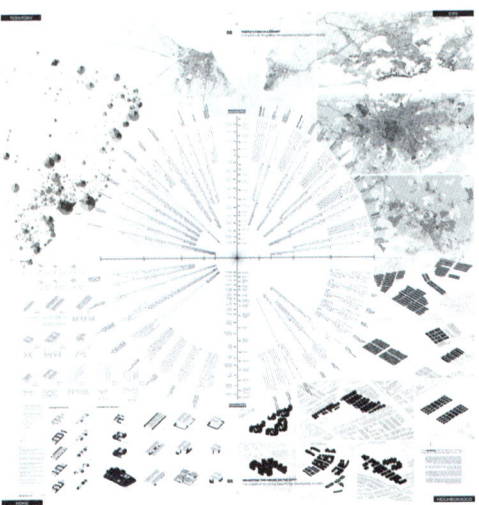

08 / Inhabiting the House or the City? The Impact of the *Minha Casa Minha Vida* housing program

How generous are the Brazilian housing programs in offering the right to the city?

The main dynamics responsible for the configuration of the above-mentioned cities were analyzed, showing the vast machine of the Brazilian real estate market and the intense impact of the *Minha Casa Minha Vida* (My House My Life) housing program, the initiative that built the largest number of low-income dwellings in the country.

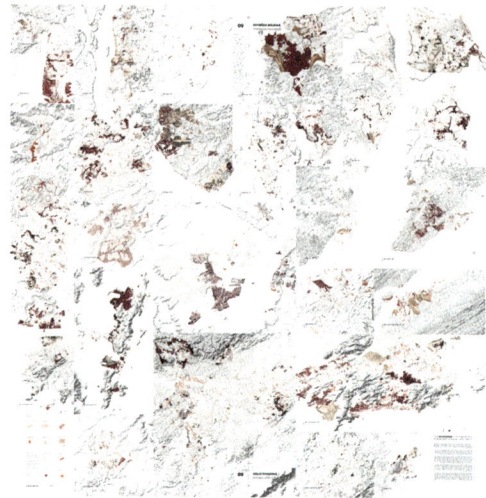

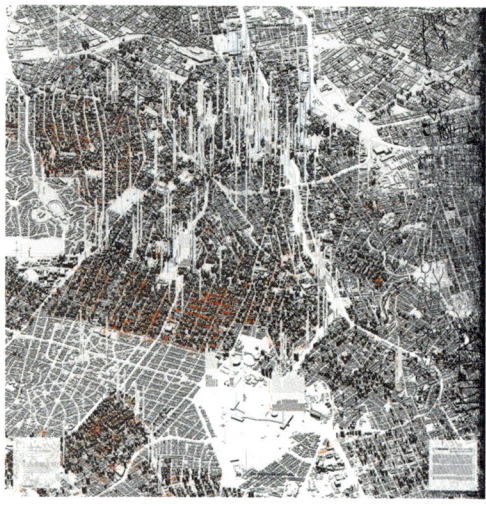

09 / Solid Divisions: Borders within the City

How unrestrained is the trespassing of limits between disparate urban fabrics?

Going down to the scale of the city, the real, physical walls that divide the urban landscape and reinforce Brazil's socio-spatial segregation were examined.

10 / The Encryption of Power: Disobedience and Exclusion in the City

How liberating can *Pixo* be in revealing the city's power logics?

Reaching the scale of the building, the phenomenon of *Pixo*—pixo tagging as a tangible representation of the wall as a space of confrontation—was studied.

Walls of Air - *Fundação Bienal São Paulo* Ph. Imagen Subliminal

"The choice of a cartographic language was made with the aim of escaping from traditional exhibition models, saturated by realistic images, as well as combining the use of drawing—the architect's main tool to represent space—with advanced geo-referencing tools."
—The Curatorial Team

△ LA PAZ

△ TRINIDAD

THE DOSSIER

WALLS OF AIR. A BRAZILIAN PAVILION

Fragment 3: Map is not the Territory; a Retraced Border

Maps for the Indo-Pacific Region

FAKE INDUSTRIES

Fake Industries Architectural Agonism, an enterprise founded by Cristina Goberna Pesudo and Urtzi Grau, speculates and inquires into the sudden invention of the Indo-Pacific region. Through four 'traditional' cartographic acts, produced in collaboration with the Masters of Architecture at the University of Technology Sydney, they document and design political, physical, historical, and conflictual contingencies of the region in an attempt to decolonize the tool.

PROJECT: Developed in the Masters of Architecture at the University of Technology Sydney, with Ben Feher, Hana Lee, Thoi Yen Ngo, James Stuart, Rachel Wan, and Callum Woo, and under the guidance of Fake Industries Architectural Agonism / EXHIBITIONS: 3rd Istanbul Design Biennial "Are we Human?" accompanied by sound pieces by Leopold Lambert, Miguel Rodriguez-Casellas, Joni Taylor, and Grupo TOMA / TEXT: Urtzi Grau and Ben Feher

The 2013 Australian Defence White Paper "Indo-Pacific Strategic Arc" formally shifted the country from the Pacific to the Indo-Pacific region. That year, Australia officially moved to the Indo-Pacific, a region created *ex-proposito* that expands from the West Coast of South America to the Gulf, from Southeast Asia to Africa's East Coast. The new region had been theorized in diplomatic circles since the 1950s, yet it was the increase of maritime trade and the emergence of the BRICS's[1] economies in the 2000s, China's regional hegemony, and the post-2001 geopolitical reorganizations that pushed Australia to be the first country to recognize it and relocate there.

During the last five years, the region has been under construction. The existence of the Indo-Pacific region is treated as a *de facto* reality in trade agreements, cultural exchanges, and development grants, while its actual characterization varies according to the agencies, parties, or policies involved. It is not a strange condition. A cacophony of legal definitions also delineates well-stabilized regions such as Europe. In fact, this blurry contour is not the Indo-Pacific's

most distinctive feature. Instead, it is its instantaneous nature of its provisional outline. The sudden invention of the Indo-Pacific region was a twofold operation; both an act of naming and of storytelling. But while the geographical limits of the region were stated in its name, the narratives that hold its geography together are barely in place. The region's vastness and its brief existence are the probable reasons for this absence. They are also responsible for the region's potential. The Indo-Pacific still needs to be designed.

The aim of these four maps is to construct the missing narratives of the Indo-Pacific region through and with architecture. The establishment of a new global region is a rare event. It radically reconfigures the shape, limits, and relationships of a section of the world. It is a definitive design project, and yet designers are rarely involved. Our hypothesis is that the case of the Indo-Pacific region is different. It covers an exceptional extension of fragmented territory in which

architecture's ubiquity makes an ideal *lingua franca*. Its ability to intersect with social, political, economic, technologic, ecosystemic, and spatial controversies makes architecture the ultimate vehicle to navigate and connect commonalities between local idiosyncrasies.

To grasp the scale and ambition of the topic, the project builds on Buckminster Fuller's "World Game" and Constantinos Doxiadis's "Ekistics," while avoiding their totalizing schemes. Shifting network theory through the lenses of cosmopolitism, the maps of the Indo-Pacific region become a constructive enterprise, a diverse, interdependent, and highly contingent system that does not simply discover pre-existing truths but, through specific practices and processes, helps shape them. The maps describe the Indo-Pacific Region using four traditional cartographic formats. Deeply interconnected, they address the imaginaries, the cartographies, and the constituencies of the region.[2]

1   The BRICS economies are constituted by the nations: Brazil, Russia, India, China, and South Africa.
2   The research project on the Indo-Pacific region is supported by a Graham Foundation Grant and will be included in the upcoming volume "Indo Pacific: An Instantaneous Region Volume 1, Stories, Atlases, Cartographies, and Commons."

THE MAP OF GHOSTS OF THE INDO-PACIFIC describes a region made of things that are no more. It deliberately and unavoidably uses the images that former hegemonic regimes and colonial empires produced to describe the subjects of their occupations—simultaneously revealing their own political agendas through representation. If the Indo-Pacific requires its new stories to exist, the fragments, ruins, and remains of previous histories will be its foundations. This map is therefore an atlas of extinct entities, documented but often mythical, including 737 exemplar of vanished flora, 563 examples of lost animals, 433 dead languages, 35 cities long gone, 53 pieces of obsolete technology, and 47 posthumous peoples.

THE POLITICAL MAP OF THE INDO-PACIFIC shows the region as a multiplicity of transnational agreements grouping nation-states in collections of overlapping legal entities that often link unlikely political systems. Distorting the traditional and recognizable geographic perimeters, this map unveils that alliances and borders extend well beyond nation-states to encompass overlapping territories and vast swathes of water. It also illustrates how redundant alliances produce robust frontiers; i.e. the more entities agreeing on a border, the more solid it becomes. The importance of antagonist political systems, conflicting religious beliefs, cultural concerns—mapped here using the Economist Democracy Index, the Democracy Ranking Index, the EFoTW, or the Human Freedom Index—seem to hardly influence these immaterial outlines made of multi-lateral trade agreements (e.g. GTSP, SPARTECA, among others); multi-lateral sports championships such as Pacific Nations CUP, PAN ARAB GAMES, or the African CON; exclusive economic zones, bi-lateral trade agreements, and military agreements (e.g. LAS, ACD, among others).

THE PHYSICAL MAP OF THE INDO-PACIFIC depicts the region as an island of water surrounded by land masses. Its fluid territory joins the Pacific and the Indian oceans, spanning from the East Coast of Africa to the West Coast of South America. It is in this depiction where the Indo-Pacific is perhaps more explicitly recognizable as a community of human and non-human inhabitants. The ocean is now a space of intricate design—manifesting itself through invisible infrastructures (underwater sea cables, trade routes, fishing banks), water quality (temperature, oxygenation, acidity), and hyperbolic disasters (coral bleaching events, radioactive contamination, islands of plastic trash). It is a space where marine pirates, coal conglomerates, plankton populations, water acidity, and melting ice-caps collide in an eco-systemic state of constant friction.

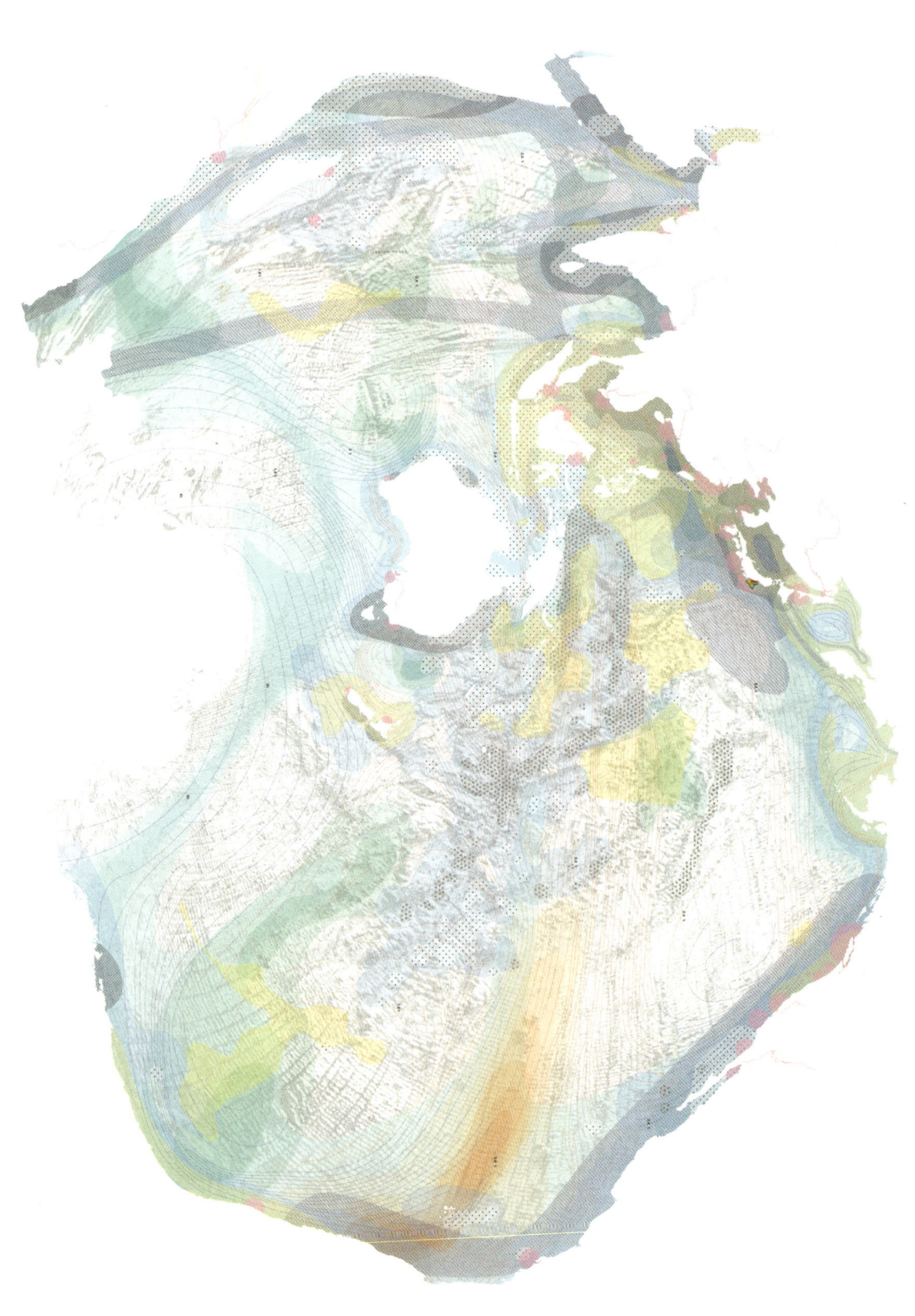

THE MAP OF CONFLICTS OF THE INDO-PACIFIC retraces the region as an archipelago of unfolding struggles involving multifarious constituencies such as exclusive economic zones, natural resources, maritime routes, cities, weaponry ranges, pirates, and natural disasters. It illustrates how the origin of this region radically differs from other similar entities around the world. The Indo-Pacific is not the result of a revolution, a fight for independence from a colonial empire, or a remedial solution to avoid another world war like in the formation of the Americas or the European Union. Rather, it is a system of conflicts and, perhaps, an attempt to learn to live with them. The current non-exhaustive list depicted in this map includes the illegal rhino horns trade between South Africa and Zimbabwe, whaling policies, the struggle between farmers and drug dealers in Kachin and Shan States in Myanmar, ISIS, the poppy fields in Iran, Afghanistan, and Pakistan, the dispute over the Senkaku and Diaoyu Islands, among others.

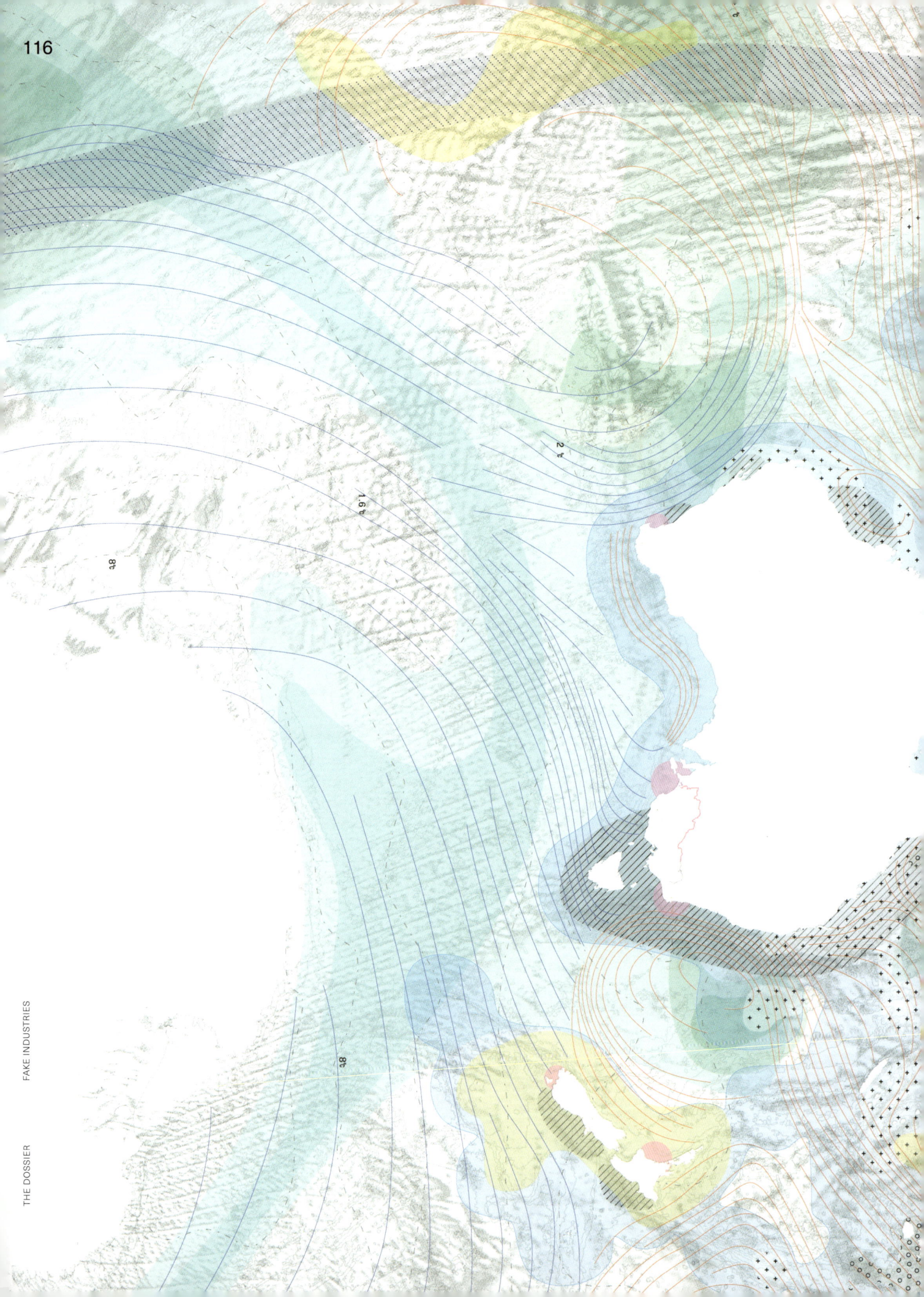

FAKE INDUSTRIES

Fragment of The Physical Map of the Indo-Pacific

IT'S A MAD, MAD WORLD OUT THERE

How Do You Picture It?

An Exquisite Corpse Game via Email

Two spies. Four agents. One mission: attempt to break into the madness, into the fragments and themes that make up the reality and fictions they live in, will live in, and create a story around it. If they can't see the whole picture, they can at least attempt to spy on it, to question it, to play it— to picture it. Uriel Fogué, Spanish architect and scholar, and NESS's editor Renee Carmichael, played spies. Each strategically contacted two agents who received prompts in the form of a phrase or an image. The agents sent a response back to the spies, who then hid part of the message and sent it to the second agent. This loop went on until the spies decided to reveal the final picture to all agents.

We are on the Planet Earth; the ice is melting, the temperatures are rising, the artificial intelligence is waiting, the fear is there, but also the possibility to create anew. No matter if it is a new beginning or the end, it is hard not to let the imagination run wild.

The Trans-Artificial Intelligence Boy/Girl Profile

The Spy ——— Uriel Fogué
Agent 01 ——— Parasite Lab
Agent 02 ——— Maria Jerez

ROUND 01 - SPY

Dear Agent 01,

As you know, it is 2018 on Planet Earth; the ice is melting, the temperatures are rising, the hate is building, the level of extinction is increasing, the artificial intelligence is waiting, the fear is there, but also the hope. No matter if it is a new beginning or the end, it is hard not to let the imagination run wild.

But... We have intercepted the following conversation: "I heard enough to realize that I am not a human being, only an instrument." "What are you talking about?"
"That's what I am. To study your reactions—something of that sort. Each one of you has a... an instrument like me. We emerge from your memory or your imagination, I can't say exactly—anyway you know better than I. [...]"

Please help us. We expect your response back before next Monday, in the form of a word or image.

Yours sincerely,
The Spy

ROUND 01 - SPY

Thank you Agent 01,

The information provided is very useful. We shall keep you informed.

Sincerely,
The Spy

ROUND 01 - AGENT 01

Dear Spy,

Attached you can find our first response. Here is an example of the 2050s series.
We were really impressed by it!

Hope you'll like it!
Best,
Agent 01

TRANS-ARTIFICIAL INTELLIGENCE BOY FROM 2050s STARTER PACK

2-Is part of the Techno Buddhism Temple

1-Squatting old homeless guy bought on the Post-Dark web

5-Lives in a Post-Zaha Hadid Jr. House

3-Took part in the 5th World War with the AI Caliphate Brigade

4-Lives solely off of this "old school" food

6-Vacations in Virtual Ibiza with their Transhuman queer friends

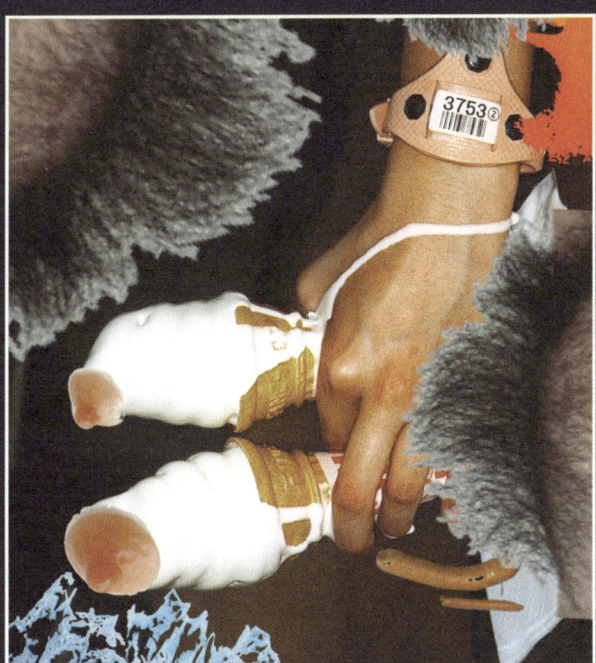

Dear Spy,

Here is the Agent 02.
Here, I send
you my image.
Let me know.

Yours,
MJ

Dear Agent 01,

We found new contents for the design of the Trans-Artificial Intelligence
Boy/Girl From 2050s Starter Pack. Please
see attached document. What do you think
about it? Can you think of any other elements
related to this last one?

Thank you.
We expect your response back before next Monday, in the form of
words or images.

Yours sincerely,
The Spy

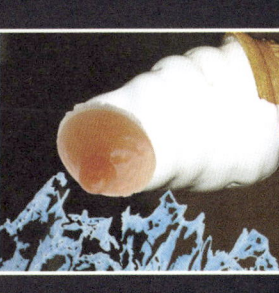

Dear Agent 02,

As you know, it is 2018 on the planet earth; the
ice is melting, the temperatures are rising, the hate
is building, the level of extinction is increasing, the artificial intelligence is waiting, the fear is there, but also the
hope. No matter if it is a new beginning or the end, it is hard
not to let the imagination run wild.

Hence, we are designing the Trans-Artificial Intelligence Boy/
Girl From 2050s Starter Pack.
Can you help us by suggesting any elements that, in your
opinion, should be included in the pack?

Thank you.
We expect your response back before next Monday, in
the form of words or images.

Yours sincerely,
The Spy

ROUND 02 - AGENT 01

Dear Spy,

Actually, the frozen-tit-cream you sent to us is a common element with the Neomillennials Lover Boy 2050's starter pack... Enjoy!

Best regards,
Agent 01

NEOMILLENNIAL BOY FROM THE 2050s STARTER PACK

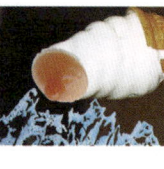

1 - Wears the presiliconocene 2000s look

2 - Eats frozen-tit-cream with nostalgia for the time when people had mothers

3 - Burns paper sticks for his sleeping capsule fragrance

4 - Still use engineered nutrition like Soylent

5 - Is a collector of primitive art

6 - Rejects molecular transport and only uses vintage electrical contraptions

ROUND 02 - SPY

Dear Agent 01,

Many thanks for your indispensable collaboration. We proceed to transmit this information to the rest of the team. The information provided by you will remain secret, until further notice.

Yours sincerely,
The Spy

ROUND 02 - SPY

Dear Agent 02,

The frozen-tit-cream has been identified as an element in common with the Neomillennials Lover Boy 2050's starter pack. Please see attached document. What do you think?

Thank you.
We expect your final response back before next Monday, in the form of words or images.

Yours sincerely,
The Spy

NEOMILLENNIAL BOY FROM THE 2050s STARTER PACK

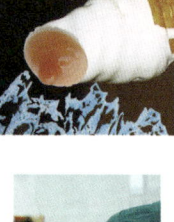

1 - Wears the presiliconocene 2000s look

2 - Eats frozen-tit-cream with nostalgia for the time when people had mothers

3 - Burns paper sticks for his sleeping capsule fragrance

Dear Spy,

Here you have a stolen photo from the data taken during 12 hours with the camera of superimposed moments, included in the "Neomillennials Lover Boy 2050's starter pack," incorporated in one user's lenses over his opaque silicone eyes.

Yours,
Agent 02

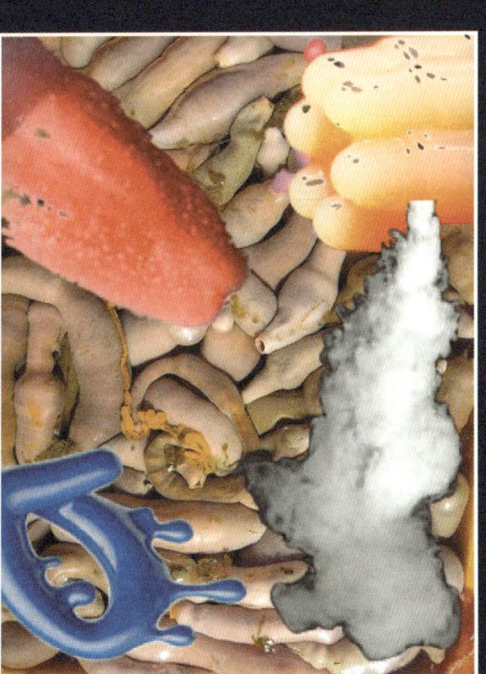

Dear Agent 01,

Many thanks for your indispensable collaboration. We proceed to transmit this information to the rest of the team. The information provided by you will remain secret, until further notice.

Yours sincerely,
The Spy

AGENT 01

PARASITE 2.0 was founded in 2010 by Stefano Colombo, Eugenio Cosentino and Luca Marullo. It is based in Milan and Brussels. The group investigates the status of human habitat acting within a hybrid of architecture, design, and visual art. They are the 2016 winners of YAP MAXXI. Their works have been exhibited at the XX Chilean Architecture Biennale (2017), the Shenzhen Architecture Biennale (2015), and at La Biennale di Venezia (2014 and 2012). They have published the book Primitive Future Office. They are professors at the NABA Nuova Accademia Belle Arti Milano and at the MADE Program-Accademia di Belle Arti R. Gagliardi in Siracusa. Parasite 2.0 is represented by Operativa Arte Contemporanea Gallery and Galleria Corraini Arte Contemporanea.

AGENT 02

MARIA JEREZ (Madrid, 1978). Her work travels between choreography, cinema, and visual arts. Since 2004, she has made pieces that explore the relationship with the viewer as the space in which the modes of representation are put into crisis. From "El Caso del Espectador" to her last pieces "Blob" and "Yabba" this relationship has mutated from a place of understanding of the atrical and cinematographic conventions, that is, from the expertise, to the intentional loss of references where the artist, the piece, and the spectator behave towards each other as strangers.

All images provided by the agents (Parasite Lab and Maria Jerez).

IT'S A MAD, MAD WORLD OUT THERE. HOW DO YOU PICTURE IT?

2

Internal Tensions:
To X and Beyond

The Spy ——— Renee Carmichael
Agent 01 ——— Jesse LeCavalier
Agent 02 ——— Sophia Al-Maria

"'The very fact that we allow all of this power to escape might be taken as a sign of our prodigal nature,' the authors surmised, 'or even of our lack of an ethic concerning environmental pollution in our galaxy.' Moreover, the repeating peaks and valleys of our planet's radio signature might strongly imply the uneven economic development that characterizes human societies, and the political, territorial, and cultural divisions that characterize human civilizations."[1]

To start with an idea is to start with an error. Galactic Footprint is an oxymoron, something earthly while at the same time 'otherly'—out there. As spy, I wanted to start with this vertical tension. What results is many other tensions, personal and systematic, mathematical and embodiment, x and σ...

1   Paglen, Trevor. "Some Sketches on Vertical Geographies." 2016. Full version of the text available at: e-flux.com/architecture/superhumanity

Hi Spy!

Happy New Year!

Please find my first round contribution attached. Sorry that it took a bit longer than planned!

Agent 01

Dear Agent 01,

We are very happy to have you as part of Mad World Pictures!

With that being said, I would like to give you your very first prompt and to start the first round. If you could reply within a week that would be great. I will then forward part of your response to Sophia, and so on.

ROUND 1, PROMPT 1:
Galactic Footprint

I will happily leave it in your hands. You can find the instructions attached.

Looking Forward,
The Spy

GFOC

Galactic Footprint Offset Credit
Application
Preclearance Formcard

[FOR AGENCY USE ONLY]

Name:

Locator ID:

FICO:

Previous GFOC Applicant (Y/N)?

If 1, GFOC ID:

The Galactic Footprint Offset Credit program is an administrative initiative to incentivize reduction of thermospheric debris through a combination of measures, including reduction of use, increased stewardship, and investment in new satellite and terrestrial forms of data reliance and exchange.

This form helps determine eligibility for Galactic Footprint Offset Credit (GFOC). Please complete the following statements: (1) for YES and a (5) for NO. Indicate your total in the area designated.
If your score is ≤ 10, you are eligible to apply for GFOC.

- I participate in a Chapter of the Debris Zone Adoption and Maintenance Corps

  If 1, indicate Chapter Number ____

- I / my household subscribes to Terrestrial LAN

  If 1, indicate SUBSCRIPTION INDEX ____ and LOCATOR GRID ____

- I have completed Reliance Reduction Training at a certified Attention Center

  If 1, indicate CENTER ID ____ and DATE (MM/DD/YYYY) __/__/____

- My place of residence is in a Subsurface District

  If 1, indicate Location ID and District Number ____

- I have Data Exemption Status through a certified Moral or Religious Center

  If 1, indicate Center Number ____

Worksheet total ____

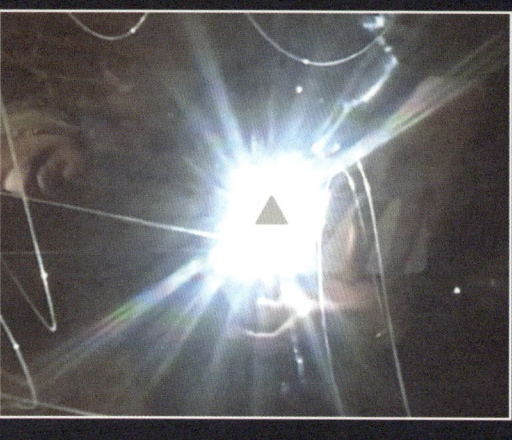

Hi Agent 02,

How are you?

I have the first response back. It came in the form of an image. Thus, you will find your first prompt attached.

You are free to respond as you want, a short text (around 50-100 words), an image, etc., etc. You can take it in any direction that you feel like... whatever inspires you.

If you could send back your response within a week that would be great so that we can keep the momentum going.

The Spy

Hi Spy.

This image is called "σ in this sphere I am everywhere the center."

Agent 02

Hi Agent 01,

Without further ado, here goes your next prompt:

$\sigma = 200$.

σ = standard deviation.

σ makes the sound of a hiss.

Is it mathematical, 200 standard deviations as a measure of an amount of variation in a set? Or is it more colloquial, 200 deviations within the standard (the norm)?

Thank you and I am here if you have any questions!

Looking forward,
The Spy

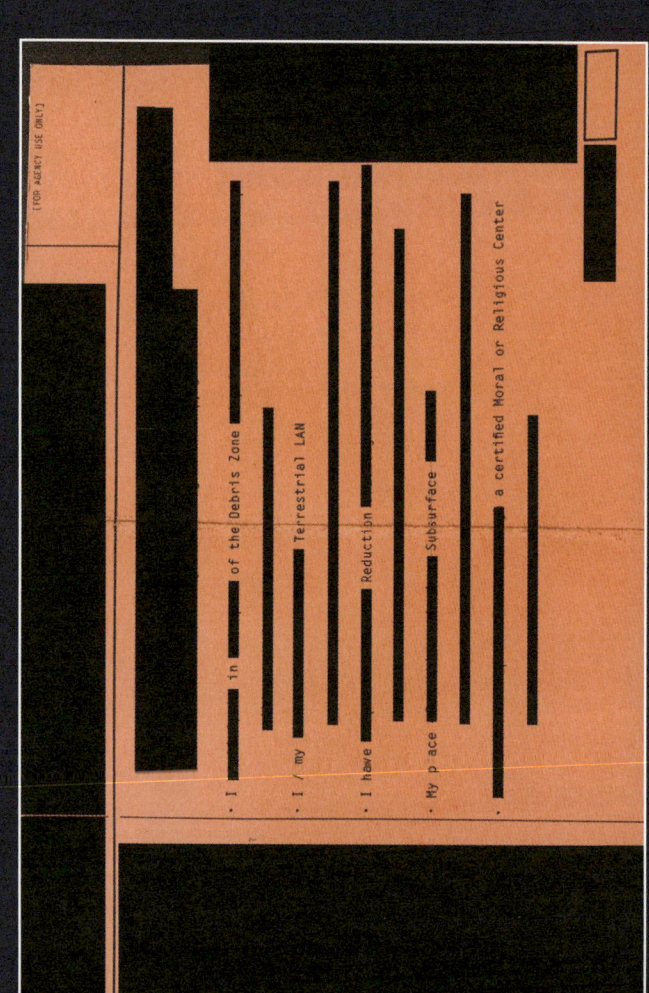

[FOR AGENT USE ONLY]

• I _____ in _____ of the Debris Zone

• I / my _____ Terrestrial LAN

• I have _____ Reduction

• My p-ace _____ Subsurface

• _____ a certified Moral or Religious Center

Hi Spy,

Here's my next round below.
Warmest greetings,
Agent 01

Six sigmas make a standard system, a system for reducing deviation. All the way down to 0.0036% error. Middle managers relax on this basis. Empires are built on this basis. Statistical repeatability like this is the basis for calculation, for forecasts, for prediction, for the "taming of chance."
But standard deviants interfere. Those unpredictable frictions and wrinkles and seams that predictably appear.
The squeaky wheel gets the grease. But what if they are all squeakers?

There's always something, they say.
Expect the unexpected.
Hurry up and wait.
When the going gets tough, the tough get going.
It is what it is.
Let X equal X.

Hi Agent 02,
How are you? I have a new prompt for you!
Do you remember what X equals?
Those unpredictable frictions and wrinkles and seams that predictably appear on the surface.
Are they marks of our own growth or do they speak of a larger texture beyond us?

Thank you!
The Spy

The Spy
is still waiting
for agent 02 to
respond. It must be
lost in the memory of
X, or perhaps in the
texture beyond...

AGENT 01

Jesse LeCavalier is a designer, writer, and educator whose work explores the architectural and urban implications of contemporary logistics. He is the author of "The Rule of Logistics: Walmart and the Architecture of Fulfillment" (University of Minnesota Press 2016). He is associate professor of architecture at the University of Toronto John H. Daniels Faculty and the Daniel Rose Visiting Assistant Professor at the Yale School of Architecture.
LeCavalier was one of five finalists for the 2018 MoMA PS1 Young Architects Program and was the recipient of the 2015 New Faculty Teaching Award from the Association of the Collegiate Schools of Architecture (ACSA). His work has been published widely, including contributions to Cabinet, AD, Public Culture, Places, Art Papers, and Harvard Design Magazine.

AGENT 02

Sophia Al-Maria is an artist, writer, and filmmaker living in London. She is contributing editor of Bidoun, and guest editor of The Happy Hypocrite – Fresh Hell, issue 8 (Book Works, 2015). Al-Maria's memoir, The Girl Who Fell to Earth (Harper Perennial, 2012), was translated into Arabic and published by Bloomsbury Qatar in 2015. In 2016 Al-Maria presented "Black Friday," her first U.S. solo exhibition at the Whitney Museum of American Art, New York, and was nominated for The Film London Jarman Award. In 2018, Al-Maria exhibited "ilysm" at Project Native Informant, London, and was Whitechapel Gallery's Writer in Residence—her exhibition "BCE" (Whitechapel Gallery, January–April 2019), draws on a year of performances and readings presented with Victoria Sin. Forthcoming exhibitions include Tate Britain, London (2019), and Julia Stoschek Collection, Dusseldorf (2020).

Documents

"The world has become more and more specialized and architecture is one of the few disciplines that still has the capacity to work in very encompassing ways. It can take extremely complex problems, analyze them, and begin to produce a form that represents not only the issues at hand, but that starts to propose solutions to these larger issues. Architecture can describe and represent that process and the potential solutions verbally and visually. That is a combination and a range of capabilities that in a complex world we undervalue and underutilize."

—MM

Michael
Maltzan
Architecture

To Build a Culture

Michael Maltzan in conversation with Daniela Freiberg

In 1988, a recently-graduated New York-born architect moved to Los Angeles with the strong conviction that he had an opportunity to make significant contributions. Almost thirty years later, his office works on a variety of contexts, programs, and scales worldwide that reflect a committed goal: to prove that architecture can be present for the widest range of ways our cultures are built. Not just in our cities nor buildings, but within our societies. His recent projects include a new site for the largest public collection of Inuit Art in Canada, housing projects that respond to a significant homelessness crisis, and pieces that create new urban landscapes for a city in constant change such as LA.

SWITCHING COASTS

DANIELA FREIBERG
Before speaking directly about your projects, we would like to know about your career. You switched coasts. Why did you make the decision to open your office in LA?

MICHAEL MALTZAN
I was born in Long Island, New York. Specifically, in Levittown, which is a typical North American postwar suburb. I lived there until I was probably ten or eleven years old. My father had a job that transferred him to different cities a number of times, so we lived in a few places: in Ohio, Upstate New York, and eventually in Connecticut. I went to undergraduate and graduate school in the Northeast. First to the Rhode Island School of Design (RISD), and to the Harvard Graduate School of Design (GSD) after that.
When I was at the GSD, I had a design studio with Professor Robert Mangurian, who was a LA-based architect. As part of that studio we visited the city and I thought it was the most fascinating, dynamic place I'd ever been in and connected with. I was about 25 years old.
I felt that I had a sense of the city, that I understood something fundamental about it. I felt very connected to it and I couldn't wait to come back. One of the things I realized afterwards is that Levittown and LA are both postwar suburbs. There are a lot of similarities to the way that space and buildings were made, the way you move through the city, the relationships of the spread-out parts of the city, the sprawling nature of it. All of those things were

very familiar and, in a way, comforting to me. I understood it enough to feel I could work here.

DF   And how long after that visit did you decide to move to LA?

MM   That visit to LA was in the middle of my graduate school education. After finishing, in 1988, my wife and I moved to LA. I worked in the city for seven years before establishing my own office.

DF   What other inspirational moments or people from your past encouraged you in this profession?

MM   My undergraduate education at RISD was extremely important to me. Architecture at RISD is within the context of the Fine Arts and Design School. We were immersed just as much in the history of art as we were in the history of architecture. Both of those histories turned out to be very important to me. Many of my friends and colleagues at school were architects but also painters and sculptors, graphic designers and fashion designers. I think that background, that contact and connection with other disciplines, helped me think about how architecture relates to culture and our contemporary moment. This continues to have an effect on my thinking and my work until today. It has an effect not only on the work, but also on how we understand the places where we may work. It gave me a different sensibility and a different way of thinking about the influences of each particular context. We moved to LA at a time when a lot of artists were also moving here, as well as a number of people I had gone to school with. LA had an incredible sense of openness and possibility, there was an opportunity to make things that felt unlike any other place. For a young person that combination is very powerful and extremely motivating. That experience, that culture connected to the city, has been one of the biggest influences on my career.

ON HOUSING

DF   In a recent presentation you mentioned that "housing is nothing less than the microcosmos of the city itself." Although your office deals with multiple scales and programs, your approach to housing is a chapter in itself. Could you explain to us your principles for developing these commissions?

MM   I've been interested in housing from the moment I began studying architecture. To some extent it was because during that time there was a real fight between competing ideas in school. It was kind of 'the end fight' between postmodernism and modernism, which brought with it a resurgence in the interest around the former.
      Housing was a fundamental program of modernism. One of its earliest and most notable inventions was the idea that housing was a thing for experimentation, for being able to say something directly about the way that you make the places we live in. When I eventually came to LA, one of the things that struck me was that the city was largely defined by the places we live, not multi-family houses, not denser housing, but the single-family house. Arguably, until 1970s and 80s, the majority of buildings here that had real architectural experimentation were single-family houses. It wasn't institutions or museums or those kinds of civic and public buildings. That was very compelling to me.
      This city has continued to evolve and change, like a lot of contemporary cities, and it is under a lot of pressure from things like density, affordability, mobility, and multi-family housing. Regarding those pressures, the potential for denser and more urban housing had started to become a real question mark in the city, and I thought back to a lot of the inventions in modernism around the subject. I wanted to do housing because you can say something about the way a culture and a city is evolving through the way you approach housing either in small iterations or sometimes wholesale reinvention. That is where that idea of the microcosmos of the city comes from. Housing is both defined by the evolution of the city, as it is by the way in which you can say something about the city. Housing has many of the same mechanisms of a city: it is the place where you live, where you play, nowadays where you work, where you build

community, or where you try to find yourself as an individual. All of those different social operations are very similar to the way in which we navigate our lives in the city, just in a more condensed way.

DF   We know that LA has a significant homeless problem and your office seems to deal with it by proposing new and more collective models of intervention. Could you tell us about that approach and process?

MM   Around the time that housing was really at the top of my thinking, we were approached by a group called Skid Row Housing Trust (SRHT) which is a nonprofit housing developer who focuses on building housing for homeless individuals and on working to find solutions around homelessness. The Trust knew a project that I had done called Inner-City Arts (ICA), which is very close to where the SRHT offices are located. ICA is a nonprofit school for children that primarily come from disadvantaged educational and economic backgrounds. At that time, SRHT had been building transitional housing, where people would live for a short time and eventually leave. These buildings were like long-term hotels for individuals, a bridge between living on the street and eventually finding a home of their own. Transitional housing was an important step for individuals to get off the street, but you only lived there maybe a few nights, a week, maybe a month—it was a temporary solution. They had some success but very often people were ending up back on the streets. They realized that what was missing was a stronger, supportive structure for those individuals. They needed to build a more permanent solution to try to help that community. Those two new goals: to generate permanent places for people to live and to have supportive services on site, which were a very new concept at the time, led the Trust in their search for a new approach and a new partner to work with. They asked us to help them reinvent the type of housing they were doing. That is how we first got involved.
      The very first project was called Rainbow Apartments. The goal was to make permanent, supportive housing with the supportive services in the building itself. If a resident needed a doctor, or a mental health provider, or counseling, or vocational training, those services would be brought into the building so they didn't have to go back on the streets and navigate many of the problematic things that tended to pull people back into homelessness.
      Secondly, the new model would be built as permanent—not temporary—housing. If you got an apartment, then you could expect to live there for the rest of your life, it was your home. That was the beginning of what has already resulted in four completed buildings and an early design for a fifth one.

DF   When was that first collaboration for SRHT? You have mentioned that you received feedback from the people living there, so you have information to help you consider how the projects can evolve over time.

MM   The first project, Rainbow Apartments, started at the very end of 2003, and finished in 2005. That project was followed by New Carver, Star, and Crest Apartments. Each was an evolutionary step in developing this new model, not only in terms of their design but also their location in the city, the projects are not just on Skid Row[1] but are now more and more citywide because homelessness is citywide. But they also evolved as we got more and more feedback from the people who live there, and they've continued to evolve as the city has changed as a whole.
That iterative process is useful to look back at as an evolving story of how we see architecture's role in these projects—not only dealing directly with the homelessness crisis, but also in the approach to a city that is transforming as rapidly as LA.

DF   Does SRHT exclusively work with you, or do they work with a number of architects that have different approaches to the homeless problem?

MM   Yes, they have been working with some very good architects over the years. It was really their belief in architecture's ability to help change the model that was so compelling when they contacted us. I was invited to their office to talk to them, and because they are a nonprofit and didn't have a lot of money, they were very tentative. They said, "We are interested in working with you, would you be interested in working with us?" And I was jumping up and down because I couldn't wait to do housing, this was my first chance. I said yes, yes, yes!
What was interesting was that, as I drove back to the office, I actually got a little bit worried. We had a lot of different projects at the time, many of which were museum projects. I worried that no one in the office would want to work on this project. My concern was that they would want to work on the more 'classically' important projects, especially the younger generation in the office. Over the next two weeks, every time I would go and get a cup of coffee in the office, somebody would come up to me and say, "Hey, I heard

The Skid Row Housing Trust is committed to preventing and ending homelessness in greater Los Angeles. It provides permanent supportive housing so that people who have experienced life in the streets, prolonged extreme poverty, poor health, disabilities, mental illness and/or addiction can lead safe, stable lives in wellness. skidrow.org

we got this housing project and if there is any chance, I would like to work on it. It really interests me." I realized how much housing speaks to something very fundamental in the architect's psychology.

DF   What kind of feedback do you receive from the people living in these buildings? I imagine you entered into a process not just in terms of architecture but also in regards to the humanity underneath as well.

MM   People still want to see the building very regularly, and there are a lot of tours and visits so all of us in the office tend to be there in more informal ways. You inevitably have conversations with the people who live there. It is more natural, as opposed to a more scheduled way of having conversations. There is a very structured feedback as well, because SRHT not only develops the buildings, but operates them. Since they manage them, they are constantly getting feedback from the residents. They have a whole management arm to run the buildings which means that when something is not working they hear about it, and when something is working very well, they hear about it. The Trust stays very much in touch with the way the building is operating and the changes in each of the buildings, beyond the specifics of the site and the context. Many of the changes in the buildings have evolved based on that feedback. For example, in Star Apartments, we were asked by the community to put a laundry room on each floor as opposed to having them together, in one place, on one floor. The community wanted more convenient access. In Crest Apartments, we went back to having all of the laundry facilities together in one place because that community wanted to see each other more often. That is one of the beauties of housing: that something as simple, as pragmatic, and as normative as the laundry room ends up being an extremely important social and programmatic part of the project. It is not that different from the history of the way that the kitchen has evolved from the 19th century to current houses, and what it tells us about changing norms, socially and environmentally in the way we live.

DF   Related to these discussions, what tools do you use in your design process? How do you consider these realities, given SRHT's programs and budget requirements?

MM   Maybe part of the answer is in the story of Rainbow Apartments, the very first project we did with the Trust. When SRHT came to us with a program, the first thing we did was an analysis of the site, trying to adhere to a basic minimum number of apartments in a very quick preliminary study. That set a lot of the metrics: how many apartments can you fit on the site, how do you think it may organize the other social or community parts of the building—almost as a developer would approach the project. It was important to

Sixth Street Viaduct, City of Los Angeles, Bureau of Engineering, Michael Maltzan Architecture, Inc. / HNTB Corporation.

try to get that part right because you live with those metrics all the way through the project.

We started the project when the economy was very, very hot. The costs and prices of things were continuing to escalate, and the type of construction contract the project had was called a 'cost plus contract,' which meant that whatever it cost the contractor to buy the materials to put the work in place was the cost that we could pass on to the trust. It wasn't a fixed budget, and because the economy was so overheated the prices were continuing to rise—to go through the roof! The cost of the building went over budget, and we kept having to pull things out in the middle of the construction to try to reduce costs and keep the building on budget. This went on week after week after week, until finally we were having arguments about whether you painted one side of the window sunshades or both sides of the window sunshades. At the end of the project, when it was done, many of the elements that as an architect you would normally point to and say, "those are the architectural elements of the building," had been lost, literally everything, the building had been ripped to the bone.

I was very anxious that the final building would be too harsh, too reduced, but within weeks a community started forming there, and grew in a very vibrant way. What I realized was that the things that were the most fundamental to the building were still operating in very powerful ways. Those were really the kind of things that you first learn as an architect: the scale of spaces, the kind of relationships between the different programmatic elements, the sense of accessibility within the building, the connections within it. It made me step back and reevaluate our approach quantitatively. What were the most fundamental needs for the building, and what were the things that still operated at a very profound level of architecture?

Following on what we had learned with Rainbow Apartment's success, we have taken those lessons to each subsequent project. What are the most fundamental aspects of the building? We begin our design process thinking about that.

TO WIDEN THE SCOPE

DF   Well, that in a way points directly to the role of the architect. Given your experience, where are we standing now and where do you think we are going?

MM   Clearly it is a very complex time. We are looking at questions around affordability, density, accessibility, mobility, equity—all of which architecture has some relationship to and is uniquely suited to grapple with.

We have done a wide range of work in the office, housing is a part of it. We do institutional projects, commercial projects, more and more infrastructure, which is a growing interest. One of my goals for the office is to continue to try to prove, even if just to myself, that architecture has the capacity to be present in the widest range of ways in which we build our cultures. Not just in our cities, not just in our buildings, but literally in our societies and cultures. And all

Above and below: Winnipeg Art Gallery's Inuit Art Center render. Courtesy of MMA

of these pieces: affordable housing, housing for the affluent, museums, infrastructure, are part of that equation. I don't think that one is more important than the other, but the full range is something that as architects we need to continue to fight for and try to demand a role and a position in the conversations around what that mix is. How do cultures continue to build and how do they continue to define themselves? In the past, architecture has proven that it is an important part of that larger equation. The capacity and ability of architects and architecture is something we need to continue to advocate for. The world has become more and more specialized or filled with specialties, and architecture is one of the few disciplines that still has the capacity to work in very encompassing ways. It can take extremely complex problems, analyze them, and begin to produce a form that represents not only the issues at hand, but also one that starts to propose solutions to larger issues. Architecture can describe and represent that process and the potential solutions verbally and visually. That is a combination and a range of capabilities that in a complex world we undervalue and underutilize.

DF   Your elasticity with commission types is reflected in housing, as well. You develop affordable projects with the same detail as affluent projects. In his key text, "Transparency," first published in 1964, Colin Rowe and Robert Slutzky elaborated on the concept as a fundamental principle of spatial organization. In fact, exposure and dissolution of the wall was a very modern idea. Talking about the

Pittman Dowell residence, you make a parallel between transparency as the great spatial problem of the Modernists, while mentioning simultaneity as the most important spatial problem for architects today. How does it feel to build next to such an iconic house, site, and spirit such as Neutra's?

MM   It was terrifying because Neutra has an iconic presence in Southern California and in Modernism as a whole. The Serulnic residence was a perfect encapsulation of his version of modernism, and the idea of a fully transparent border between inside and outside. Neutra's house was sitting on the site above us, as if Neutra was always looking down, making sure we weren't causing too much trouble. It was like your 'modernist parent' making sure you were not making a mess in the backyard.
While talking to Lari Pittman and Roy Dowell, the original owners of that house, we realized that that idea of a

complete transparency is very much a modernist idea but not necessarily a contemporary one. In our contemporary lives we are confronted more and more with this idea of constant exposure, a virtual transparency. The kind of psychological effect of that constant exposure is substantial. I thought that the issue at hand was one of simultaneity: the idea that we are in many places at the same time. It's a relatively new phenomenon, and it is arguably the defining spatial challenge of our time. The Pittman Dowell house was trying to not only propose an alter ego to Neutra, but it was also about trying to explore how to transform this idea of transparency into a positive form and space that recognizes the complexities of this new reality.

DF   MoMA Queens was your first arts and culture project, was it not? Now, the largest public collection of Inuit art,[2] the Inuit Art Centre, is being developed in Manitoba at the Winnipeg Art Gallery. In what stage is this project? Does the Arctic Topiaries project directly relate to it?

MM   MoMA wasn't the first art project, but it was a very early and certainly a very important project for me and for the office. About the Inuit Art Center and Arctic Topiaries, they definitely relate to each other. The Winnipeg Art Gallery's Inuit Art Centre is under construction right now. Every year, Winnipeg has a large winter festival. They host a competition for warming huts that are built out on the river where people skate. With the museum under construction, we thought it was appropriate to get involved, so this year we took them up on their invitation to do a warming hut. Our design, Arctic Topiaries, relates to the Gallery in terms of its form, but it was also interesting to try to use the knowledge and technology that the Inuit have: using snow as a material. Like all building processes, it was quite interesting to become more immersed in the protocols and limitations of it. I saw an equivalency between the site for the huts and an abstract garden landscape, really almost a fantasy of a French garden with their abstract, highly geometric topiary on large abstract plains. There was a similarity to me with the abstraction of the big white plain in the Arctic and this river landscape. The huts were built in January 2019 and remained until they melted into the river.

ON MODELS AND MATERIALS

DF   In your essay "After Narrative, Beyond Mimesis"[3] you explain the role of models in your office's design process. Could you expand on that?

MM   The physical model has always been extremely important to me. I think it is because, even though the drawings are very important, the model enables us to get a sense of the thing that we are making in physical three dimensions. It is a very

personal way in which I connect to the work and to the design. Working in physical models also goes back a to this question of simultaneity that we were touching on with Pittman Dowell. When we experience a building, that experience is built from both seeing what is directly in front of you, but also from our perceptual sense of what is around us, what we just saw, and our anticipation of what we are about to see. On the screen, even if it is a digital model in three dimensions and you can move around it, it is still a two-dimensional representation of the thing in front of you. It doesn't really represent all of the other relationships of the spaces and forms that are inherent in a building. When you are working on a physical model, I find you have a more complete sense of the thing that you are looking at directly, and you have a sense of what is behind it and what's below it and what's above it. You hold all of these relationships in your mind simultaneously. In the same way as when you move through a building, you are very conscious of not only where you are but where you are heading, and what you have already seen, including your experiences of approaching the building or the space. For me the model provides a more complete physical and temporal understanding of the specific place where you are standing. The design feels like more of an experiment to the ultimate goal, which is the building itself.

Arctic Topiaries. Ph. Jacqueline Young

At the start of the design we begin generally at a smaller scale, sometimes very crudely. Those are our working models, but we do finished models for presentations. We often have large scale mock ups of different parts of the building or different materials on the building site. Those are continuations of the model process. I don't really think that the model is completely separate in the design process from the final building. It is part of a continuum. That changes for me though once the building is built. What I value most in process models are the imperfections in them. All of those imperfections and the ability to intentionally misinterpret those mistakes is very useful in producing ideas. They suggest not a perfect idea, but a number of different possibilities, and are how a building is actually built. I feel like all those process models are freed from having to stand in for the actual building. They are released from that responsibility and freed to become something else.

DF Wood is the most common material used in LA, however in the case of the Star Apartments, you used prefabricated modules and for the Moody Rice Center for the Arts, you used a special brick. When you start working on a project, what is your approach to materiality?

MM We built a lot in LA using wood as the primary framing and structural material. I don't have an inherent love for that technique, but it is ubiquitous here for many logistical, cultural, and economic reasons. When I began working in LA, I thought it was important to embrace or at least accept that reality, and to see how far we could go with it. It is the same with the plaster exterior material we have used a lot. It exists everywhere here. It has a long history in LA building. A good challenge is to see how much you can continue to evolve something and give it new life.

I have always been very suspicious of materials. The reason for that is that at times architects rely too much on the cultural values placed on certain materials to produce a kind of short hand understanding of the value of a building. For instance, if you use a very fancy material, people immediately respond to that by thinking that there is a real value to the architecture.

I wasn't concerned with trying to produce architecture through material at the beginning of my career. I was interested in the three-dimensional form and spatial relationships formed by the building and preferred the buildings to be very abstract, in order for those spatial relationships to carry most of the meaning.

That started to evolve, and I became more and more interested in materials that have a slightly more fugitive quality to them. Materials that change with your perception or seem to change with phenomenological changes that occur around the building. For instance, the way the light changes the color or the contrast or the depth of a material on the façade.

Some of that interest can be traced back to growing up in a place like Levittown. When most people look at those places they think of them as being really monochromatic, incredibly mundane places with very little richness to them. I developed a different perception of the characteristics of the place, sometimes very subtle, sometimes very nuanced, sometimes a little bit abstract. There were differences there,

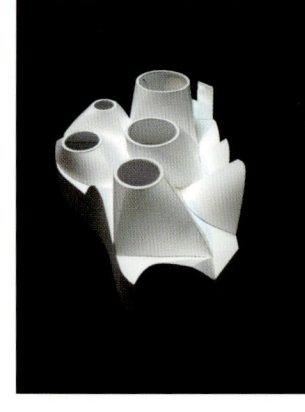

Fresno Metropolitan Museum Model (above). Santa Monica Museum of Art at Bergamot Station Art Center Models (right). Ph. Courtesy of MMA

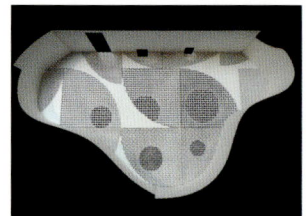

but differences that were happening at a very subtle level of perception. It wasn't bold or apparent and you had to work harder to see it. I think the way that I approach to materials today, the way I try to put them together, is by understanding that they are animated by the characteristics of the place, and that that is very likely tied to those early experiences and observations of a place like Levittown.

Look at the Moody Center—the brick has a dimensional relationship to the traditional brick which is used across the Rice University Campus, but the material, a magnesium-oxide brick, has this quality that changes quite significantly over the course of the day. When the sky is overcast it has an almost silver metallic appearance; when the sky is very blue, the brick gets this kind of blue sheen to it; at other times when the light starts to become less intense, the brick seems to become a very deep black. Something as seemingly fixed as a brick can have a mutable and extremely variable quality. It demands that you work with it...it challenges your perception, and that is a quality that I look for in materials.

TO SET PRIORITIES

DF In many of your projects you are creating new urban landscapes. The Sixth Street Viaduct is an example, but some housing projects, such as One Santa Fe, also work as an important piece for the city. In that sense, to finish our conversation, what do you consider to be the priorities for LA?

MMA Office. Ph. Marc Goodwin

MM   If you look at the most pressing priorities, they are certainly around confronting the challenge of density. The city is getting more and more dense. Density is also creating another priority which is how to address affordability for those living in the city. Density is having a significant effect on many different generations' abilities to live here and will certainly have an effect on the future of how the city evolves. It is having an effect on mobility, which in the past has been a way that the city has dealt with affordability. If you couldn't afford to live in an area, you moved a little bit further outside the center, and you drove to wherever you worked. That is becoming harder and harder as well. Density is having social effects on different neighborhoods that are becoming increasingly gentrified, putting real pressure on established communities that are very often moderate to lower income communities and are in danger of being displaced. Resource management is also being driven by density and affordability.

LA has always been a place that has invented itself in response to whatever type of development and change was happening in the city. It has invented a way of dealing with its environment, it has invented a way of dealing with distance and the car, it has invented a way of even portraying itself in media. Much of this innovation was possible because the city has had an extremely open, creative culture. With these new pressures, one of the greatest challenges for LA is to try to invent its future on its own terms as opposed to merely importing other models from more traditional cities. In the face of this extraordinary pressure, how do we, as a culture, continue to invent responses to the challenges that face us? Responses that are uniquely our own. If we can do it, then I think we keep that culture of creativity and invention, which is fundamental in LA as it moves forward. We have the potential to really add something to the conversation: how do you address new and pressing urban challenges in an unexpected and imaginative way, that hopefully has some resonance for other cities around the world.

1   Skid Row is an area of downtown Los Angeles that is known for containing one of the largest populations of homeless people in the USA.
2   Inuit art refers to artwork produced by the people of the Arctic previously known as Eskimos.
3   Maltzan, Michael. "After narrative, beyond mimesis". Originally published in Riedijk, Michiel. "Architecture as a craft": SUN architecture, 2011.

CLIENT: Rice University / PROGRAM: LEED Silver Academic facility dedicated to the advancement of transdisciplinary collaboration between the arts, sciences, and humanities / BUILDING AREA: 50,000 ft² (4645 m²)

RICE UNIVERSITY MOODY CENTER FOR THE ARTS

PHOTOS: Iwan Baan

HOUSTON, TEXAS. 2017

The Moody Center for the Arts (MCA) at Rice University in Houston, Texas, is a state-of-the-art facility dedicated to the advancement of transdisciplinary collaboration for students between the arts, sciences, and humanities. The facility houses diverse instruction, production, performance, and exhibition spaces. As a collaborative platform, the MCA extends and enhances existing campus resources in the service of project-based initiatives that seek to bring together students and practitioners from varied academic and professional disciplines. Within the interior, flexible studios work similarly, bringing diverse programmatic functions into contact with one another and extending views out toward the campus.

The emphasis on transparency and circulation extends to the building's exterior, with most of the building's first floor along the principal elevations and clad in floor-to-ceiling glass. Arcades created by the second floor's cantilevered form shade walkways below, while the building's brick-clad upper story appears to levitate. Many of the Moody's design elements reinterpret characteristics of the university's historic buildings. For instance, the exterior cladding is a manganese ironspot brick that shifts colors by reflecting the area's environmental conditions. While the building's brick is similar in scale to the traditional brick elsewhere on campus, the Moody's brick may take on a black, purple, silver, or pink hue.

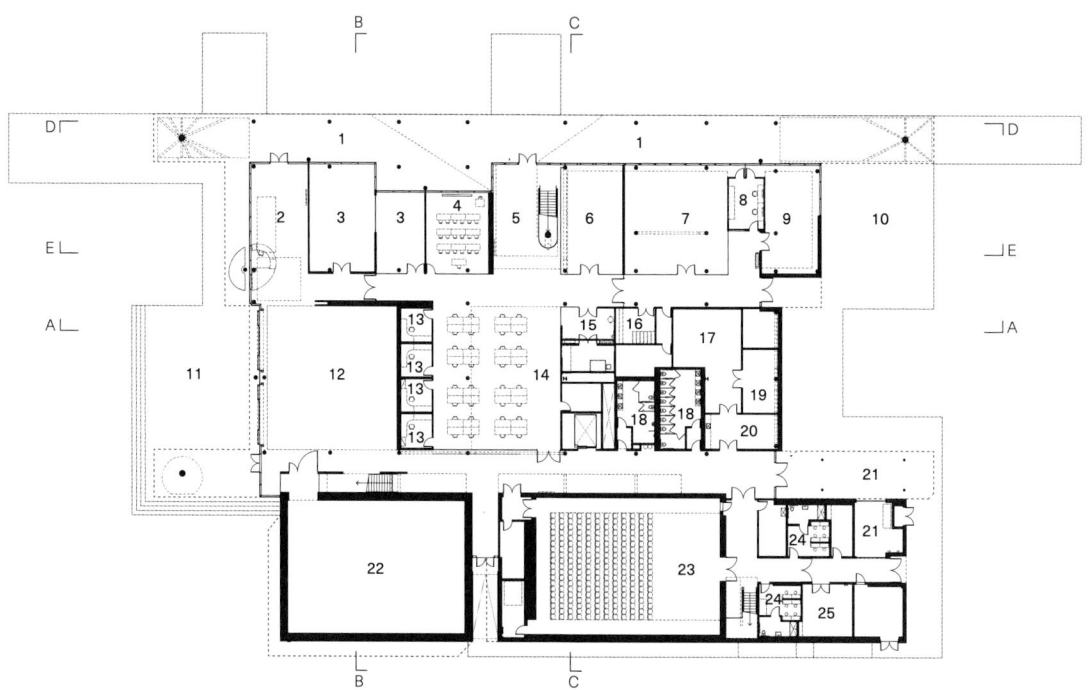

First Floor

1. North Arcade
2. Entrance Gallery
3. Media Arts Gallery
4. Classroom
5. Vertical Gallery & Lounge
6. Rapid Proto-typing Lab
7. Woodshop
8. Shop Manager
9. Metal Shop

10. Assembly Mock Up
11. Lantern Terrace
12. Central Gallery
13. Office
14. Creative Open Studio
15. Paint Shop
16. Shop Storage
17. Art Storage
18. Restroom

19. Art Preparation
20. Storage & Catering
21. Loading Dock
22. Skylight Gallery
23. Studio Theater
24. Theater Dressing Room
25. Theater Storage

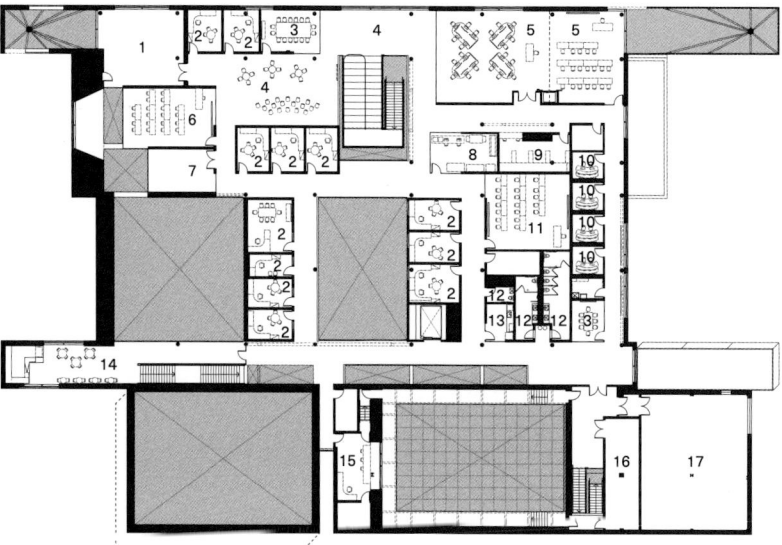

Second Floor

1. Large Module Studio
2. Office
3. Conference Room
4. Break Out Area
5. Open Studio / Double
   Classroom

6. Classroom
7. Artist's Studio
8. Media Lab
9. Technology Library
10. AV/Editing Room
11. Digital Classroom

12. Restroom
13. Faculty Break Room
14. Cafe
15. Theater Control Room
16. Technology Storage
17. Mechanical Room

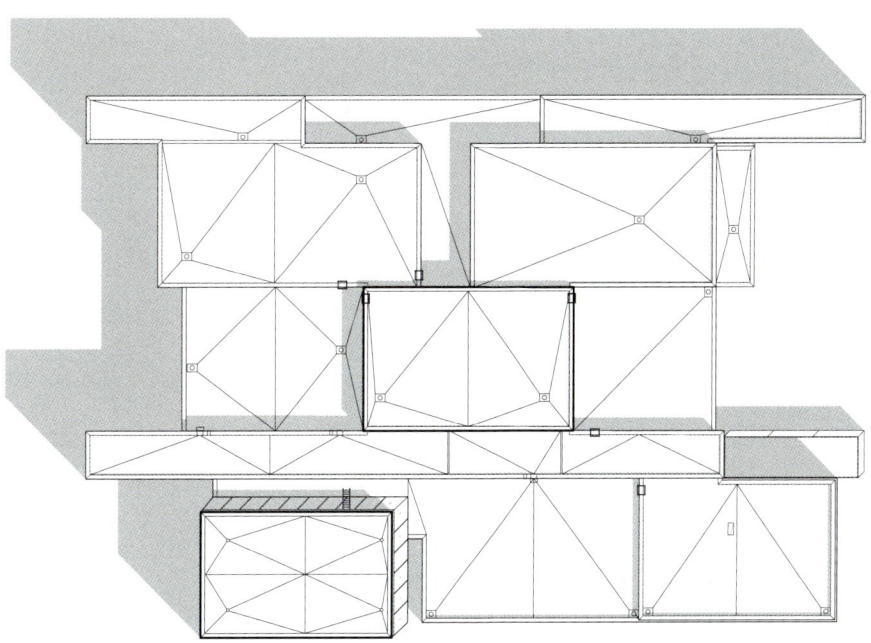

Roof Plan

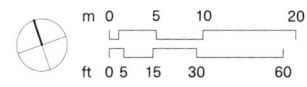

Featuring a high degree of visibility, the space is expected to serve as a platform for group collaborations, performances, and art exhibitions. The transparency affirms its artistic mission to foster connections between disciplines while leveraging the constant hum of activity to energize the core of the building.

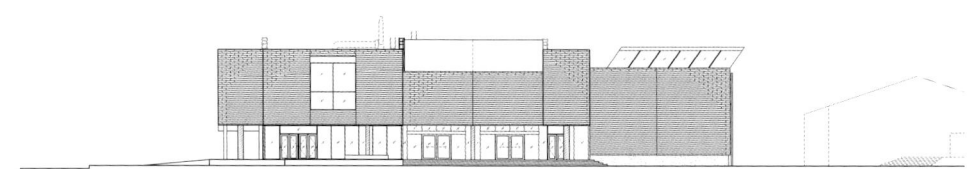

West Elevation

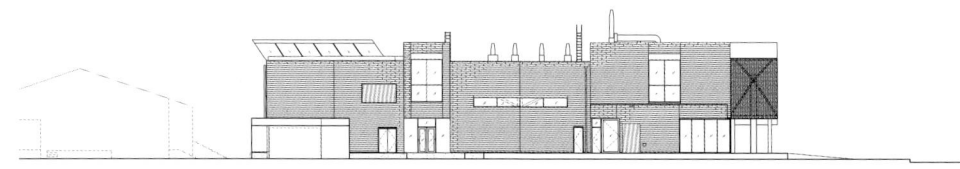

East Elevation

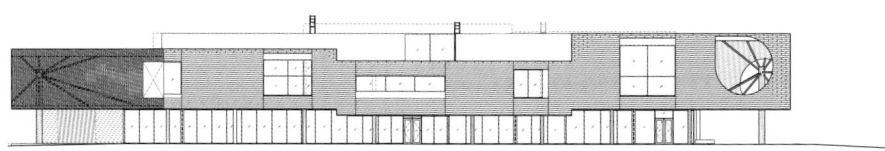

North Elevation

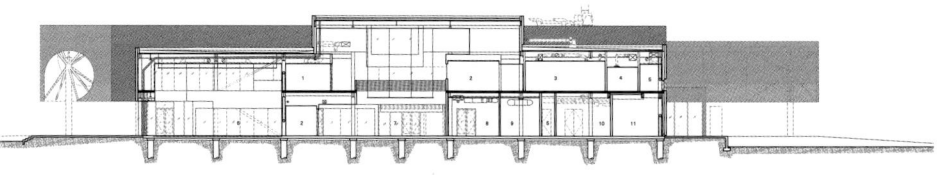

Section A-A

1. Executive Director's Office
2. Office
3. Digital Classroom
4. Audiovisual Editing Room
5. Hall
6. Central Gallery

7. Creative Open Studio
8. Paint Shop
9. Spray Booth
10. Shop Storage
11. Art Storage

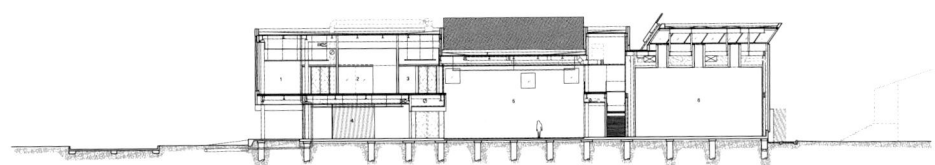

Section B-B

1. Large Module Studio
2. Classroom
3. Artist's Studio
4. Media Art Gallery
5. Central Gallery
6. Skylight Gallery

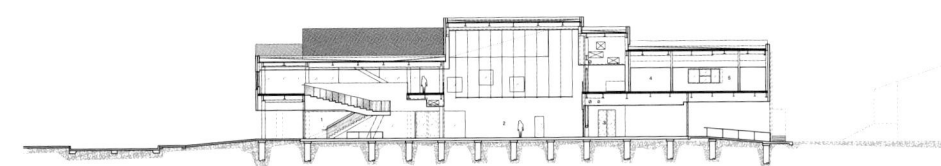

Section C-C

1. North Entry - Vertical Gallery
2. Creative Open Studio
3. Corridor
4. Dimmer Room
5. Control Room

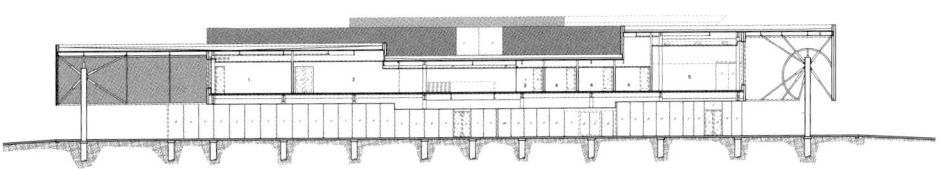

Section D-D

1. Double Classroom
2. Open Studio
3. Meeting Room
4. Office
5. Large Module Studio

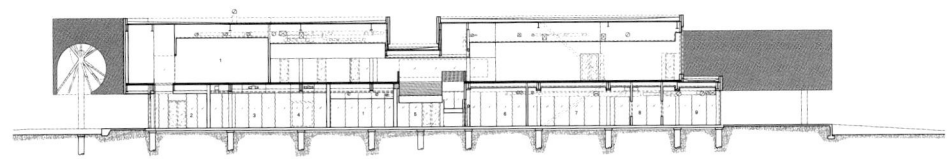

Section E-E

1. Classroom
2. Entrance Gallery
3. Media Art Gallery
4. Large Module Studio
5. North Entry - Vertical Gallery
6. Rapid Proto-typing LAB
7. Woodshop
8. Shop Manager
9. Metal Shop

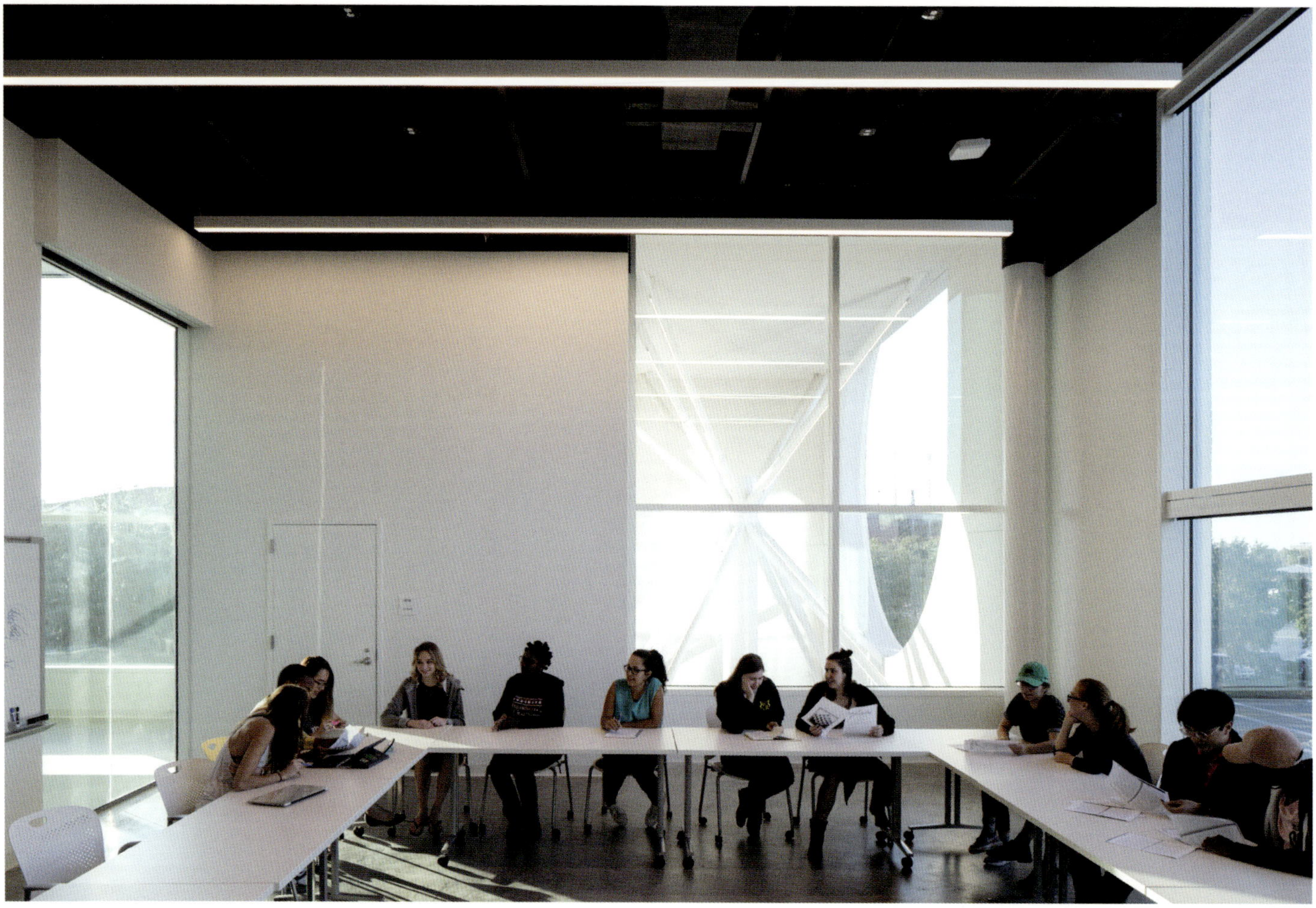

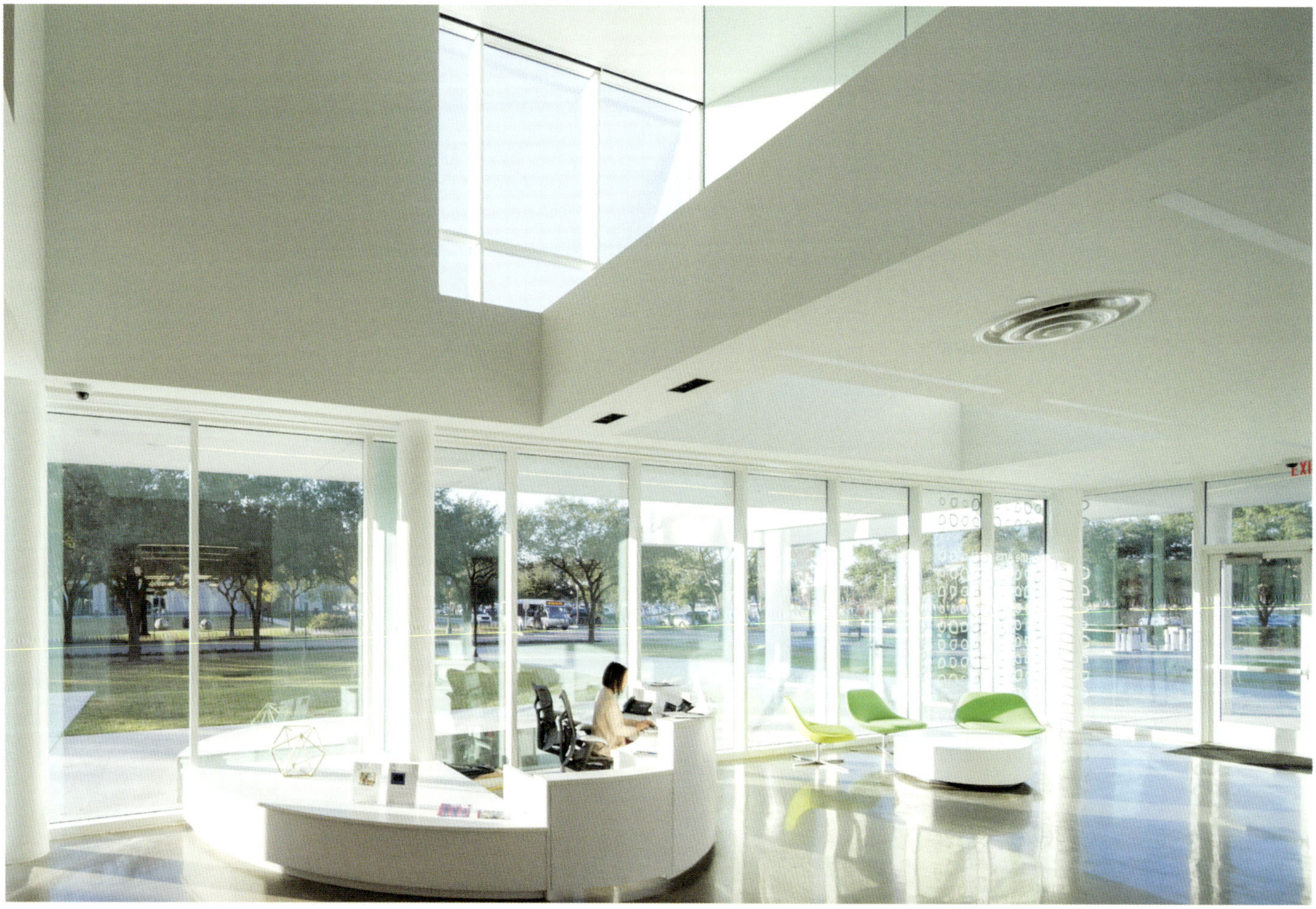

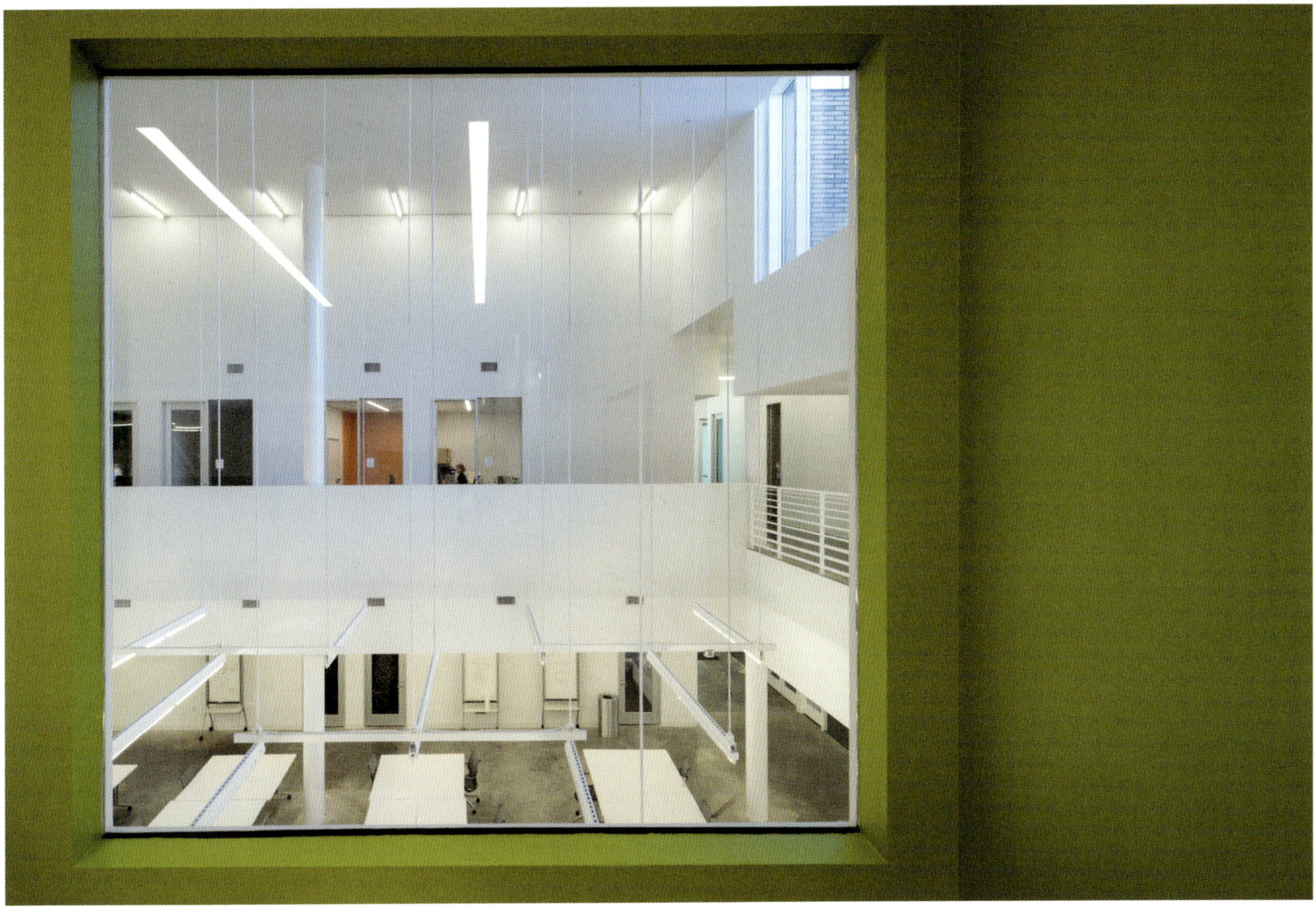

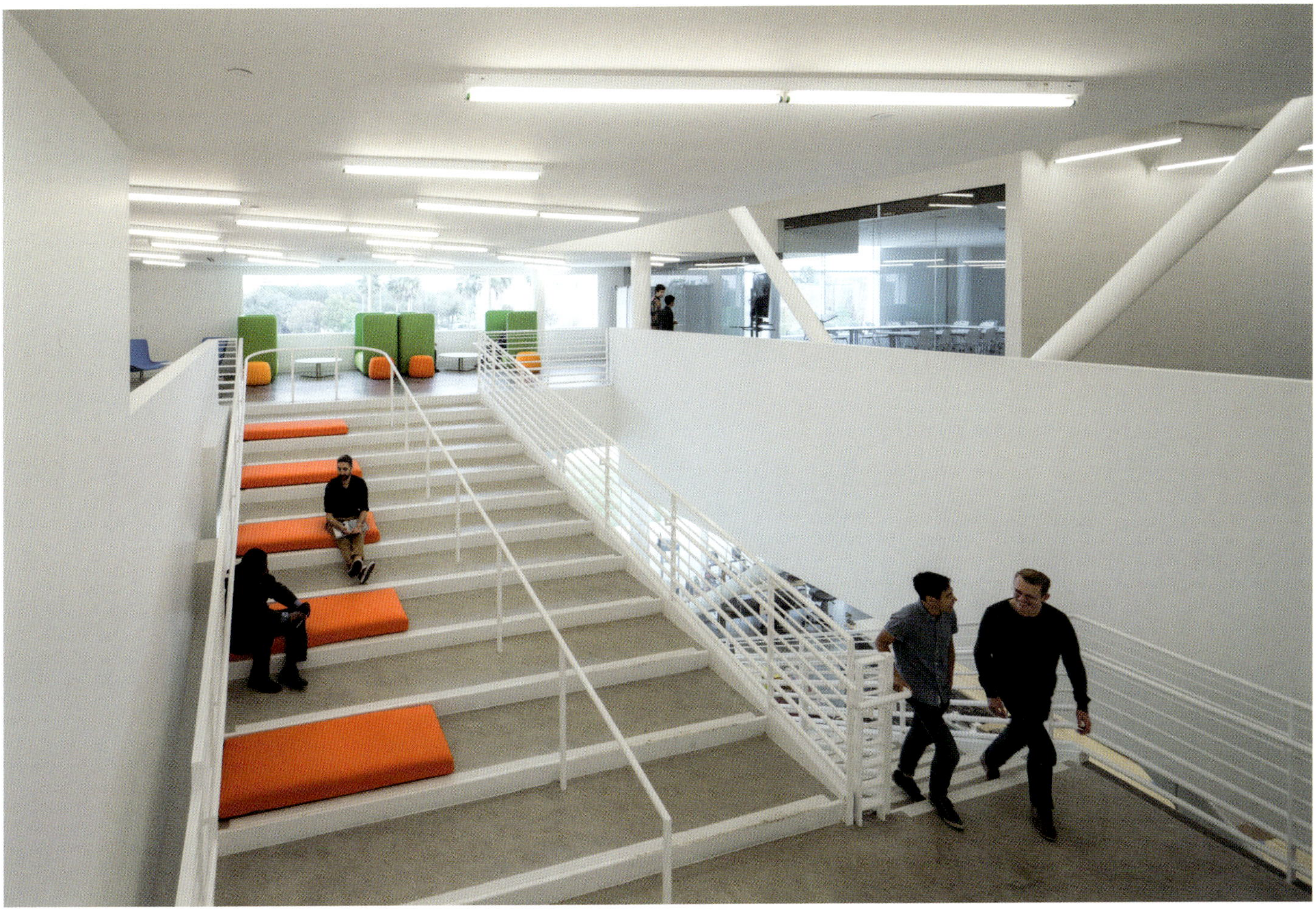

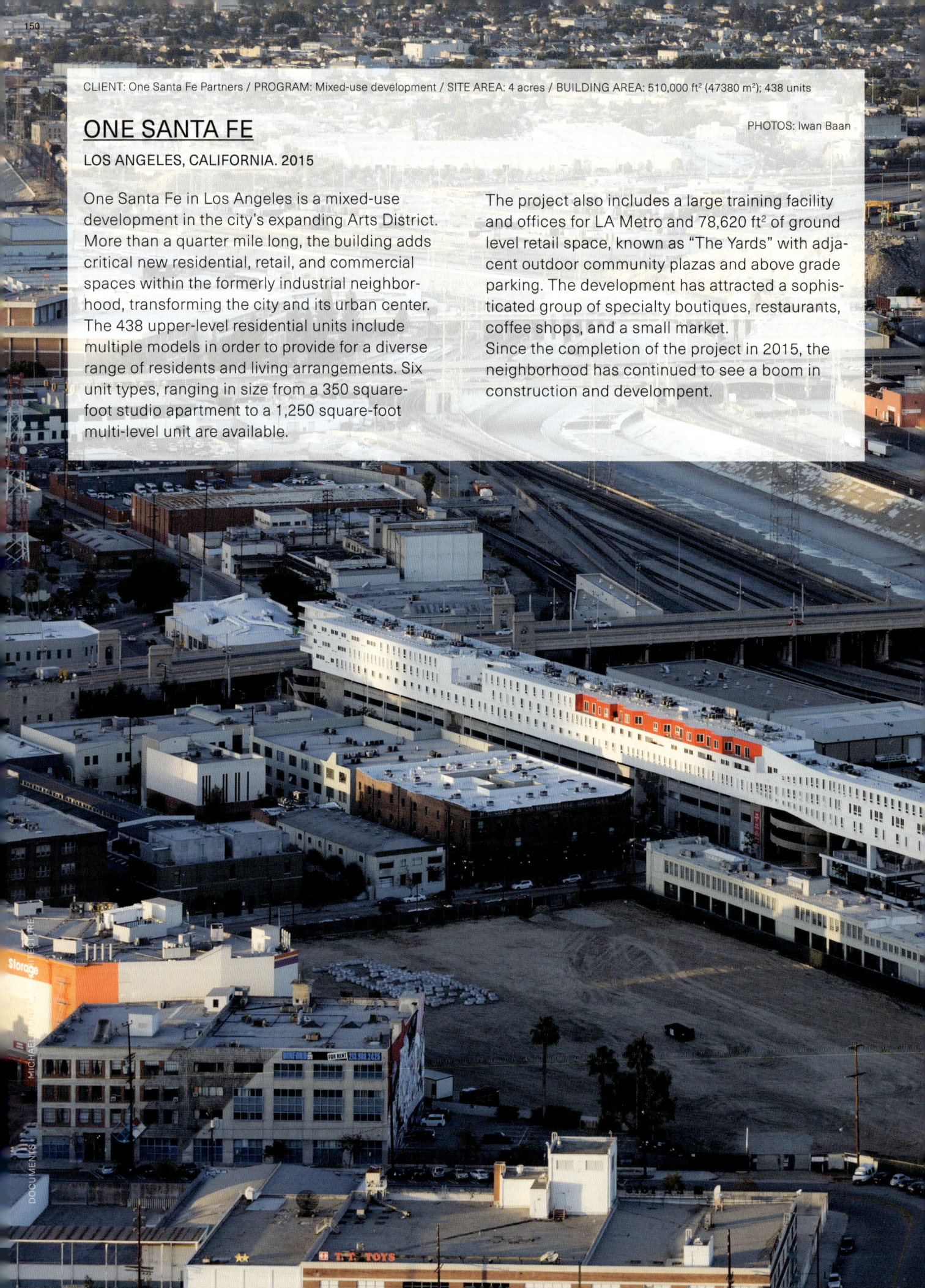

CLIENT: One Santa Fe Partners / PROGRAM: Mixed-use development / SITE AREA: 4 acres / BUILDING AREA: 510,000 ft² (47380 m²); 438 units

ONE SANTA FE

PHOTOS: Iwan Baan

LOS ANGELES, CALIFORNIA. 2015

One Santa Fe in Los Angeles is a mixed-use development in the city's expanding Arts District. More than a quarter mile long, the building adds critical new residential, retail, and commercial spaces within the formerly industrial neighborhood, transforming the city and its urban center. The 438 upper-level residential units include multiple models in order to provide for a diverse range of residents and living arrangements. Six unit types, ranging in size from a 350 square-foot studio apartment to a 1,250 square-foot multi-level unit are available.

The project also includes a large training facility and offices for LA Metro and 78,620 ft² of ground level retail space, known as "The Yards" with adjacent outdoor community plazas and above grade parking. The development has attracted a sophisticated group of specialty boutiques, restaurants, coffee shops, and a small market.
Since the completion of the project in 2015, the neighborhood has continued to see a boom in construction and develompent.

The building's length of more than a quarter mile echoes the strong, linear forms of the surrounding regional infrastructure, including the Los Angeles River, adjacent rail lines, and the former freight depot building that now houses SCI-Arc.

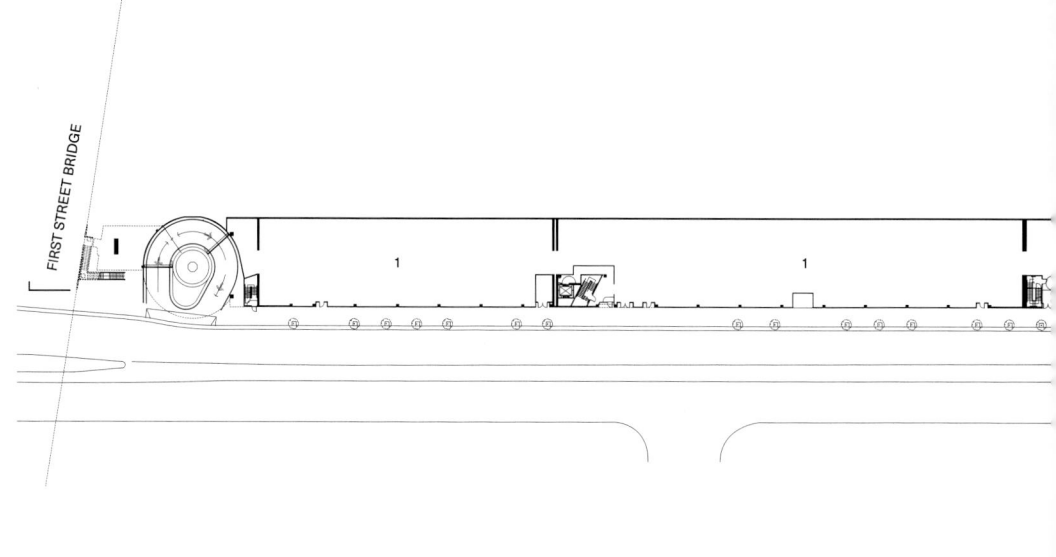

Ground Floor

1 Commercial Offices
2 Grocery
3 Retail
4 Cafe
5 Surface Parking
6 Outdoor Courtyard
7 Restaurant

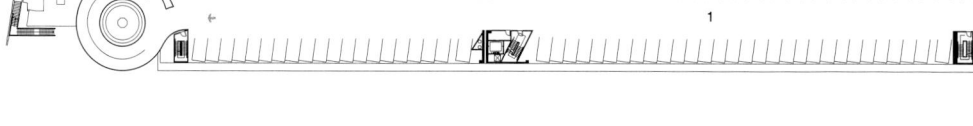

Second Floor

1 Parking
2 Community Room
3 Pool
4 Exercise Room
5 Outdoor Terrace

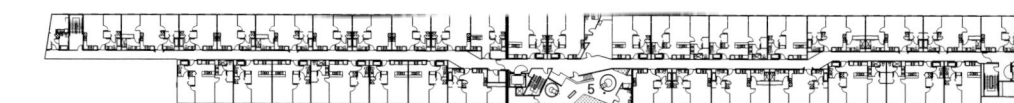

Fifth Floor

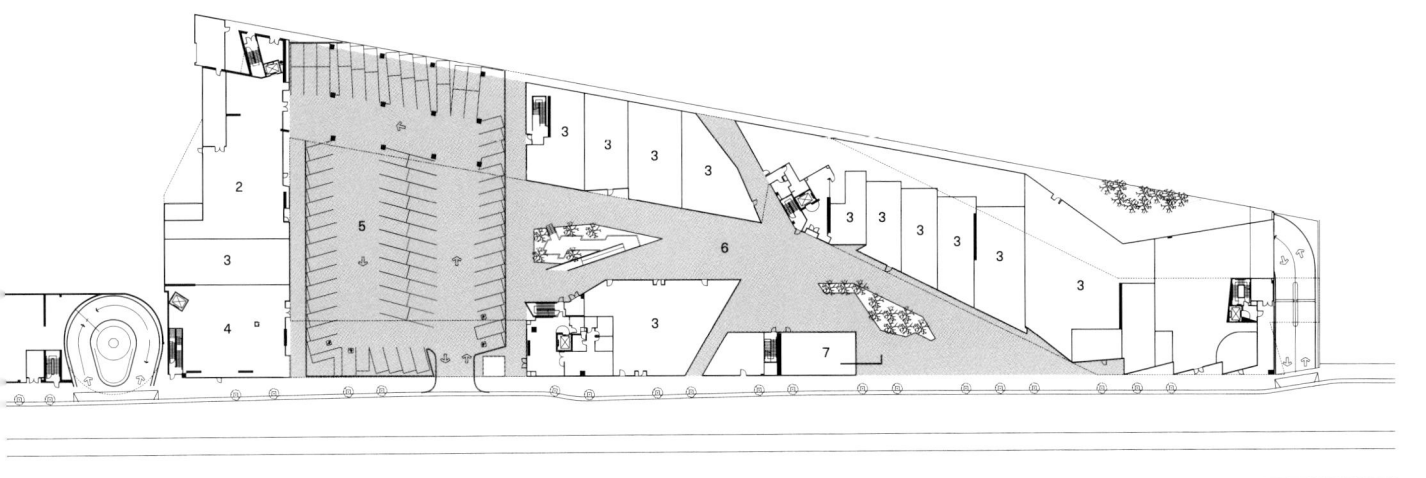

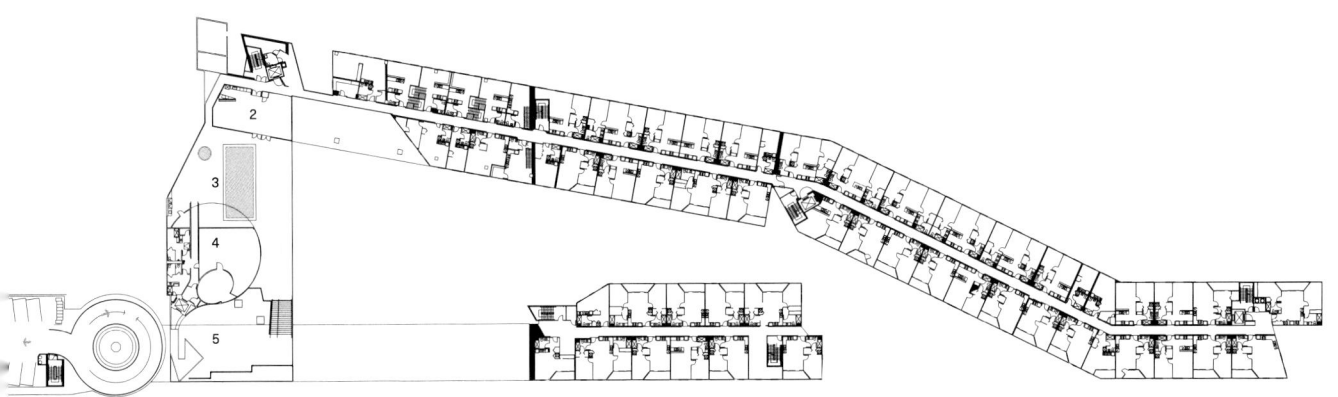

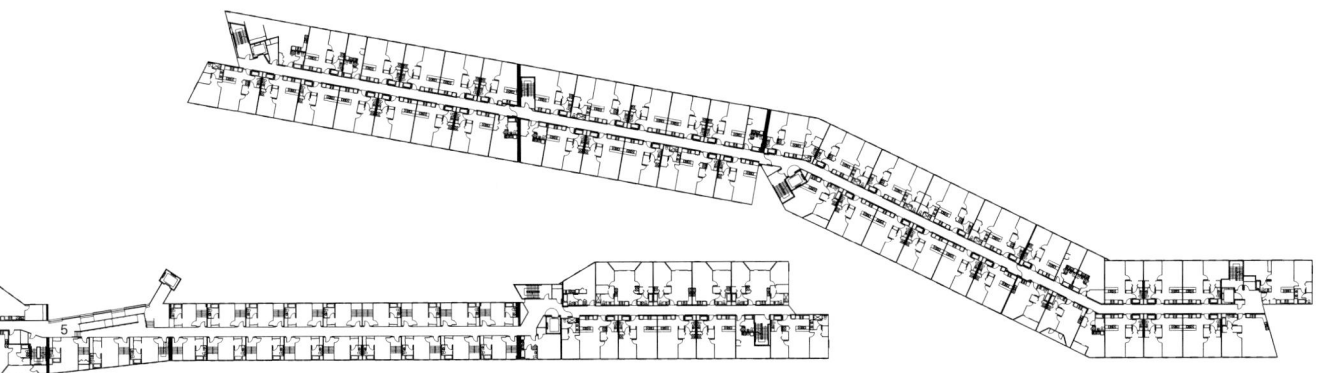

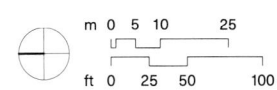

m 0 5 10 25

ft 0 25 50 100

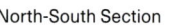

North-South Section

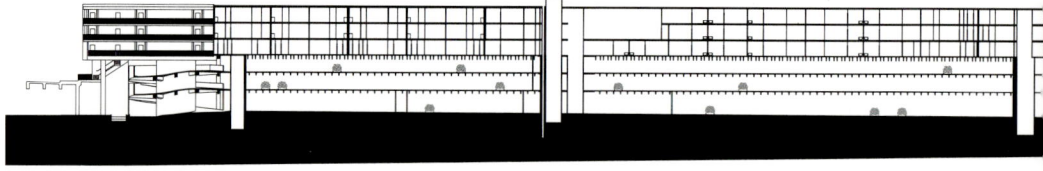

West Elevation

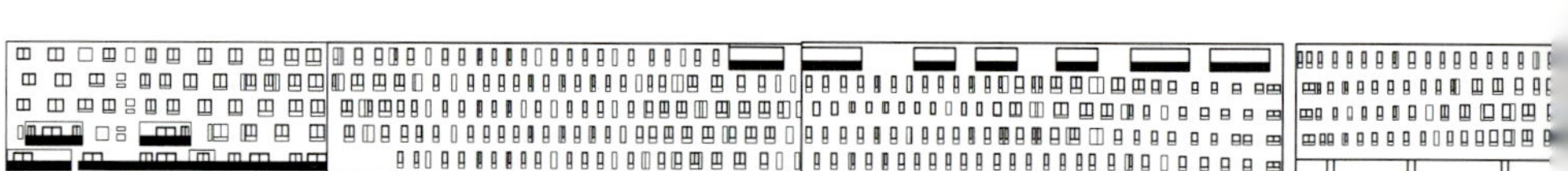

East Elevation

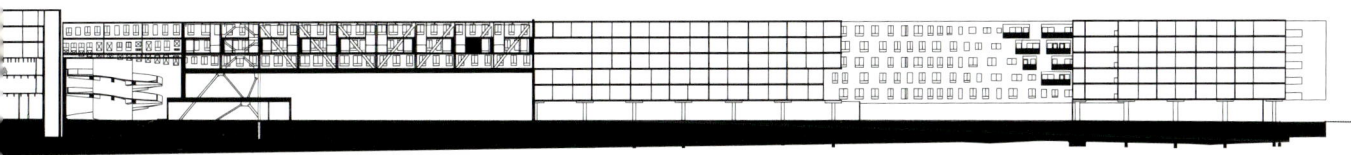

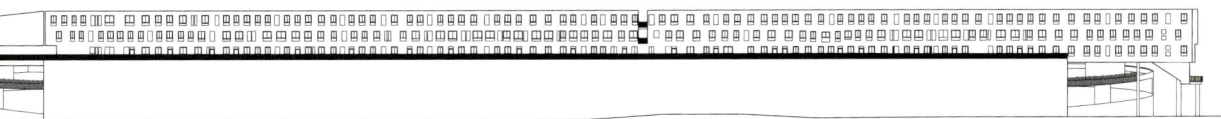

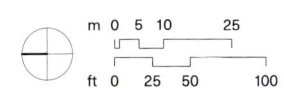

CLIENT: Lari Pittman and Roy Dowell / PROGRAM: Private Residence / SITE AREA: 6 acres / BUILDING AREA: 3,500 ft² (325 m²)

PITTMAN DOWELL RESIDENCE

PHOTOS: Iwan Baan

LA CRESCENTA, CALIFORNIA. 2009

Located fifteen miles north of Los Angeles at the edge of Angeles National Forest, the Pittman Dowell Residence is sited on six acres of land originally planned as a hillside subdivision designed by Richard Neutra. Although three level pads were cleared only one house, the 1952 Serulnic Residence, was built on the site. Over the years, the current owners have developed an extensive desert garden and outdoor pavilion on one of the unbuilt pads. The new Pittman Dowell Residence sits on the last clearing, circumscribed by the sole winding road which leads to the Serulnic Residence on the bluff above.

Five decades after the original house was constructed in this once remote area, the city has grown around it with an accompanying change in both the visual and the physical context. Similarly, the evolving contemporary needs of the artist occupants required a new relationship between building and landscape that is more urban and

contained. Inspired by geometric arrangements of interlocking polygons, the new residence takes the form of a heptagonal figure; its purity is confounded by a series of intersecting diagonal slices through the space.

Bounded by an introverted exterior, living spaces unfold in an array of shifting perspectival frames from within and throughout the house. These perspectival manipulations begin at the level of the room, collapsing and distending space through a series of non-parallel walls that never fully enclose the space of a room. Instead of using doors, a level of privacy is maintained by layering space and limiting view access. An irregularly shaped void caught within these intersections creates an outdoor room at the center whose edges blur into the adjoining living spaces. Movement and visual relationships expand and contract to respond to the centrifugal nature of the site.

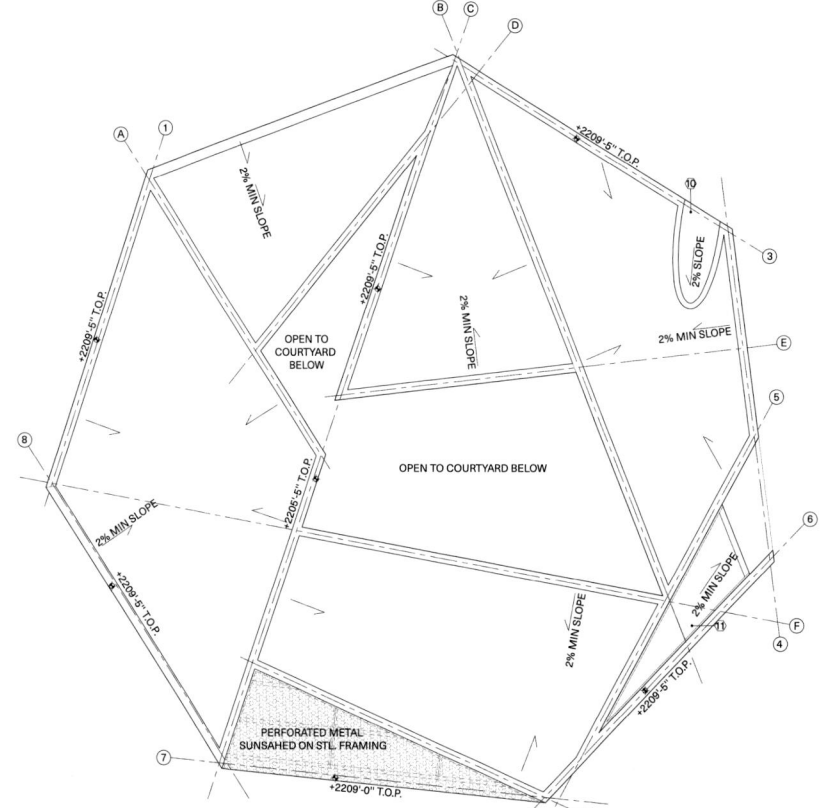

Roof Plan

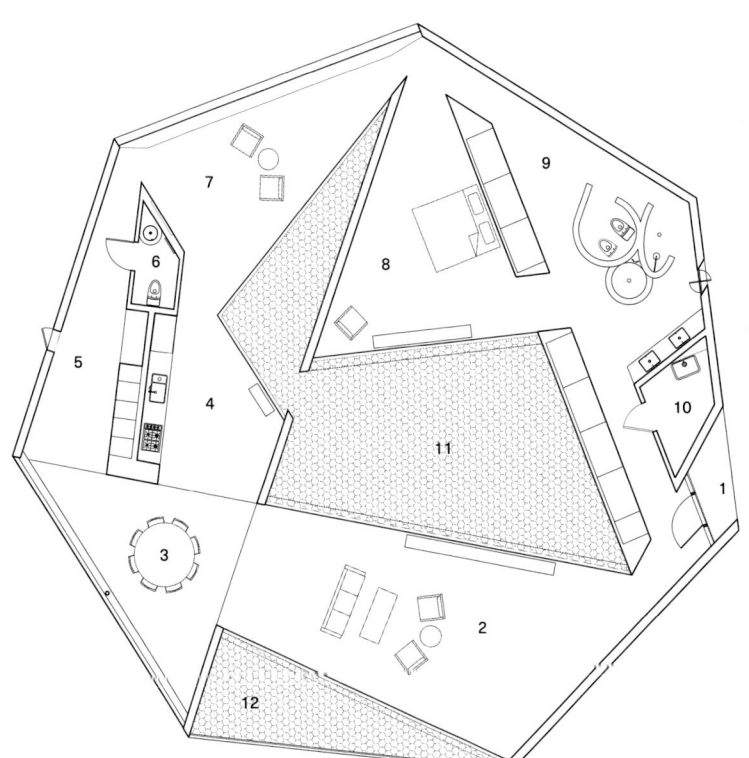

Floor Plan

1 Entry
2 Living Room
3 Dinning Room
4 Kitchen
5 Office
6 Powder Room
7 Library
8 Bedroom
9 Master Bath
10 Utility Closet
11 Courtyard
12 Balcony

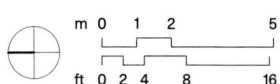

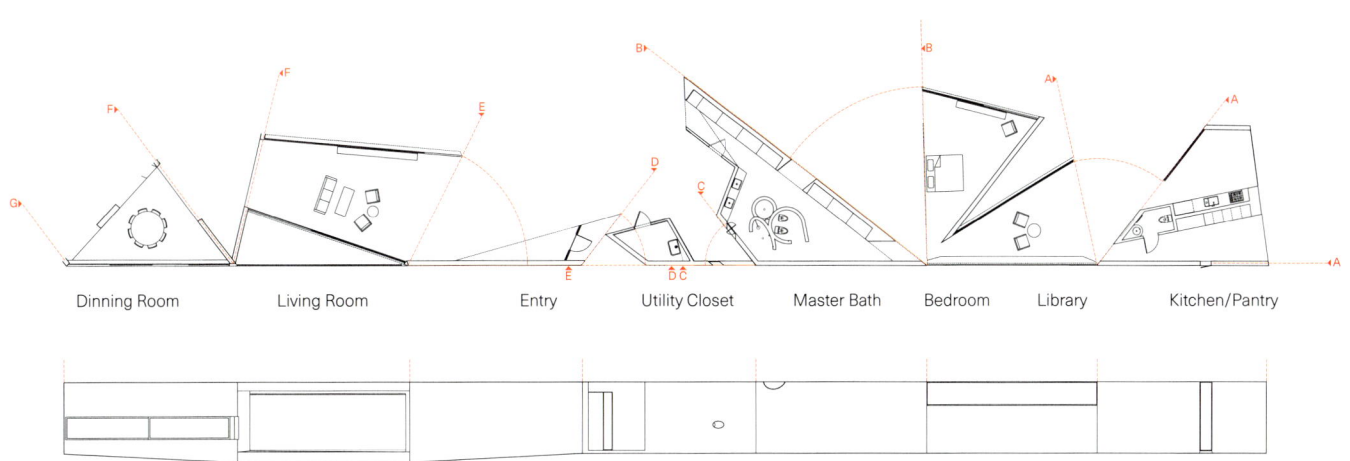

Dinning Room   Living Room   Entry   Utility Closet   Master Bath   Bedroom   Library   Kitchen/Pantry

Unfolded Elevation and Plan

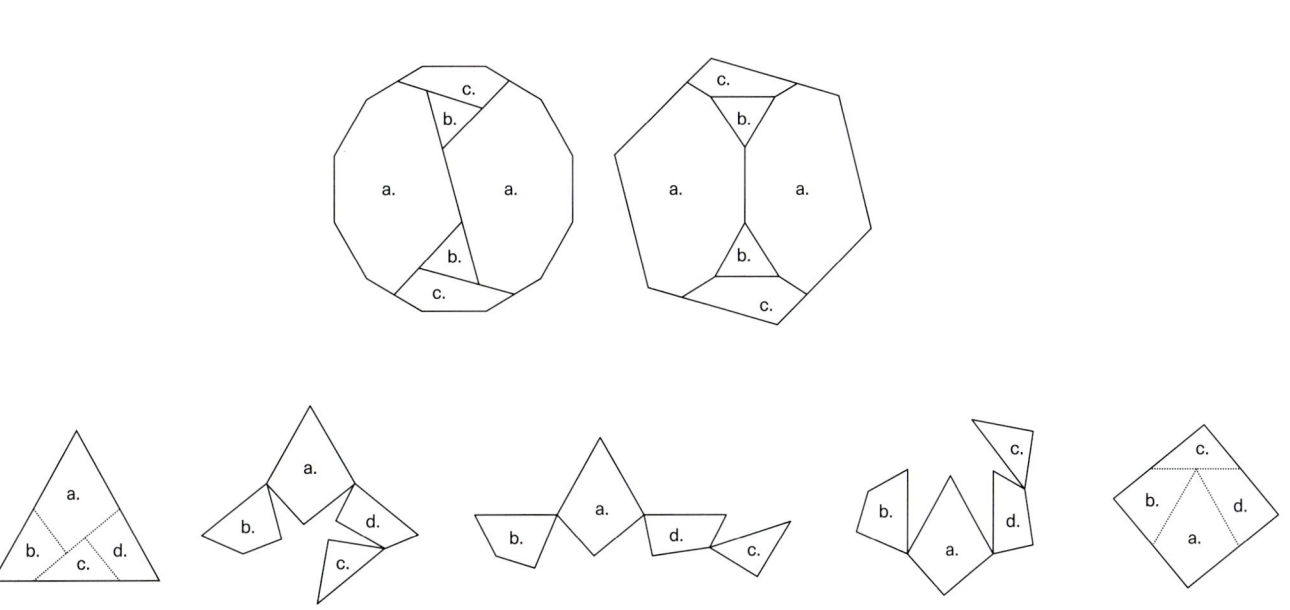

Dissections - diagram of the mathematical concept

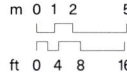

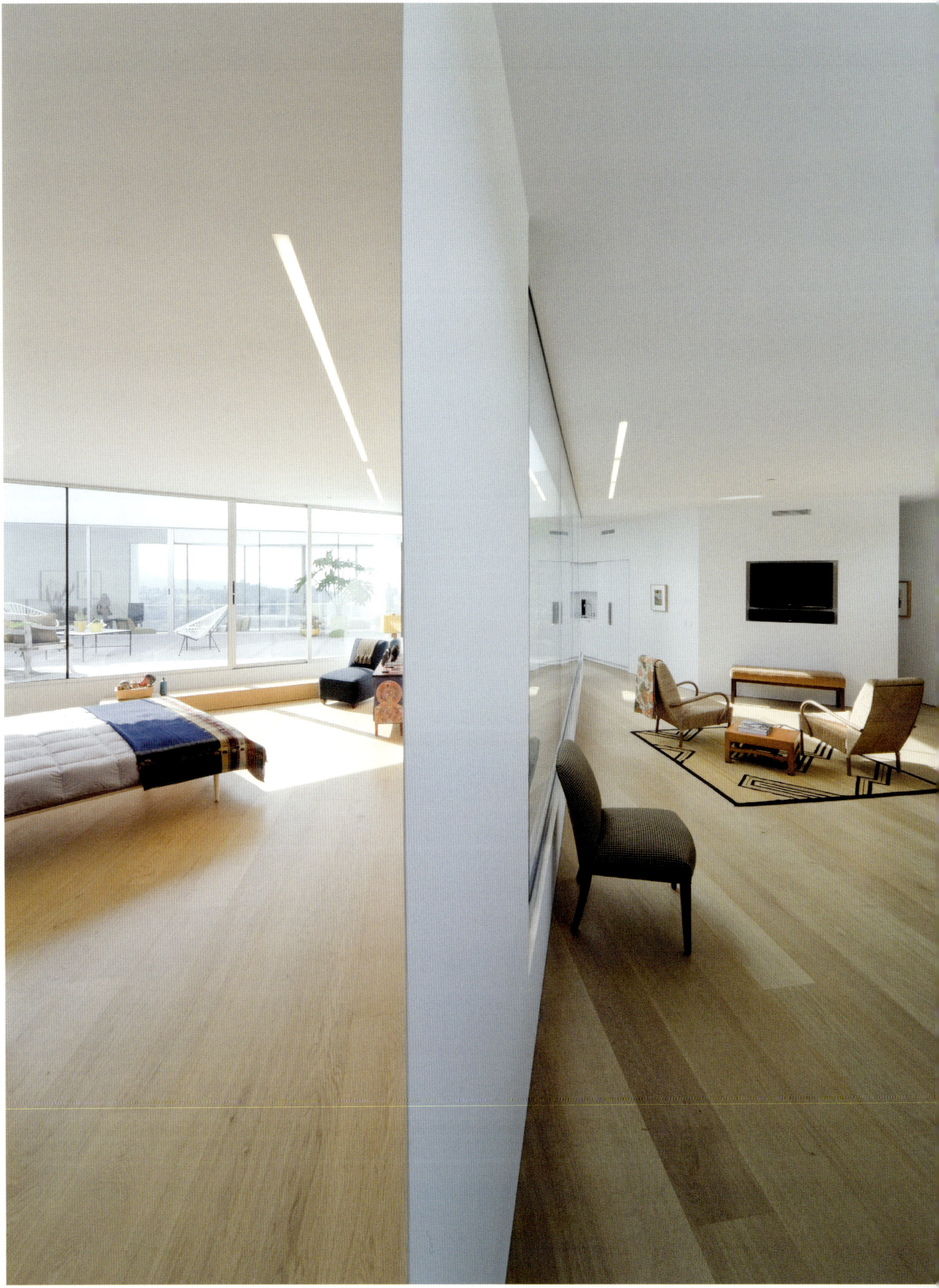

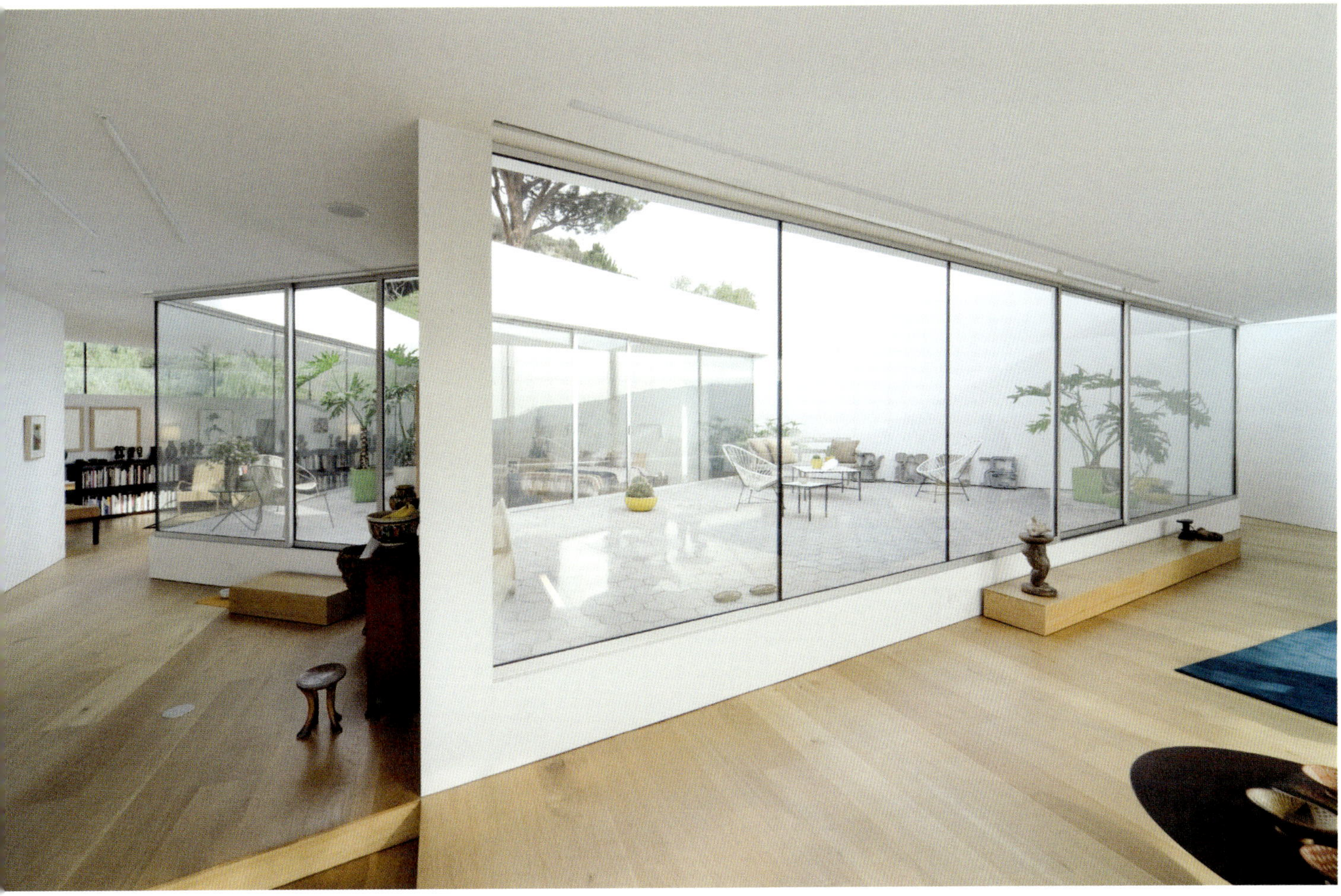

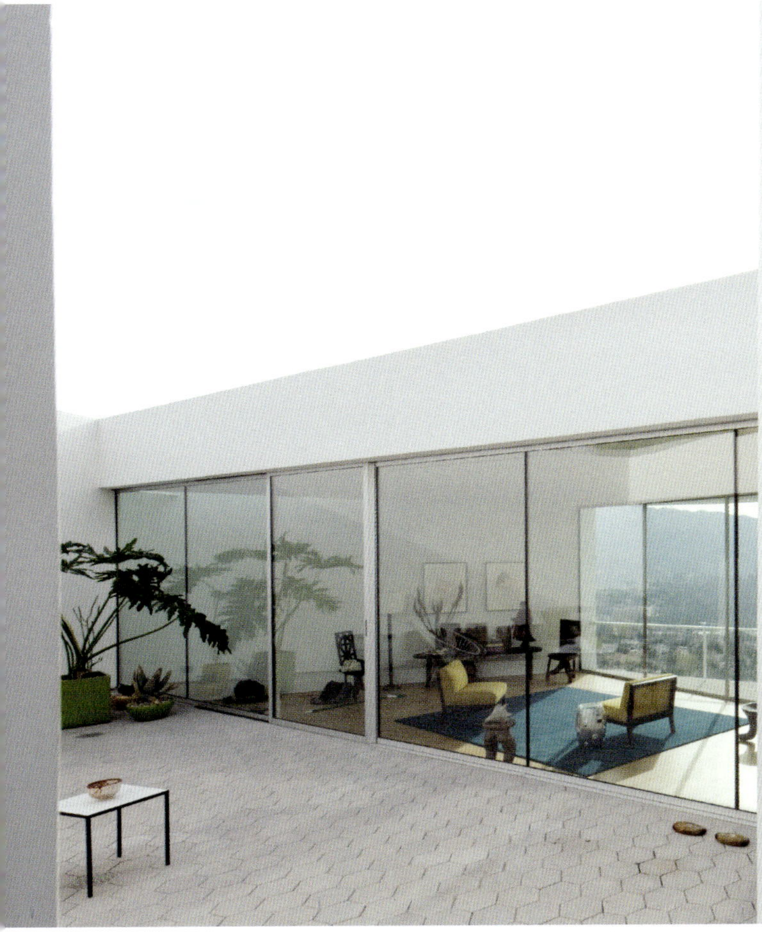

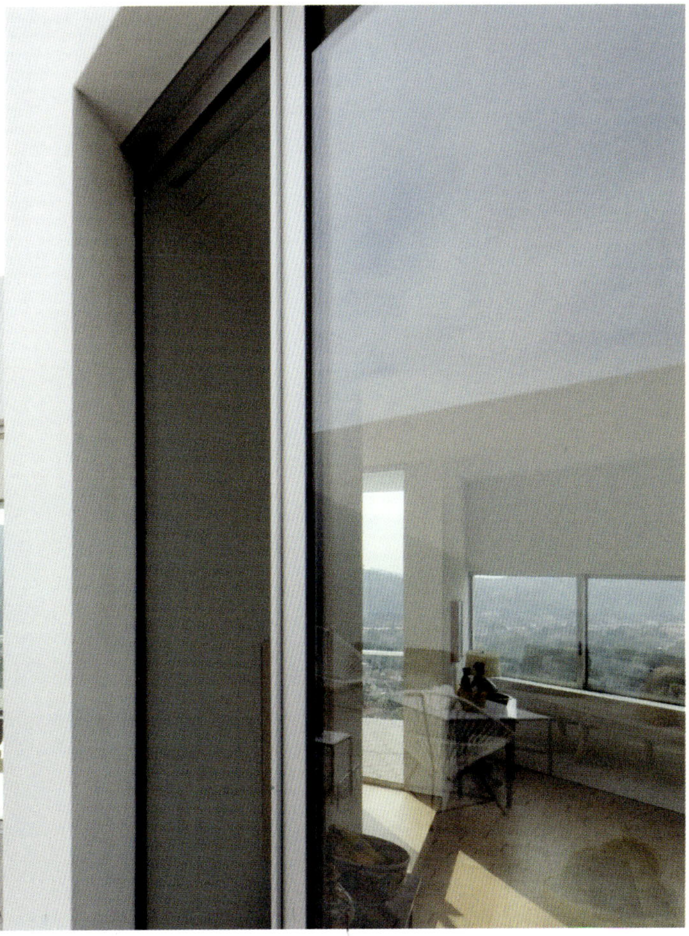

"The Pittman Dowell house was not only trying
to propose an alter ego to Neutra's project, but
it was also attempting to transform the idea
of transparency: in our contemporary lives we
are confronted more and more with this idea of
constant exposure, a virtual transparency."
—Michael Maltzan

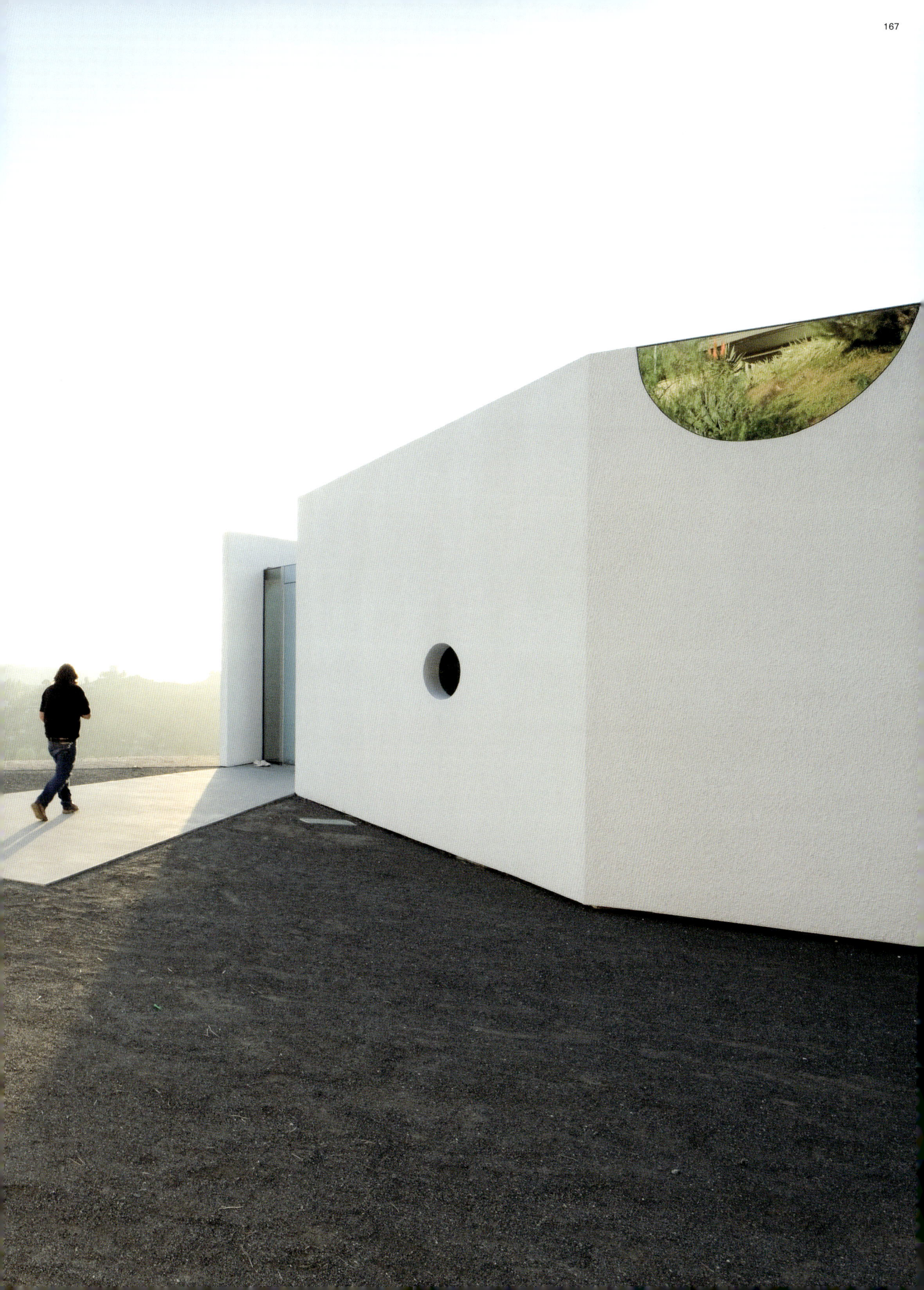

Architecture and Policy

Three projects against homelessness

Since 2003, Michael Maltzan Architecture has been carrying out an extremely committed work together with the Skid Row Housing Trust to contribute concrete solutions to the Los Angeles homelessness problem. Together they have already finished four buildings and a fifth is in process. Maltzan's designs make a powerful statement about the role that innovative, affordable, and safe supportive housing and health resources can play in downtown Los Angeles. His buildings not only accommodate but also offer communal spaces for tenants, assisting residents in their transition and encouraging them to reconnect with each other.

Skid Row Housing Trust is a private association that seeks to provide housing and a permanent support system to those who have experienced homelessness, prolonged extreme poverty, poor health, disabilities, mental illness, and/or addiction. One of the most significant things about their work is that they have managed to design a kind of public-private cooperation, where the state supplies a part of their health budget for the construction of homes. This initiative also provides medical and social assistance.

Their strong belief in architecture's ability to help change the model—from transitional housing to a more permanent solution—led them to contact Maltzan's office. Here, we present three of the developments that resulted from this partnership.

1 CREST
APARTMENTS

2 STAR
APARTMENTS

3 NEW CARVER
APARTMENTS

CREST APARTMENTS

1

The Crest Apartments transformed an existing open site in suburban Los Angeles into a 64-apartment complex for formerly homeless veterans. Located on a busy thoroughfare near two freeways, the project introduces a new density in the neighborhood with easy connections to public transportation and area resources. The client's permanent supportive housing model includes individual efficiency apartments with on-site social services and community spaces. The building's arching form stretches the length of the site, creating a sheltered courtyard with tiered terraces above that include open-air outdoor corridors and an expansive ground level landscape zone. The low points of the mass touch down at both the front and back of the site, ensuring a strong volumetric relationship to the smaller scale single-family residences behind the property and the larger commercial façades running along the boulevard.

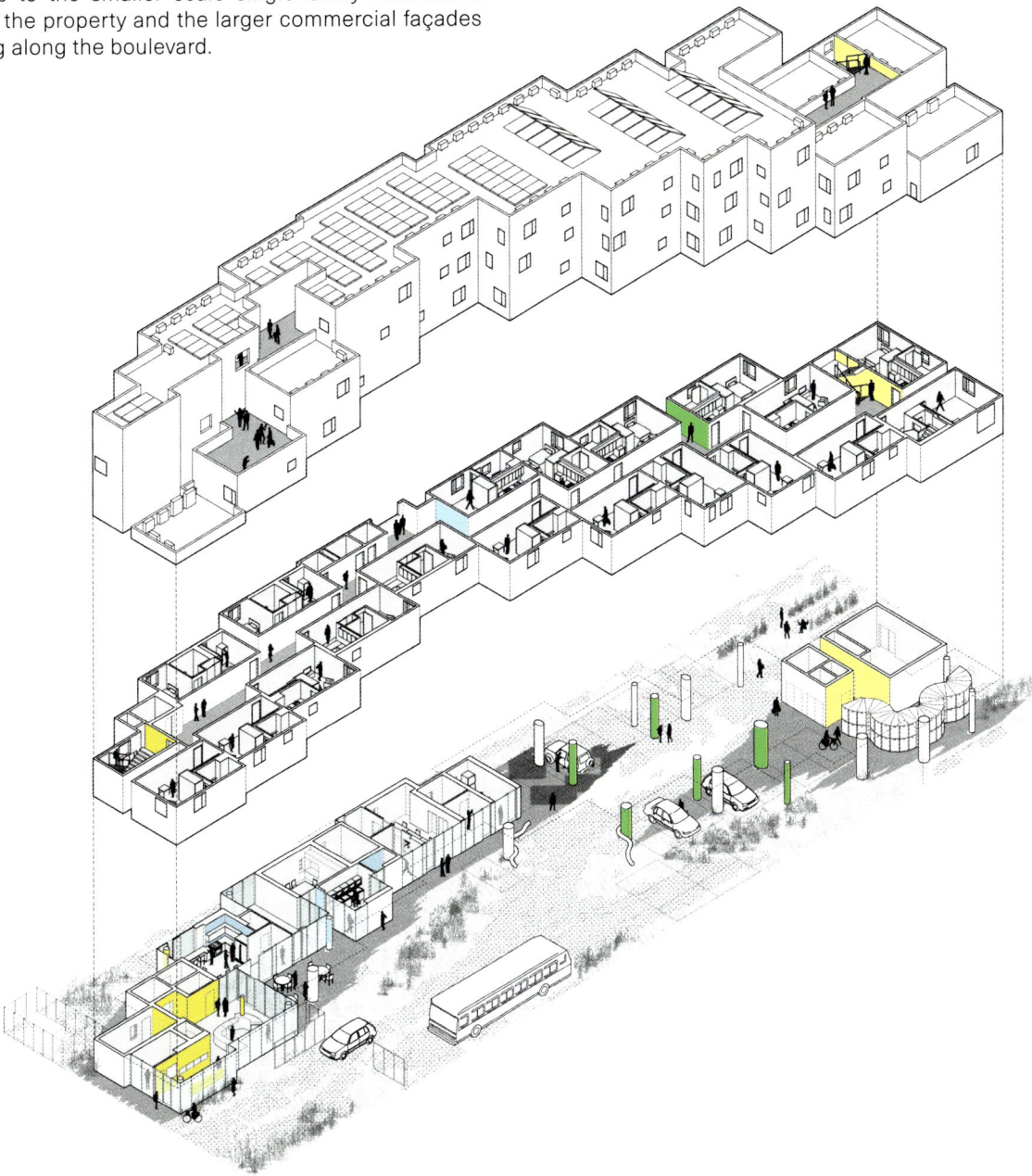

LOCATION: Van Nuys, California / TYPE: 64-unit affordable housing project with shared community spaces, social service offices, and community gardens / SIZE: 45,000 ft² (4180 m²) / STATUS: Completed 2016 / LEED STATUS: LEED Platinum for Homes

STAR APARTMENTS

2

Star Apartments transformed an existing one-story commercial structure in downtown Los Angeles into a new LEED Platinum facility with 102 apartments and support services for homeless individuals. Providing spaces for both permanent housing and supportive services, it is organized around three spatial zones stacked one upon the other: a commercial zone at street level; a second level for community programs; and four terraced floors of residences above. Star Apartments is the first affordable housing project in Los Angeles to incorporate modular construction. As a way to minimize construction waste and reuse existing resources, the design retrofitted the shell of the existing building into the new ground level development. Modular units were built off-site and delivered to the site where they were craned into place on the new tiered structural concrete podium.

1. Lateral Frame + Floor Plates
2. Prefabricated Modular Units
3. Moment Frame / Tray
4. Community Programs
5. Circulation Infrastructure
6. Street Level Retail + Entry

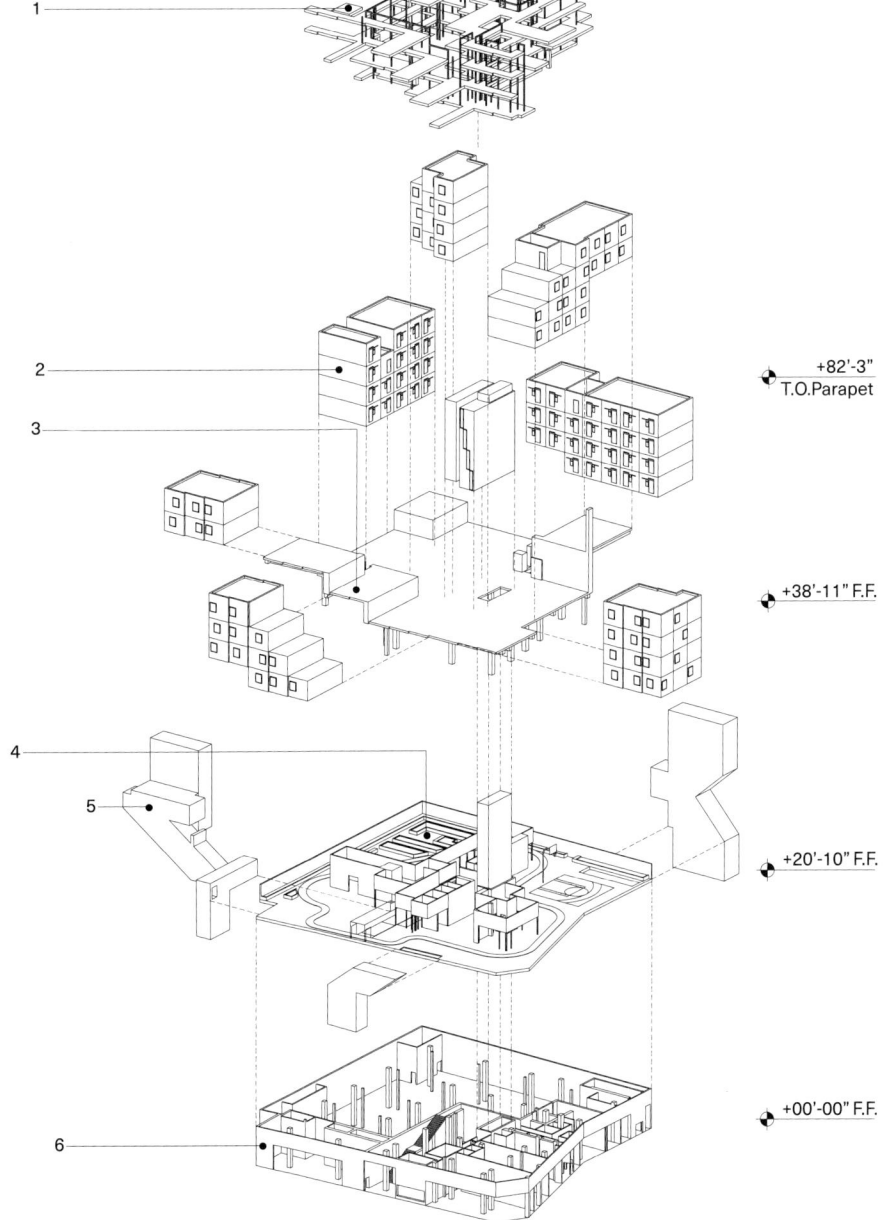

+82'-3" T.O.Parapet

+38'-11" F.F.

+20'-10" F.F.

+00'-00" F.F.

LOCATION: Los Angeles, California / CLIENT: Skid Row Housing Trust / PROGRAM: Affordable Housing, Social Services Counseling, Community Activities, Market-Rate Retail / BUILDING AREA: 95,000 ft² (8825 m²) / NUMBER OF UNITS: 102 efficiency studio units / CONSTRUCTION: Type 3 (wood) over Type 1 (concrete) / STATUS: Completed 2013

NEW CARVER APARTMENTS

3

The New Carver is a 97-unit permanent supportive housing apartment building in Los Angeles' revitalized downtown. The six-story building's circular plan and façade incorporates a subtle pattern of color, light, and shadow. Its core is a broad staircase and open courtyard that provides public open space for residents and allows natural light and fresh air to reach each apartment. Other public spaces include a community kitchen and garden on the ground floor, a lounge and laundry room on the third floor, and a roof terrace with panoramic city views. By incorporating communal spaces into the plinth beneath, the project encourages its residents to reconnect with each other and the city beyond. The six-story circular form emerges from the path of the Santa Monica Freeway. Confronted with a significant level of ambient noise from passing automobiles, it creates a sound buffer by minimizing the building's area directly opposite the freeway.

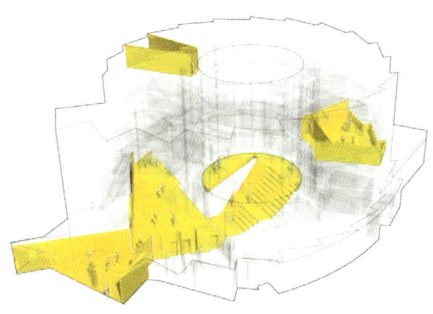

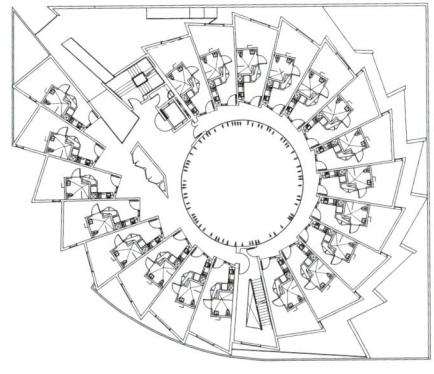

LOCATION: Los Angeles, California / CLIENT: Skid Row Housing Trust / PROGRAM: Affordable Housing, Efficiency Units / SITE AREA: 16,105 ft² (1500 m²) / BUILDING AREA: 53,000 ft² (4924 m²) / STATUS: Completed 2009

Founded in 2000, Ensamble Studio is a cross-functional office led by Antón García-Abril and Débora Mesa, that fuses architecture, engineering, landscape design, and material research. It is based both in Madrid and Boston.

Becoming a 'Master Builder,' as they prefer to be called, is a hands-on commitment that combines meticulous planning with childlike curiosity. Opposites do unite in their practice, where prefabrication and onsite experimentation merge in a poetical outburst.

Antón García-Abril in Ca'n Terra. Ph. Iwan Baan

Ensamble Studio

Débora Mesa at Beartooth Portal. Ph. Iwan Baan

Beyond Design

Antón García-Abril and Débora Mesa interviewed by Pablo Gerson

On a late summer afternoon, Pablo Gerson arrived at the Cyclopean House. Finished in 2015, this project is Ensamble Studio's second building in the United States, and also their second home. In 2012, Ensamble Studio founded the POPLab, Prototypes of Prefabrication Research Laboratory, at the Massachusetts Institute of Technology (MIT) and were contacted by clients for what would become Structures of Landscape at the Tippet Rise Art Center in Montana. Both events made moving to North American soil imperative, but they would not abandon their European office—rather, they expanded it, enlarging it into a factory. It is precisely this tension between industrial prefabrication and artisanal construction, or between the caveman and the robot, that accurately characterizes their architectural doing.

THE STUDIO, THE LAB, AND THE FACTORY

PABLO GERSON

I would like to start with some essential questions: how did you form your studio? When did you begin to work together?

DÉBORA MESA

Antón founded the studio in the year 2000. I joined in 2003, at the beginning, when they were very connected to the world of art, just completing a great deal of work, many competitions. I was still studying architecture and I joined part-time, working in a few projects out of the Madrid studio. The third leg of Ensamble Studio, what in Spain we call, *parejador*, is Javier Cuesta, who joined Antón from the beginning and is the soul of the construction side. We were a rather small office and it was a time in Spain when the system of competitions made work accessible to young architects; there was a lot on offer, which made for a fruitful beginning.

ANTÓN GARCÍA ABRIL

And now that nearly twenty years have gone by—lately I have been thinking a lot about the past—I realize that what we built was not an architecture office. What we founded is a group that builds buildings, which is part of what it means to be an architecture office, but is not

exactly the same thing. In reality, everything that Débora has said is not entirely true. What is true, is that I am older than her [laughs] and that, before, I was doing projects like *Arquitecto Antón García*—we made the *Escuela de Estudios Musicales* in Medina del Campo, Spain. When we began, Ensamble Studio and *Materia Inorgánica*, our developmental business, we decided that we would begin to build our projects, which today, twenty years later, is logical, because technology is inviting this connection between project and object. To be capable of constructing our work, we had to be builders, and to be builders we needed a business, and to have a business we needed partners. And so, well, let's say that the system jumpstarted from there. Before then, we made projects, and after, we started making buildings. It is a significant change. Ensamble Studio's first endeavor was the SGAE headquarters in Santiago de Compostela (2007), where we were the architects, the engineers, the constructors, the artists, the ones who conducted the tests. We did it all, we were everything, we were a full-service operation. From that point on, all of the other works were done in the same way, even those that for their scale, dimension, and location did not permit us to contractually serve as the contractors. Gradually, almost by habit, we took on an executive role that transcended the work of the architect who designs the plans and supervises. We do not supervise, we execute. Débora moved to Santiago to live and become what in the United States is called the Design Chief or Project Manager. That kind of integration was what captivated us. For example, in the United States works are not executed in this way, quite the opposite: the American model is based on the fragmentation of knowledge, not to hyper-specialize it but to divide it up, for reasons that are favorable to architecture. *Ensamble* is the Spanish-ization of the French *assembler* and of *ensamblaje*. We bring together the semantics of tectonics, which has to do with our understanding of architecture as a tectonics of putting things together, and the idea of a group, of an integral group, in which we are capable of 'giving' a building, not of designing it. That is our origin and it is where we are positioned now; we have taken a turn, but it is exactly where we are now.

PG   What brought you to Boston, to Cambridge?

AGA   Adventure could be a good answer. To make an arts center in the Rocky Mountains, the Structures of Landscape project in Montana (2015) on the other extreme of the earth, and to go there to execute the project represented a unique opportunity, and we went with our family. It coincided with an invitation from MIT to start a laboratory that would give us the chance to consider the integration of the architect and the circumstances surrounding a building from a technological perspective. The lab that we established, POPLab (Prototypes of Prefabrication), in a way already had its task laid out for it, because prefabrication has two problems to resolve. In the first place, the cultural stigma: we have to redress the idea that prefabrication is equal to the mass production of low-cost Soviet barracks. We have worked hard on the cultural stigma, transforming prefabrication into a thing of intellectual, formal, and spatial sophistication. The house Hemeroscopium (2008) is an example of that manifesto because it creates a language based on pieces 'off the shelf' from different markets: a beam here, a slab here. We did some interesting projects in the POPLab that developed that language: the Suprablock (2014) and the Urban Shelve (2013), which, from a speculative point of view, work in a typological and/or cultural line. Second, we realized there is an opportunity right now—in the United States they are making buildings with investments that are expensive but inefficient and of poor quality. Those of us who have seen the world a bit realize that in countries without the economic potential and level of opportunity of the United States, there is far better architecture. One has to go to the campuses of Harvard or UCLA to find something. We realized that there are circumstances that have generated this condition, and we decided that our American adventure had to take a look at this way of understanding architecture. We understood that—in this, MIT inspired us—now is the moment in which technology joins perfectly with design and responds to something that has not yet been made visible in the market. So, these last five years that we have been in charge of the

laboratory have been a time of reflection. We have done very significant work, and we have realized that architecture requires a connection between data and material. It is a technical connection that the architect needs to lead. We have the tools, and what has not yet been developed is a protocol for practice that allows all of this to be executed. What in the academic field was called the 'revolution of the fab'—of digital manufacturing in the nineties and, in the last twenty years, developed at the linguistic, formal, and cultural level—now has to make a jump to the street. This is what we want to dedicate ourselves to doing over the next ten years, but we have needed this adventure for its change of context, of perspective. For us it has been very enriching.

DM   Our practice has always been quite experimental because we have formed unconventional ideas and wanted to build those ideas. This has made it necessary for us to experiment to resolve uncertainties before turning to action, before beginning construction. We were very interested in coming to the United States, to MIT, to understand what research means in an institutional, organized environment, with the possibilities of projection. In these five years we have learned a lot, but we have not ceased to be people of action; times and protocols do not match what we are used to doing within our profession.

AGA   What has changed our perspective as Europeans? We always understood research to be an intimate task, linked to an almost personal experience, to creativity, but we have realized that this is not the case. Research is the spark of an economic engine, one that usually begins in the university and its surrounding garages and has to jump to the street, immediately. That is the American method of research, which is exactly what we are doing. MIT is an engine to get things out on the street. There is another MIT that contains academic research behind the walls, comfort, and warmth of the school. That is not the case for us. We are from the street and we always have been. Everything we have learned from entrepreneurship over these five years has been extraordinary. How does the capitalist system work? What does society expect in order to validate an idea? The concept of authorship in the North American context is completely different from the Latin one. In the European context, and mainly in the Latin world, the author is the one who gives his name: authorship reflects a respected person. In the North American Anglo-Saxon context, the author is non-existent or irrelevant, and yet, nevertheless, there are concepts associated with intellectual property that transform into capital. You have to think how these types of economic games—which are so relevant to constructing a building that costs 200 million dollars—affect architectural design. The world has evolved very quickly, and architecture has to respond if it is to serve the society we have. All this without forgetting the deep mysteries of space, construction, matter, and architectural principles that have been maintained throughout history. Now, the history within which we must work has accelerated algorithmically. It is an incredible thing that the technology accessible to us today is not being used in the construction industry. That puts the architects in a very precarious situation.

These years at MIT have allowed us to understand context, to make a couple of buildings—the house we are in right now is an incredible example. This is exactly what we live for, to build this room, but it was not easy. The house, in reality, does not have great tectonic complexity: they are galvanized profiles, not welded but bolted; it is a dry construction, it is fiber cement. Obviously, there is nothing 'catalog,' but we have not invented anything special either, we just wanted to use a different tectonic, another language, but it was impossible. Im-poss-i-ble. And when we found a way—very expensive. The solution: art and science, as always. We designed a first test in the laboratory using lightness as a concept and containing the tectonics of American framing with the tectonics and logic of large-scale prefabrication. It is a meeting between two worlds that are rarely found together, but that allowed, on the one hand, to build this space, which, without being a structural audacity, differs from other spaces in the domestic sphere. On the other hand—and this is the most important thing—we built it in Spain and we transported it to the United States. Thus, we opened a channel of vision that is globalized, technological, and offsite. To do this we had to assemble an importer. Prefabrication is always a local industry: it is prefabricated in Toronto and in two days the piece is in New York; it is not manufactured in Toronto and taken to Chile, because that would mean a truck that crosses the Andes and the Amazon jungle. I am talking about bringing a finished piece, ready to go. I did not know that industry, and we made all the effort: it was ten percent design and the rest was logistics and assembly. The assembly, the vehicle that transcends the design, can have all these kinds of variables.

We also realized another thing. In the United States you do one thing and they ask you for a second one. Now, to do the first one is very difficult because everyone is subjugated by the past, what has been tried, what is safe. Risk capacity in this society is high, but they always ask you—and this happens in Europe as well—to do an A type building, to make another A type building, and this is redundant. If you are capable of breaking this routine and making the type A, automatically there is a market for type A. This room was a moment of revelation. The laboratory inspired us to work in dry with light elements, we tested them; we had a beam there for a year going cold, measuring its oscillations to see how it behaved. Pure, hard research. Immediately we did a spin off, which in this case was not-for-profit, and

we transferred that technology, that experience, and that knowledge to whoever was going to manufacture our house, which in this case was also us. This has had a very important impact on our way of seeing architecture and especially on our way of understanding the American context. This experience, this adventure, which takes time, because in architecture everything is slow, gave us a project for MIT, a project for Tippet Rise Art Center, and this house, which has allowed us to develop an unprecedented, new form of conception of the labor of the architect.

We are now working on the next rendition of this, which is to transfer the parameters and constructive systems, made by engineers and designers in code for manufacturing, so as to communicate to either the welding machine or automated arm. If the intermediate engineer or the contractor is the only one who transfers the data to the material then we, the architects and designers, are dead. In fact, we will be going back to study in Madrid: we are building the *Ensamble Fábrica*.

DM   We have grown and grown: we have gone from an office with computers to the model laboratory and, now, to an entire factory.

AGA   It is almost an industry with a prototyping space large enough to accommodate a three-stop station of forty feet, which is the logical maximum of an international transport. It has two tracks with two automated robots on both sides and an automated bridge. Soon we will be able to serve an industry—but not with a design, that to me seems very fragile, but with a product. At the factory, we as designers are able to transmit ideas to this gadget, which will be the welding of this little screw. It is not a renunciation of architecture, but in order to reach this technical revolution, we must be clear—technically and culturally—for the people who will receive a semi-automatic system to assemble. It should be said—this is not going to be an architecture without soul, without design, redundant, repetitive; on the contrary, it is the same architecture that is in the hands of the architect, but it is now capable of being delivered in pieces, like a car, neither more nor less. We patented a truss system and we are going to do hybrid prefabrication, where the shuttering mode can be automated; it is hoisted dry and it is concreted up. Right now, we are doing it with a hopper, which is the most precarious thing in the world, but soon we will do it with a pressurized system. We have already begun to study how this system can build a generic tower by semi-automating the assembly.

The technological basis of our protocol is to undo the *Maison Domino* as a principle. The modern movement, which today still dictates how a building is made, determines first the skeleton, then the façade and, once closed, the interior layout and the installations—great, you have a building. It gives a formal and linguistic freedom in the façade that is fantastic, but the most important thing is still that the skeleton

Building process of SGAE headquarters in Santiago de Compostela. Ph. Roland Halbe.

is made first. After many years of researching, building, and interpreting the market, we have come to an opposite conclusion. Automation allows us to make everything that contains a building in parts, following the code of efficiency of the tools off-site, in the factory, and then injecting the skeleton with fluid concrete at the last minute. That's what we call hybrid prefabrication. The structure of this house can be prefabricated and is stable on two to four floors, but you cannot build a tower. With the anti-domino principle, yes. In the end, it is a technological problem.

STONES AND BEAMS

PG   In the Dossier of the first issue of this publication we postulated that we must look for a certain discomfort in the contemporary discipline. Many architecture offices operate from a historical or technical component that accommodates them—that is why we chose the title "Between Cozy History & Homey Technics." My next question points to how Ensamble Studio operates theoretically. There seems to be a dilemma between Structures of Landscapes in Montana and this house, the Cyclopean House. They seem like different, or almost parallel paths, that meet in many aspects, but not in others. How do they relate to more historicist or more technical theories, to parametricism, for example, which seems to be mutating into something else? How do you see the work of your studio in relation to this disciplinary context?

AGA   We have always been working within these two parallels. These two parallels are two lines, or one delimited by its edges—it is mathematical topology—that never touch. We started our manifesto with two of our houses because

we want to keep them while we can, and I think we will never let them go. We built The Truffle (2010) and Hemeroscopium House at the same time, simultaneously. Stones and beams—we've spent ten years talking about stones and beams. Stone, something that is of the earth, that you interpret and use. Beams, something you finish, you have taken it out of a scientific laboratory context and into another. We keep doing that—exactly that—we have just changed the scale and the context. What is the union? Technology. We are positivists in that aspect. We believe that technology connects us with the deepest aspects of humanism and art and we have always said (half in jest) that we did the first 3D-printed building in the history of architecture: The Truffle, twelve years ago. Who was the printer? I was. I handled the concrete task, but the logic is the same. What interested us was the idea of a continuous task in which morphology, space, rugosity, and material expressiveness was its consequence. In parallel, we were making Hemeroscopium House. Ten years later, we are still doing the same thing, in the American context, with light beams, with pieces in the landscape that we make with the same logic, with the same semantics. Still in the research phase, we are testing the automation of the assembly of high-rise systems. We recently presented an exhibition at the FRAC Centre that we call Towers of Landscape (2017): the landscape is absolutely material; it is a landscape linked to a tower, a tower that is still abstract, not yet built, and without a place—but it already defines that possibility in some way. At the Chicago Architecture Biennial, we presented the Big Bang Tower (2017), made from prefabricated pieces. If we see each other in ten years, I hope to talk about those built projects, because that is our goal. We still do not have the technology to draw a tower, but we are already investigating how to make concrete that does not require so many reinforcing sheaths so that they can move perfectly in a context of real tectonics. We do not want to make more toys, we are talking about real buildings and vertical typological systems, which, in fifty years, are going to build the city. I think those two lines are the edges of a race that remain as they were at the start. It happens that the context and the scale have changed.

DM   We are constantly asked this question: if those two lines are absolutely different and cannot touch or be crossed, if it is something conscious, or if one is Antón and the other me. It is true that both begin at the very origin of our practice. I think it has to do with this double identity as an architect-builder, which has always led us to desire that ideas be reflected but that they retain all their essence, all their energy. This has led us to want control from the first thought, the first spark, to the materialization, and to develop a very intimate relationship with the materials. We want to understand them, not only from a mechanical

Exterior view of Can Terra, house in Menorca. Ph. Iwan Baan.

Suprablock. Image: Courtesy of Ensamble Studio.

Urban Shelve. Image: Courtesy of Ensamble Studio.

or aesthetic point of view but often an economic one, which is a smarter and more effective way to build an idea on a tight budget—as budgets have been in Spain in recent years. At Hemeroscopium House we discovered, in reality, a technology that already existed—prefabricated concrete. That jumpstarted an interest in wanting to build standard elements that are not necessarily 'standard.' We have repeated this, and when we speak of contexts that can benefit from prefabrication, from the repetition of certain elements, it acquires full meaning. With this house [Cyclopean House] we have continued to progress with completely different materials but preserved our past logics and discoveries. There is still a lot to do, because we try to jump to scale and see how we can influence or build affordable housing, at a lower price but better quality. Later, in projects like Structures of Landscape or The Truffle, the context was absolutely different, but we worked to apply almost the same vision while using the available resources. The exercise of The Truffle was how to build a landscape with the rules of the landscape, with the resources and materials that existed in the environment, and with a very reduced budget. It was a house for us, in a rural context and with a particular history, a different poetry. Poetry is born with the idea and continues in the construction. Of course, what was learned from The Truffle suddenly resonates in Structures of Landscape. Again, we find a very virgin landscape, very wild; one we have to see, from which we must learn, and with which we have

to react, in order to work. What we want is to discover what architecture can make of it, to understand its energies and reorganize them. It is not about what we can place with materials from the outside.

AGA For example, we were commissioned to build an installation for an exhibition that took place at the Cooper Hewitt Museum in New York about 'the natural.' They called us to make the garden, a wonderful garden, in front of Central Park. We took the language we developed in Montana or The Truffle to the city, which starts to pick up some of the logic of standard prefabrication. We made a prefabricated river that contains all the poetic and magmatic substance of the flow of a river that is made of concrete, which we petrified. We are alluding to the rivers that Manhattan had before the grid. Now, it is a river that flies and that technologically is a prestressed concrete beam. Here we have mixed...

DM ...the cables! [Laughter]

AGA The cables, yes. We have taken a river to Manhattan, in which the poetic aspect of the natural is mixed with the synthetic logic of a beam. These connections, these 'short circuits,' between two polar worlds are beginning to interest us a great deal. From time to time, we short-circuit the two lines.

PG In fact, my next question has to do with that. At the end of a lecture of yours at the Architectural Association in London in December 2016, you made a reference to asking for more time to move 'the rules of the landscape' to the city.

AGA We have begun to make that move with this element, a semi-artistic installation where we put the precious concepts that interest us to the flame. If Manhattan were uninhabited for ten years, the rivers would rise, and with them, all those reminiscences of the landscape: its morphology, its language.

DM I believe that all our projects give a very important weight to intuition. A good part of the inspiration for the first projects came from spending a lot of time in quarries, trying to understand how the material is transformed, how it is extracted. Of course, the union of nature, landscape, and industry is brutal. Then, there begins a thing that has been repeated in many projects, which is the idea of recycling and discovery. We discovered huge stones, rocks that were discarded because they were irregular. We wanted to build a stone wall that was structural, we did not want to use stone cladding, or anything that would remove the essence of the stone. With the budget we had, we decided to take these stones that do nothing for the stonemason and that, for us, had all the components. It was the cheapest stone and had incredible structural and aesthetic qualities, but it was waste material. Visiting a factory with a cemetery of discarded beams also [helped us] approach the prefabrication of concrete.

AGA So much so that they did not let us use them.

DM We said to the prefabricator: "would you let us use these beams?"—already thinking of Hemeroscopium House, not with the idea of prefabricating them, specifically, but with the intention of reusing the material. Even though our approach was to discover a series of elements that we wanted to reuse, by exercising prefabrication we discovered other things, other values, that maintain the same methods of construction that we already apply in other projects. With both Structures of Landscape and The Truffle, the approach, the inspiration, the intuition comes from the landscape: from using the earth as a formwork, as a support, mixing the earth with the concrete as a binder, etc. Clearly, we learn new things that perhaps are not in the landscape itself, but have to do with how to use concrete, its expressiveness, how to use constructive methods that use logic and resources in a different way.

PG In that sense, there seem to be two very differentiated views regarding technology. On the one hand, we said that architectural thinking today is not up to the technology because it still cannot be applied or is very expensive. On the other hand, there are decisions in some of your works that decisively seek where to stop the technological or industrial process—for example, when looking for the stone before transforming it into a small pebble. The two paths coexist: at once stopping industrial process at one point and demanding its advance in another.

DM The point is to understand the whole process and position oneself in the place that seems most relevant to each work. We wanted the SGAE Headquarters project to be unique, really unlike anything—sculptural, monumental, entirely built of granite, in a garden that transgressed the industrial landscape of the city of Santiago de Compostela. It was a very particular exercise, not designed to be replicated or scaled up. In contrast, in the Cyclopean House, this house, we thought of a prototype that could be scaled and built as collective housing, in which the technology had to be much more refined. We are thinking about how to create systems that are efficient, easily constructed, and that, at the same time, force or push the economy of the whole alongside its aesthetics. Of course, we do not work outside of how things are, we understand that if we do not give the best of ourselves as architects, we would simply act as artists. We try to bring together the best of art and science, understanding the whole process and playing from our position. I think both positions are just as difficult, trying to convince the stonemasons to

do things as they had been taught not to do was hard. To us, in our ignorance or naivety, it seemed obvious: "if you do not want the stones at all and you want to crush them, we can clean the quarry, we can reuse them." They did not understand. These things are lovely parts of the process: communication, and negotiation are essential to the project's success. The stonemasons knew how to work the stone, we had to form a team. Then, in a context like Boston, where there is a very consolidated construction industry, building a house with a constructive system, with widely available materials that are used differently, is also impossible. Trying to make things differently than the established way in the construction sector is very complex. It requires a lot of dedication and perseverance, you have to be very determined and very passionate for your efforts to pay off.

LANDSCAPES OF CALIBRATED UNCERTAINTIES

PG While the operation is very centered on the technical, in Montana and The Truffle a concept of nature is clearly marked out, even if it is not explicit in the discourse. Do you generate a conception of nature that is new, in disciplinary terms? At the same time, the technical aspect of this kind of work seems to be rather traditional.

AGA That's it. We have not invented any technique at all, what we have done is a total disruption of the established technique. To make concrete as one should, one must make a good form—firm and not deformed—one makes it, mixes a homogeneous concrete, in which all its parts are well mixed, pours it and, finally, once the formwork is released, it should show the perfection of all this. That's a well-made concrete wall. We wanted to do all that wrong, understanding the virtue of the wrong-doing. Doing it wrong means that you do not follow these guidelines, you break the rules; for example: the formwork can be abrasive, scratched, formally indeterminate. It does not mean one loses control: [it is done] with total control, while being undetermined in its formal aspects. The plastic that separates the earth from the liquid so that it does not leak should be tense, careful, and fantastic; we, by contrast, overlapped it, wrinkled it. The pigments should be perfectly mixed with binder; we simply throw them out, we abstract them from their pigment condition so that they become a kind of pollutant, with earth mixed in. If you are breaking each of the established rules to achieve a well-executed concrete wall, what you get is a wonder that transcends a wall. It is a material that I couldn't say is in the realm of concrete, or stone, although it is petrified. Concrete is a stone crushed beforehand and made of many small stones under control, but it is still a mineral. We have not invented a new concrete, no, we have rethought the technologies that allow us to build it: how to calculate the center of gravity of formally undetermined pieces, using the demands and control of engineering. They gave us the national prize for structural design in the United States, not because we calculated the center of gravity, but because we understood that structural engineering served the architectural idea in a very direct way and that all the poetics, the staging, were part of it.

PG   It seems that this desired indeterminacy requires very specific technical knowledge and precision...

AGA   They are things that can be done at the same time: you can play and be in control. For example, soccer is not chaos, everything is under control. The amount of influence and indeterminacy that exists for the variables is enormous and a great team is able to control all that; there are very clear rules. Now, artists are the ones who get angry with rules and take them to another level, but without losing control. The architects, however, do not play with indetermination, fluency, acting... We make projects, we project. We are able to, or think we are able to, control the whole process, and we do not let anything be exposed to physical laws, to conditions, to circumstances, which are in reality the dynamics of the project.

DM   It is not comfortable to be constantly risking determined issues. In our case, each project is an opportunity to experiment with something new. Every time, either in the project phase, or in the construction phase, or sometimes in both (as it was in the Montana project), we must control a high degree of uncertainty. We make prototypes, tests, or acquire knowledge through unusual methods to arrive at a project prepared. You asked us about how other concepts of nature are implicit in our work, concepts which we have not defined—we always focus on solving the technique, because it is what transforms an idea into an architectural space. I think there are major themes that we take from project to project. At Hemeroscopium House, the idea of working with standard elements to generate non-standard products seems fundamental to us. Above all, to understand how the industry and construction evolves so as not to keep using the same things that generate mediocre and poor-quality environments. Breaking those rules through works—however small they may be—seems relevant to us. Defining what is natural or artificial is a moving field, but in the case of Montana, very rigid categories are questioned: what is architecture? What is art? What is nature? We love how the Montana project generates a debate about whether it is architecture or art. It is difficult to categorize.

AGA   The landscape did not have an architecture that was associated comfortably with it because the Mies van der Rohe-type white box, which relates to the landscape

wonderfully, has not generated a protocol to follow during the last fifty years. What we have done now, I believe, is going to open a new path. In architecture schools they forget the rigors of language and depart from the landscape where these pre-architectures can be made. However, although this is a simple principle, it is very difficult to execute. We started it with The Truffle, because it was an illegal construction in our garden. Imagine—take The Truffle and ask for a license, they would put you in a straitjacket.

PG   Part of this question has already been answered, but you have returned to the subject: today, is there a critical view of general production, beyond what happens here in the United States, with issues surrounding constructive quality and the rest? When what you put into play in Montana begins to appear in urban areas, what consequences would there be at the level of interpretation?

AGA   It is a yearning of the unsatisfied human condition: the idea of the city and the landscape. Everyone in New York on a Friday flees, they cannot stand the city seven days a week, everyone who lives in town wants to go to the city, and vice versa. We love living in community, in urbanity, in a semi-automatic machine that takes us, brings us, raises us up, lowers us down, but we still like silence... This kind of historical dissatisfaction has had moments of particular success in very small circumstances: from the Palladian Villas, which bring a language from the city to the countryside, to the Garden City Movement or the Courtyard Houses. In Barcelona, for example, Mies van der Rohe abstracts the Japanese Garden. There are so many examples of this dissatisfaction that they are trying to replace now with technology and with language. Putting trees inside towers, which is not without its charm, is forcing one's hand, right? But it's fine. It's talking about that green city. We plug in a tree into a normal architecture because we have not yet found an architecture whose language, space, materiality, and scale connect with nature in a way that is different from the Miesian box, from the modern movement that we admire. Notice that we really do like nature: we decided to put the beams like this [points out the structural pieces of Cyclopean House], because we did not want to see anything interposed except the light of the West and that beautiful forest. But we do not live in a forest, it is an abstract view. Putting a tree here would be another abstraction. We have not yet found—it is a cultural and technological problem—a way to integrate with nature in a different way.

It is a grotesque revision, isn't it? It is the return to the cave, but with fiber optic, thermal mass, and renewable energies. We still like the cave a lot, we actually just bought one. I do not know if I have something to show you [looks for something], I'll tell you about it, and now I'll show it to you. We have found a space that we have not made ourselves, but that we are going to interpret. We are going to add some

Model of Towers of Landscape. Ph. Ensamble Studio.

layers of technology, but fundamentally and spiritually, it is a hole in the earth in which we have inserted light and a little tree, so as to have nature inside the stone. Brutal contemporaneity: we have returned to the cave. This is valid as an architectural language, it is a low resolution, rough language, one I can even imagine made with a 3D printer. It is a matter of implanting layers of mass, which technologically can recreate a concrete mass with a few tractions. This may be reminiscent of what we are proposing in Menorca.

DM   We ask ourselves about nature. A project like Montana allows one to inhabit a landscape without exploiting it, without urbanizing it; a project like this house has to do with how to optimize resources, how to eliminate waste, how to minimize the impact of construction on materials and transport. When prefabricating, the process—manufacturing, assembly, transportation—is much more efficient. Thinking about the whole process that makes projects possible is also a view of nature, in terms of how to minimize construction's impact upon it. These issues interest us in both projects: it is not to suggest that when building in Montana, in an exceptional landscape that does not cease to be an exception, we are thinking about nature and that when we build with prefabrication, we are not.

AGA   [Brings something and points to it] This is an old cave; sorry, an old mine; it is an industrial language. This is the profile of the quarry and these are the spaces that we have inside. This is a car that has been abandoned since the Civil War. Is this an architectural language? Yes! We have done a 3D scan; the argument is that nature with four strokes or actions of man becomes architecture. But you have to interpret it, of course. Anyone who sees it gets boulders, but when you clean it, it starts to be something like architecture, and the moment you scale it and light it, it becomes a building. Ca'n Terra House (2018) is the house of the earth in Menorca, Spain. We introduced a tree to incorporate nature into a dead space and cut the stone so that light comes in. We made an artistic performance. This is to sublimate the nature connected to the space, the material, to a whole concept. In the end, it is a secret garden, an oculus eight meters deep, like the Pantheon, but a natural version. Conceptually, it is the same—this is what amazes us about this project. We play with the rules of nature, which we want to manipulate and intervene in. Although it is a mine, for us, it is a natural context.

PG   Yes, almost post-industrial in this sense, isn't it?

AGA   Yes, but abandoned since the 1950s, taken over by...

PG   ...partially recovered by nature.

AGA   Of course. Every human construct will eventually be taken over by nature, if you give it time.

Reader's House

The Reader's House, developed by Germán Sánchez Ruipérez Foundation and completed in 2012, is a place for education and innovation, a place where reading is understood as an active creative process that can be implemented through an immense variety of supports, the book being just one of them. In order to give space to such a grand project, Madrid's Old Slaughterhouse—with its 148,300 m² being dedicated to a center for contemporary creation and its singular architectural presence—became the perfect site.

Within this historic complex, the Reader's House occupies warehouses 13, 14, 17b, and 17c. Office space responsible for the operation and management of the program sits in warehouse 17c; warehouse 17b becomes a multipurpose auditorium, conveniently close but independent from the rest of spaces; and warehouses 13 and 14, the most representative ones, accommodate the main public and educational activities.

The protected architectural complex required a surgery of great precision to retain its appearance and internal structure, while at the same time providing the framework for its new use. To provoke this transformation, the consolidation of the pre-existing structure—in a precarious state of stability—through the insertion of a new structure and, thus, a new order that is in close conversation with the one of the original buildings, was followed.

In warehouses 13 and 14, this new order is built by bridges, 40 ton and 23-meter-long precast concrete beams inserted through the windows of the thick masonry walls. They are able to cross the basilica-like space of the twin buildings without intermediate supports and to sew transversally what used to be independent units. These architectural elements symbolically represent the communicative spirit of the project and spatially resolve the connection between the warehouses while also serving as structural aerial streets that offer additional support. Two physical, perceptual, and functional levels are defined, configuring a mutable scenario. The lower level is open, dynamic, social, easily accessible from the street, and dedicated to exhibition and academic group activities; the upper level is a space for intimate research and study, visually connected to the larger space of the original building but sheltered by the linear structures.

The delicate metal interior structure and the masonry perimeter wall that defined the original containers, continue to define it today, and the confluence and relationship of both architectures—old and new—successfully preserve the memory of the place while continuing its life through other exciting stories.

DATE: 2006 / LOCATION: Arganzuela, Madrid, Spain / BUILT AREA: 1,596,288 ft² (148,300 m²) / PROGRAM: Education and innovation / STATUS: Built, finished in June, 2012 / PRINCIPALS IN CHARGE: Antón García-Abril and Débora Mesa / TEAM: Marina Otero, Elena Pérez, Ricardo Sanz, Alba Cortés / QUANTITY SURVEYOR: Javier Cuesta / DEVELOPER: Fundación Germán Sánchez Ruipérez / CONSTRUCTION COMPANY: Ferrovial / PHOTOS: Ensamble Studio (p. 189, 192), Roland Halbe (p. 193).

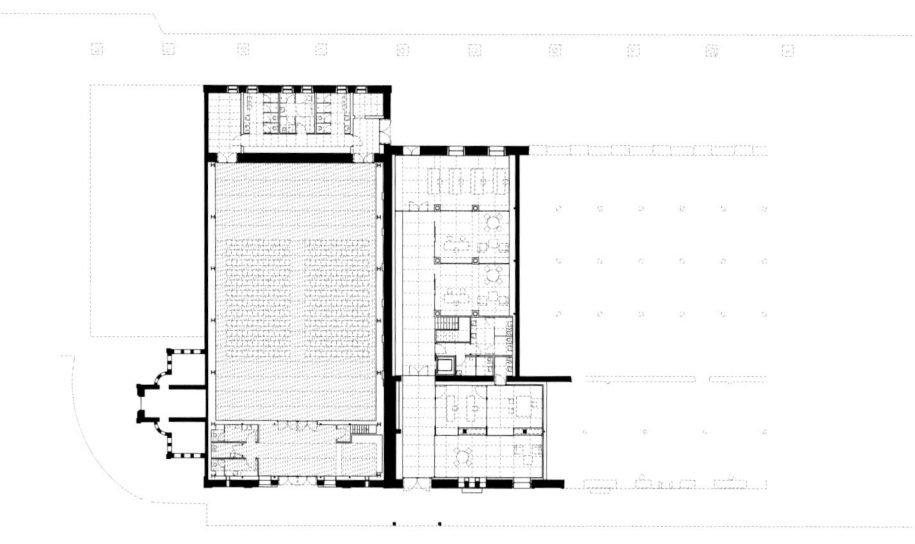

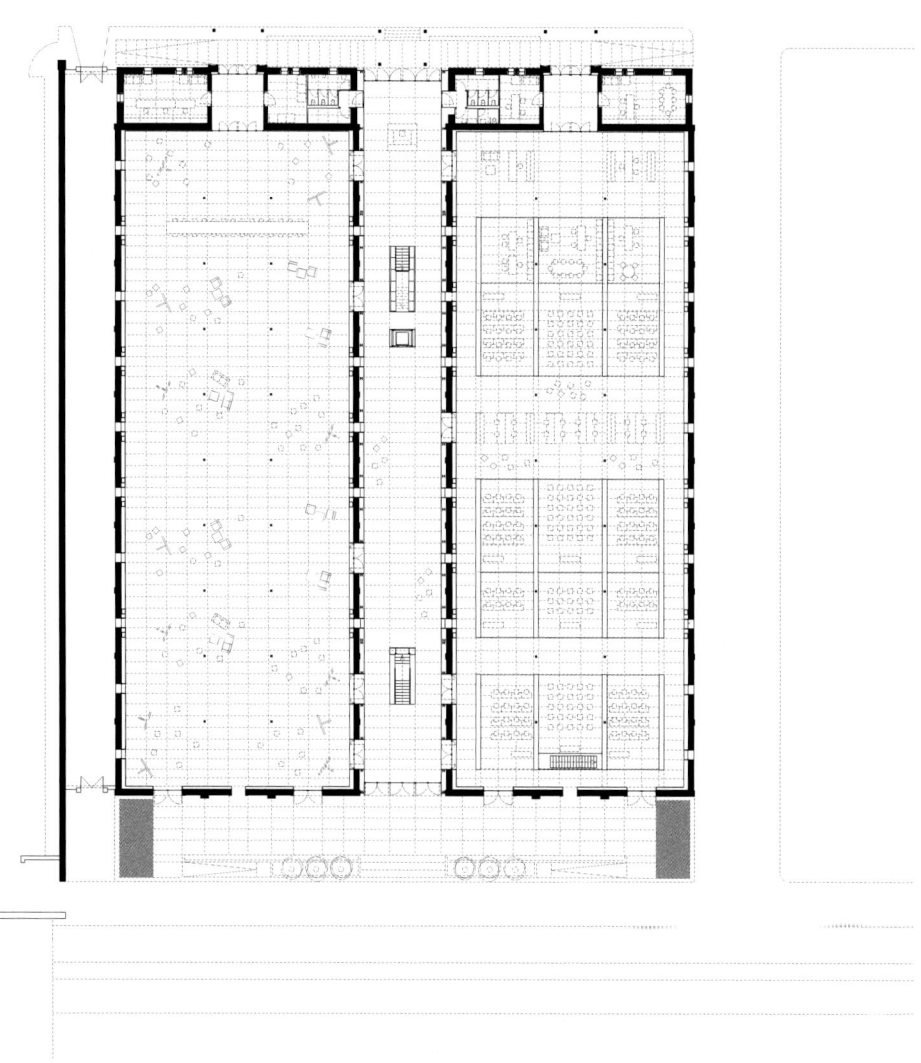

Ground Floor

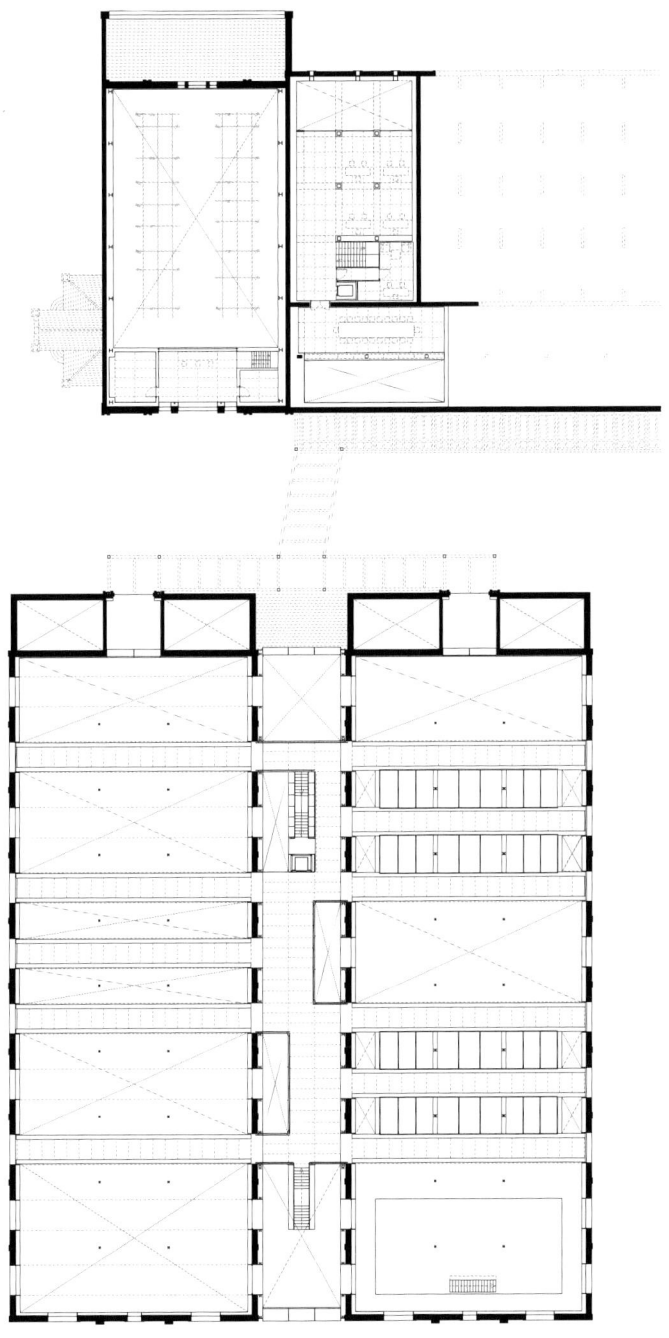

First Floor

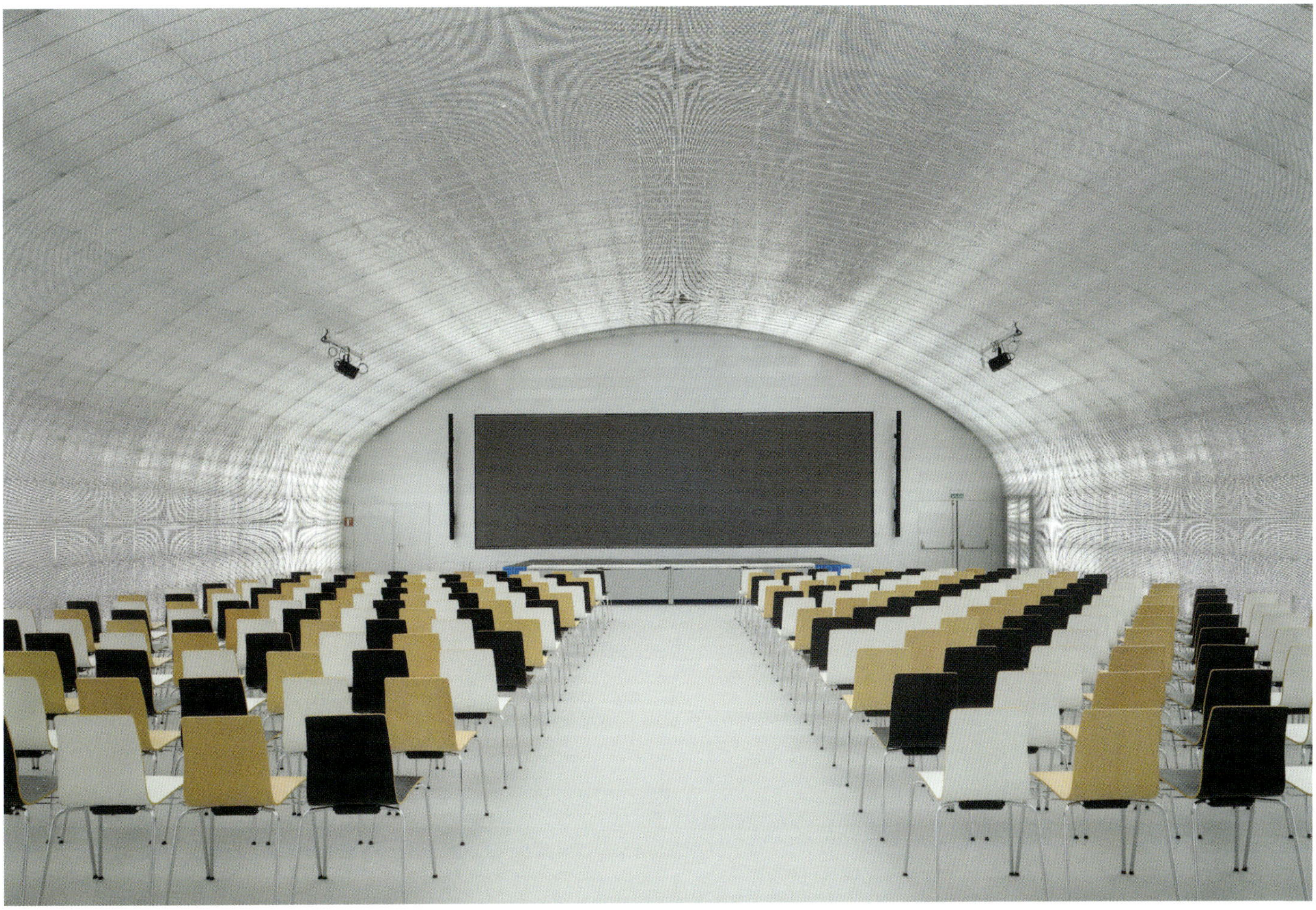

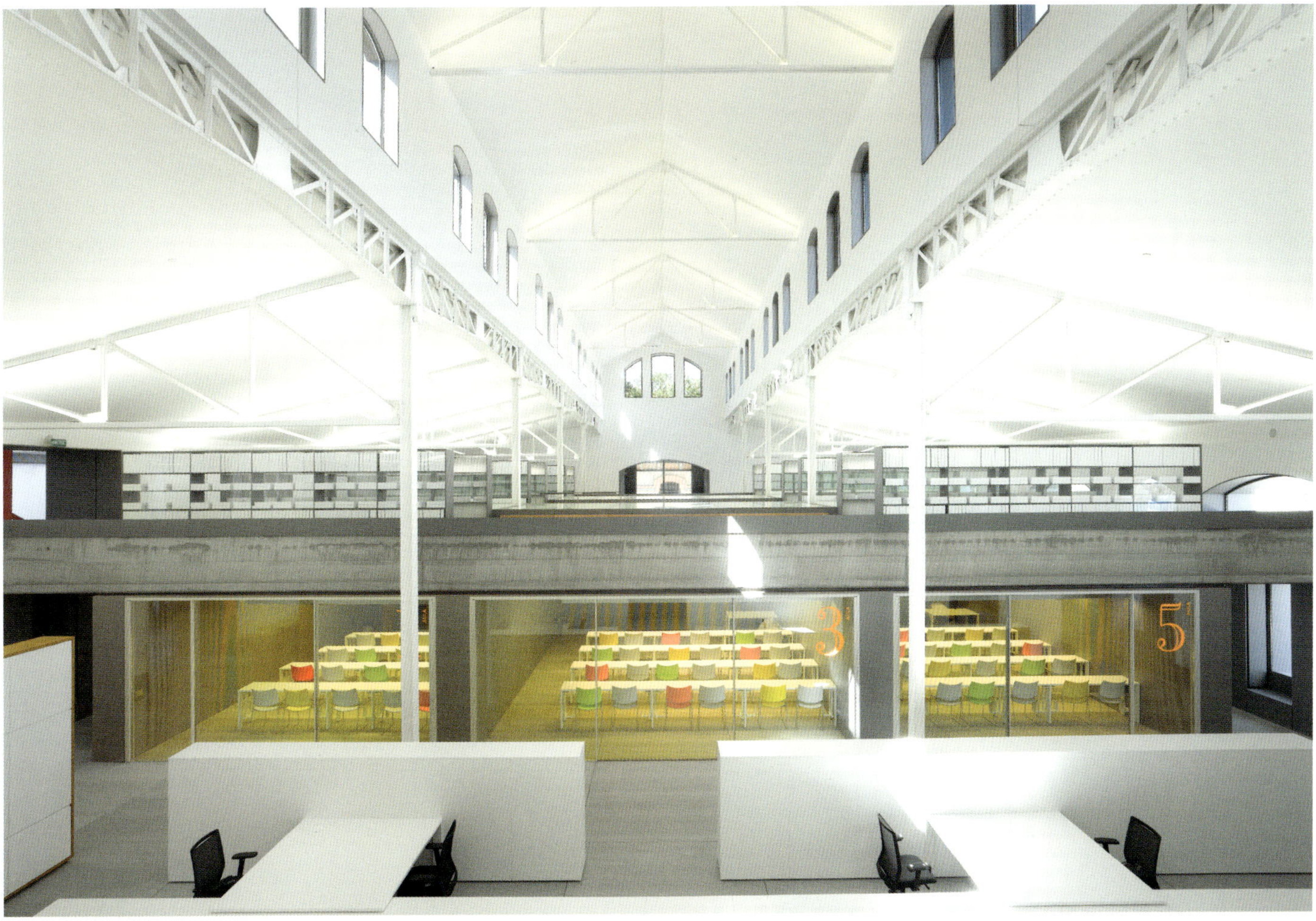
3
5

Hemeroscopium House

For the Greek, *hemeroscopium* is where the sun sets: an allusion that exists only in the mind, in the senses, that is ever-changing and mutable but nonetheless real. It is delimited by horizon, light, and time.

Hemeroscopium House traps a domestic space and a distant horizon. It does so by playing a game with structures placed in an apparently unstable balance, one that encloses the living spaces but allows the vision to escape. Heavy structures and big actions provoke gravity in order to bring movement to the space.

The order in which these structures are piled up generates a helix that sets out from a stable support, the mother beam, and then develops upwards in a sequence of elements that become lighter as the structure grows. It is made of seven elements in total. The design of their joints responds to their constructive nature, to their forces; and their strain expresses the structural condition they are under.

Through the way this structure is set, the house becomes aerial, light, and transparent. The space trapped inside is flooded with life. The apparent simplicity of the structure's joints is contrasted against the complex calculations required to reinforce them, resulting in a web of beams that is sewn by the pre-stress and post-tension of the steel rods.

The house took a year to engineer but only seven days to build, thanks to the total prefabrication of the different elements and a perfectly-coordinated rhythm of assembly. A new astonishing language is invented: form disappears, giving way to naked space. Hemeroscopium House found its equilibrium with what Ensamble Studio has ironically called the "G point," a twenty-ton granite stone; the force that acts as the physical counterweight to the whole structure.

DATE: December 2005 / LOCATION: Las Rozas, Madrid, Spain / BUILT AREA: 4,305 ft² (400 m²) / PROGRAM: House / STATUS: Built, finished June, 2008 / AUTHOR: Antón García-Abril / TEAM: Elena Pérez, Débora Mesa, Marina Otero, Ricardo Sanz, Jorge Consuegra / QUANTITY SURVEYOR: Javier Cuesta / DEVELOPER: Hemeroscopium / CONSTRUCTION COMPANY: Materia Inorgánica S.L. / PHOTOS: Roland Halbe.

"*Ensamble* is the Spanish-ization of the French *assembler* and of *ensamblaje*. We bring together the semantics of tectonics, which has to do with our understanding of architecture as a tectonics of putting things together, and the idea of a group, of an integral group, in which we are capable of 'giving' a building, not of designing it."
—Antón García-Abril

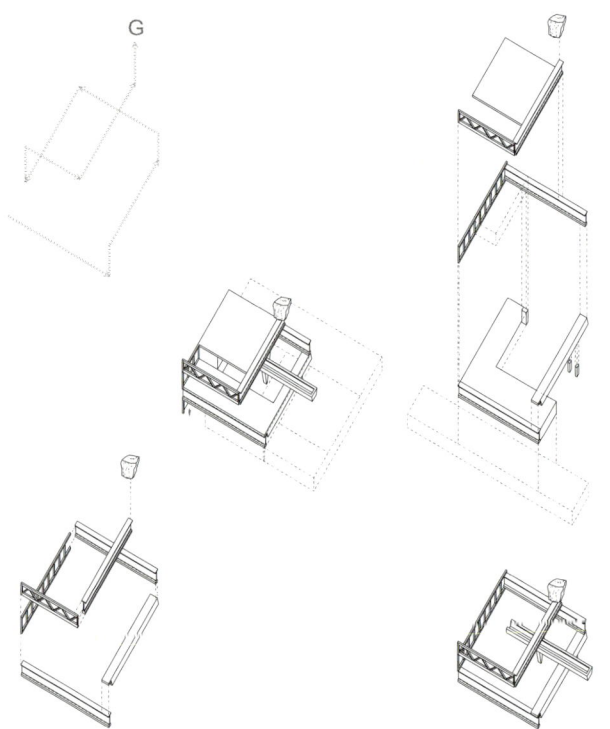

Axonometric Diagram of Structural Elements

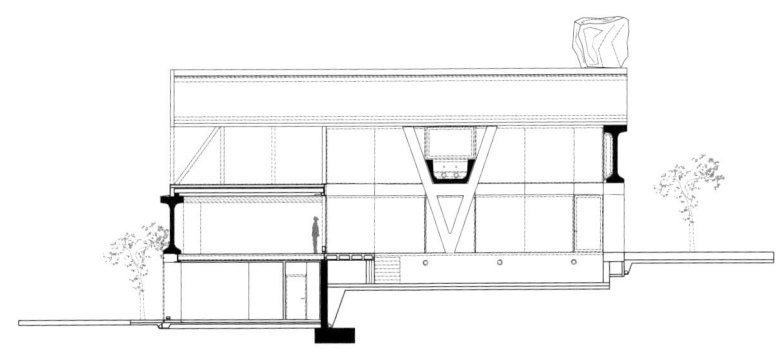

Cross section

Ground Floor

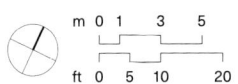

m 0 1 3 5

ft 0 5 10 20

Cyclopean House

In his first stop on the way home, Ulysses reaches the cave of the Cyclops, a fierce and strong builder who looks through a single point. And there he is, locked up, until he uses his ingenuity to escape and go where the winds take him.

Cyclopean House was built using the vigor of the builder and the ingenuity of the engineer. Its parts were manufactured in Madrid and later transported to the place where it now sits, on top of an existing garage—the ugly duckling of the area—located in a calm residential neighborhood of Brookline.

The one-story existent construction accommodates the parking, workshop, and service spaces. On top, the large prefabricated elements enclose a big room. This open-plan, double-height living area includes the main domestic activities and enables the transformation of the building into a two-story residential unit, technologically and spatially adapted to its time as well as the life of its users.

The new architecture concentrates structure and infrastructure in the perimeter: seven monumental beams accommodate the activities of cooking, bathing, storing, seating, dining, sleeping, working, and projecting. The rest of the plan is then cleared and left flexible, to be shared by different events that create temporary layouts. The seven programmatic beams configure a thick enclosure that minimizes visual contact with the exterior on the three sides that adjoin neighboring houses and opens onto the street, enabling panoramic views of the trees in front.

Complementing this one 'eye,' the beams that assemble together and embrace the space lose their mass in the points of contact where flanges touch and the web recedes to provide additional light and ventilation for the specific functions. Privacy and thermal insulation is thus guaranteed, while light and view are maximized.

To avoid overloading the preexisting structure, or having to dig new foundations, ultra-light construction systems give form to the new elements: solid cores made of foam (98% air) reinforced by steel profiles and fire-proofed by a thin layer of cement and fibers. Dry joints and material lightness enable the different elements to be produced out of site—including finishes and fixtures—easily transported by ship and trucks, and quickly put together following a rhythmic sequence carefully planned beforehand.

Unlike the heavy, cold stone that prevented Ulysses from leaving the cave, Cyclopean House is light and warm. The lightness is due to its lack of mass and its coat of air. It sits and watches without being seen, interlacing its elements.

DATE: December, 2014-March, 2015 (Design); (Construction Research & Prefabrication) January, 2015-July, 2015; August, 2015-November, 2015 (Onsite Assembly) / LOCATION: Brookline, Boston, MA, USA / BUILT AREA: 1,292 ft^2 (120 m^2) / PROGRAM: House and office / STATUS: Built / PRINCIPALS IN CHARGE: Antón García-Abril and Débora Mesa / TEAM: Javier Cuesta, Ricardo Sanz, Borja Soriano, Massimo Loia, Walter Cuccuru, Valentina Giacomini, Marietta Spyrou, Juanjo Fernández, Federica Zunino, Marian Stanislav, Chung-Wen Wu, Yannis Karababas / STRUCTURAL ENGINEER: Jesús Huerga / CONTRACTOR: Materia Inorgánica S.L. / PHOTOS: Roland Halbe (p. 205), Ensamble Studio (p. 201-202, 206).

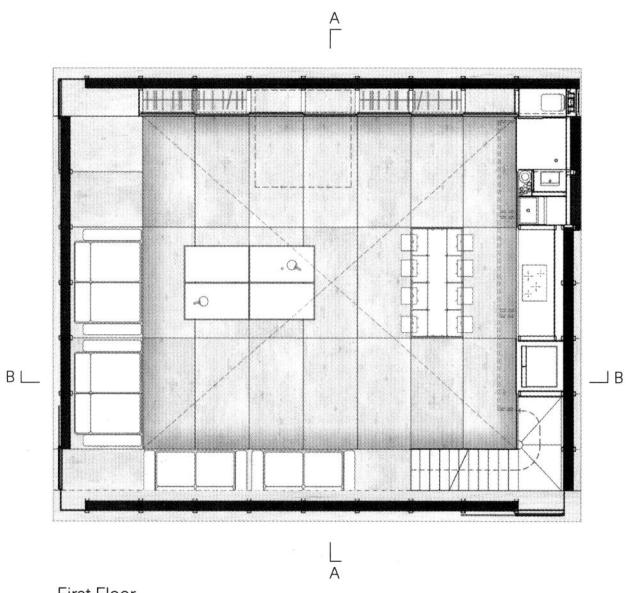

A

B

B

First Floor

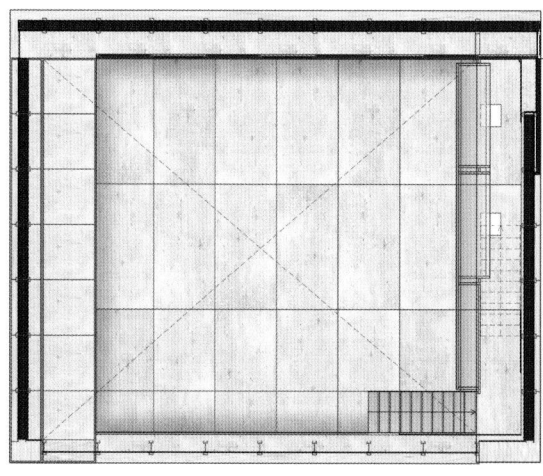

Mezzanine

A Section

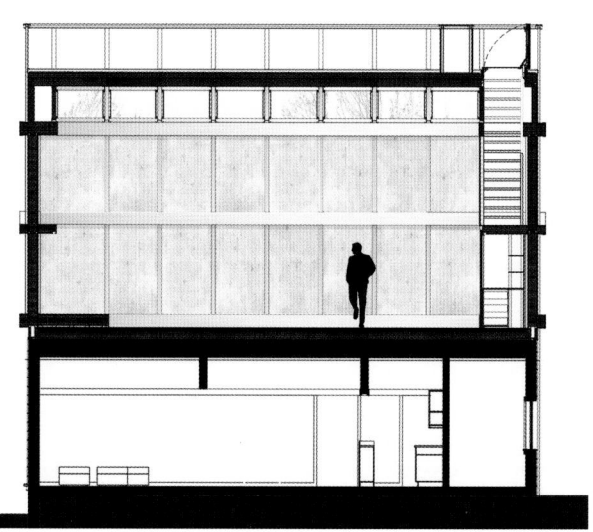

B Section

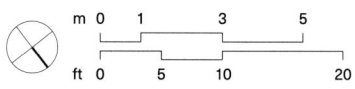

m 0 1 3 5

ft 0 5 10 20

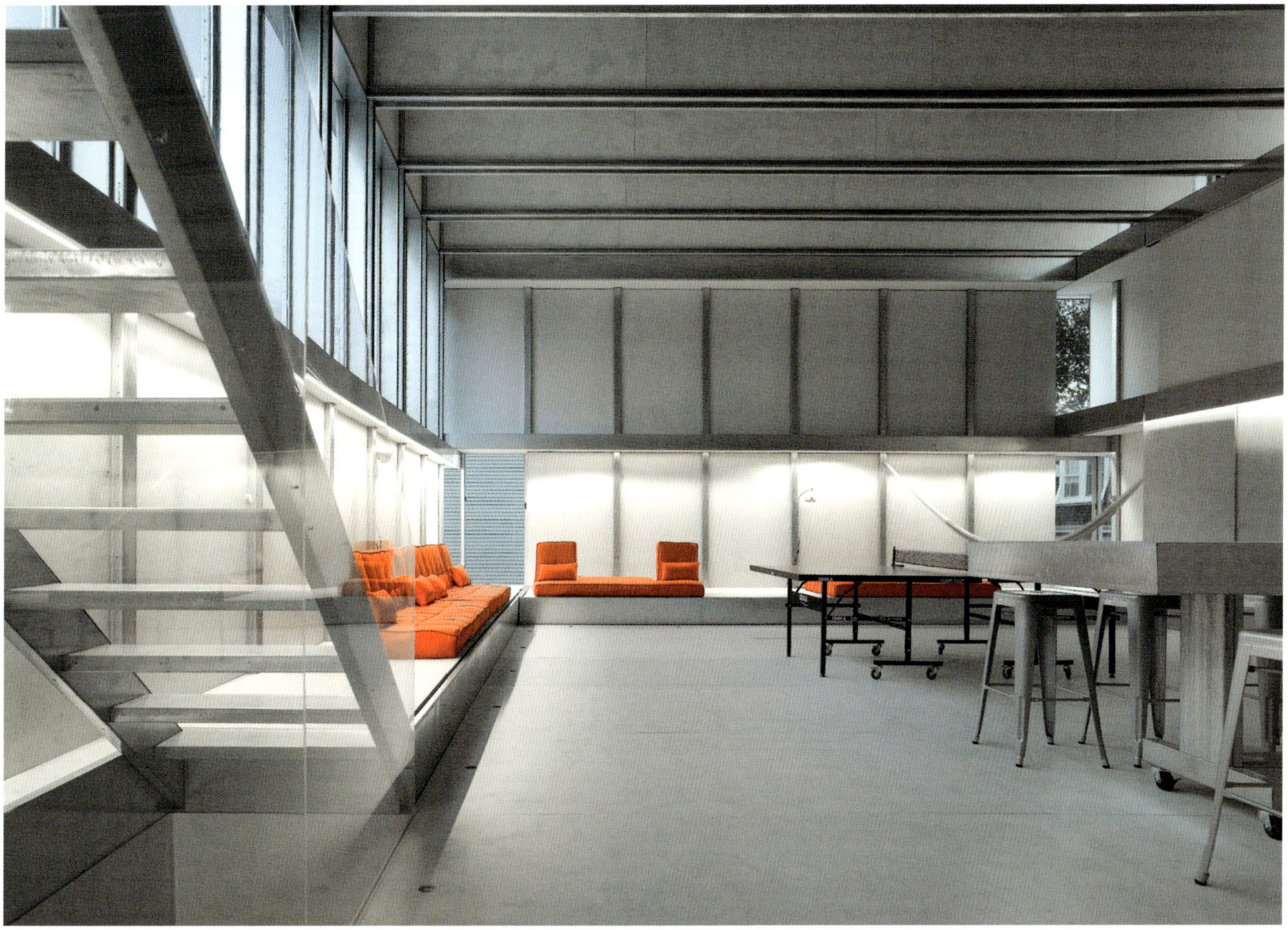

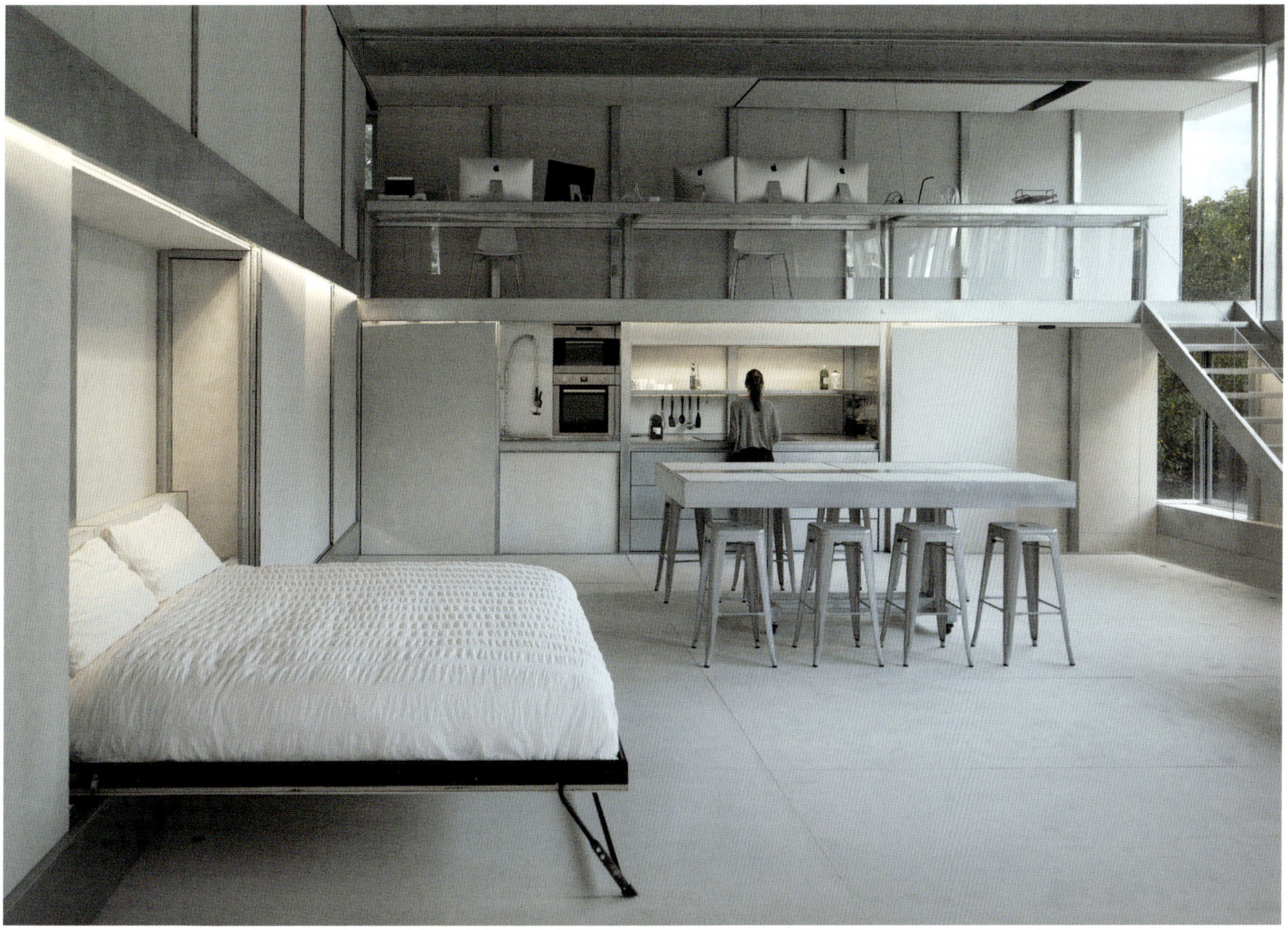

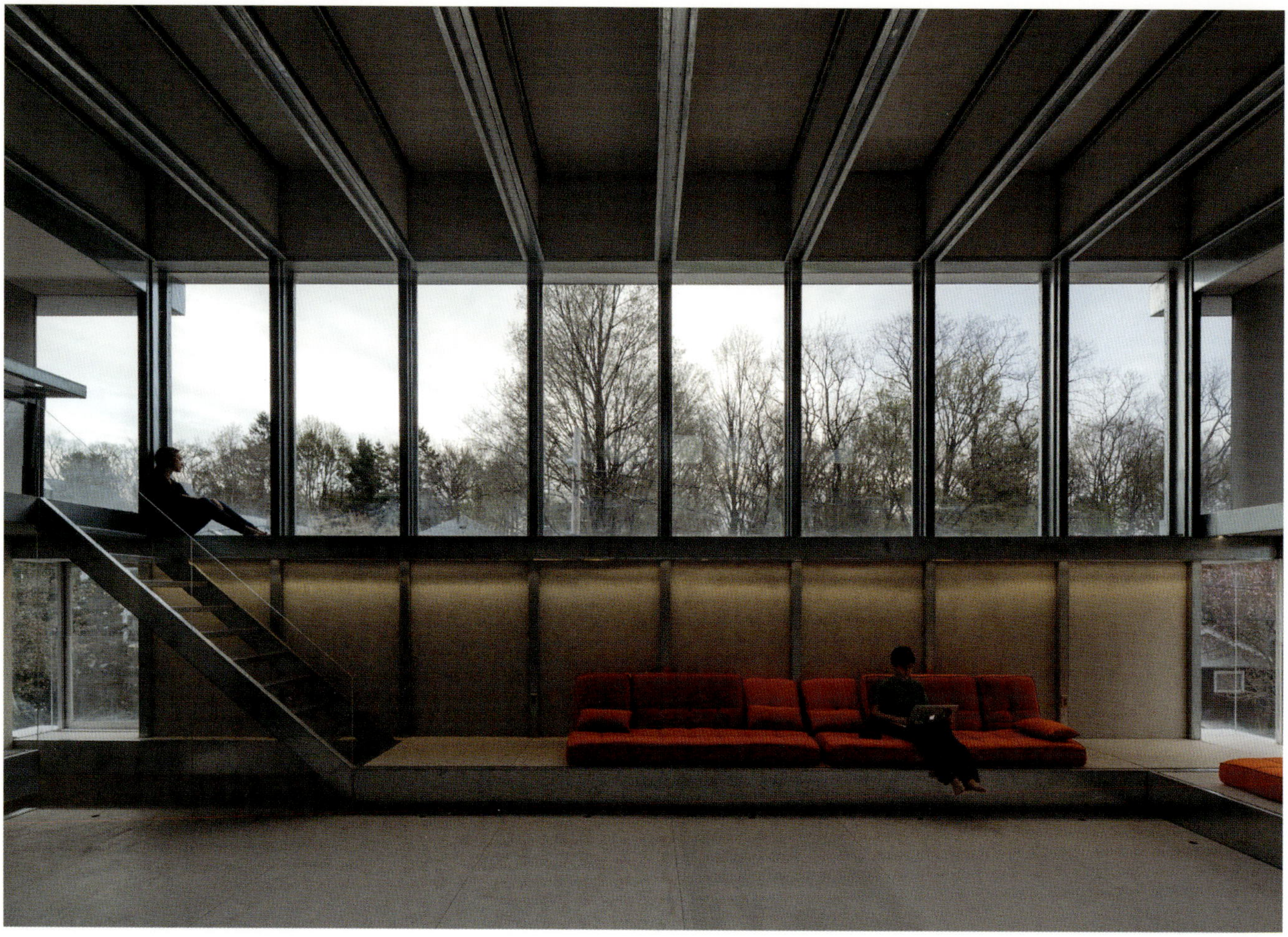

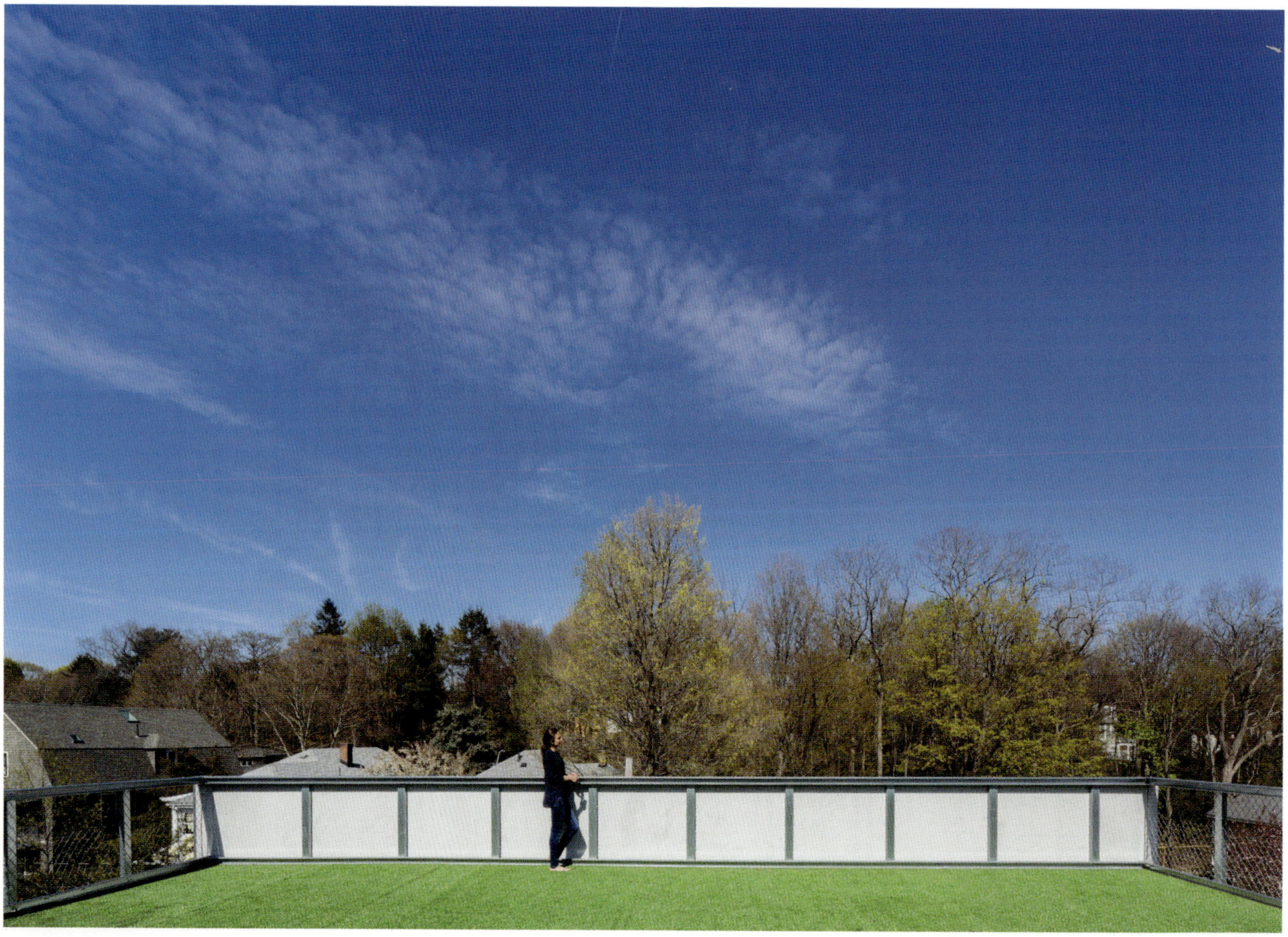

Front Elevation

Back Elevation

"We are thinking about how to create systems that are efficient, easily constructed, and that, at the same time, force or push the economy of the whole alongside its aesthetics."
—Débora Mesa

Lateral Elevation

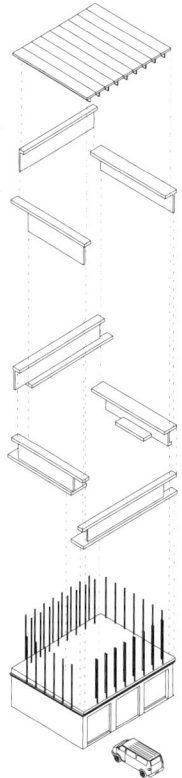

Axonometric

The Truffle

The Truffle is a piece of nature built with earth and full of air. It is a space within a stone that sits on the ground and blends in with the territory. It camouflages itself by emulating the processes of mineral formation in its structure and integrates with the natural environment by complying with its laws.

It started as a hole in the ground and, on its perimeter, piles of topsoil were removed, resulting in a retaining dike without mechanical consistency. It was filled with hay bales and concrete was poured on top to materialize the space. Time passed and an amorphous mass emerged.

The earth and the concrete exchanged their properties. The land provided the concrete with its texture, color, form, and essence; the concrete gave the earth its strength and internal structure. However, it was not architecture yet; it was just stone.

After making a few cuts using quarry machinery, the core of the stone built with hay—now compressed by the hydrostatic pressure exerted by concrete on the flimsy vegetable structure—was discovered. In order to empty the interior, the calf Paulina arrived, who enjoyed the 50 m³ of the nicest food. After a year, she had finally eaten it all up and left the space, restoring the architectural condition of The Truffle.

The architecture is surprisingly ambiguous: between the natural and the built, the mass of unreinforced concrete provides the materiality, the structural, and the spatial qualities of the space. All of these can be seen, from the amorphous texture of its exterior to the violent incision of a cut that reveals its architectural vocation and eventually leads to the fluid expression of the interior solidification of the concrete. This dense materiality, which gives the vertical walls a rustic scale, comes from the size of the bales; it contrasts with the continuous liquidity of the ceiling, which evokes the sea, petrified in the lintel of the spatial frame that looks sublimely to the Atlantic Ocean, highlighting the horizon as the only tense line within the interior space.

The program and dimensions of Le Corbusier's "Cabanon" were recreated to equip the space. It is this precedent that transforms The Truffle into an enjoyable living space in nature. The architects had to manage a high degree of uncertainty as they followed their desire to build with their own hands a piece of nature, a contemplative space, a little poem.

DATE: August, 2006 / LOCATION: Costa da Morte, Spain / BUILT AREA: 270 ft² (25 m²) / PROGRAM: Vacation house / STATUS: Built, finished February, 2010 / PRINCIPAL IN CHARGE: Antón García-Abril / TEAM: Débora Mesa, Ricardo Sanz, Javier Cuesta / DEVELOPER: Materia Inorgánica S.L. / COLLABORATORS: Tongadas & Zuncho Dolorido, SL., Galicorte, Macías Derribos, Suministros Zurich, Ganadería Paulina, Franchetau / PHOTOS: Ensamble Studio (p. 209) , Roland Halbe (p. 210-213).

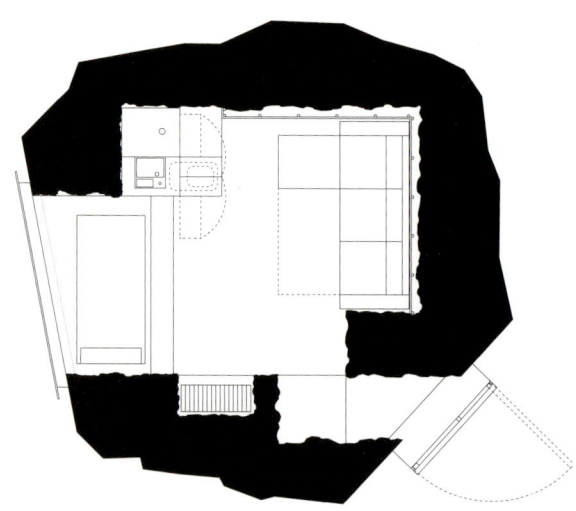

Ground Floor

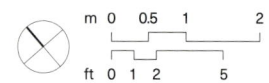

Construction Process

Structures of Landscape

Located at the edge of Yellowstone Park in Montana, Tippet Rise Art Center—with an extension of over eleven thousand acres of wilderness—was born as a new destination for the arts, a place where music performances and large-scale outdoor sculptures play a major role. The challenge of finding a coexistence between the local fauna and ranching activity and the added artistic and architectural interventions fueled research for this project.

Ensamble's early experiences with the quarry and projects like The Truffle were the precedents that made the architects appreciate and learn from the preexisting natural conditions. Once again, they go back to primary elements in order to configure site-specific architectures that are in harmony with nature. Working with earth, rocks, and studying their formation logic, different techniques and processes were developed to manipulate the structural, acoustical, and thermal properties of the local materials used. At the same time, geological transformation processes—sedimentation, erosion, weathering, crystallization, compaction, metamorphism—were reinterpreted to cultivate structures made of landscape, made from landscape; structures that stir and reinforce existing matter, using highly engineered processes while, at the same time, welcoming unpredictable results.

The procured forms have been twinned with those taken from the land that previously contained and supported them during a state of rest, the land from which they retain a memory and imprint, but also to which they introduce new meanings and tensions. They are Structures of Landscape because they are born from it and give it order, transforming matter into inhabitable space and unfolding a new constellation of programs among the plateaus, ridges, canyons, and hills of brutal beauty that compose the site.

Structures of Landscape enable habitation without exploitation as well as intimate relationships with the environment. They resonate with the immensity, the roughness, the silence, and the magical loneliness of the place, amplifying its values. Ensamble's actions are thus placed in an ambiguous position between nature, architecture, and art.

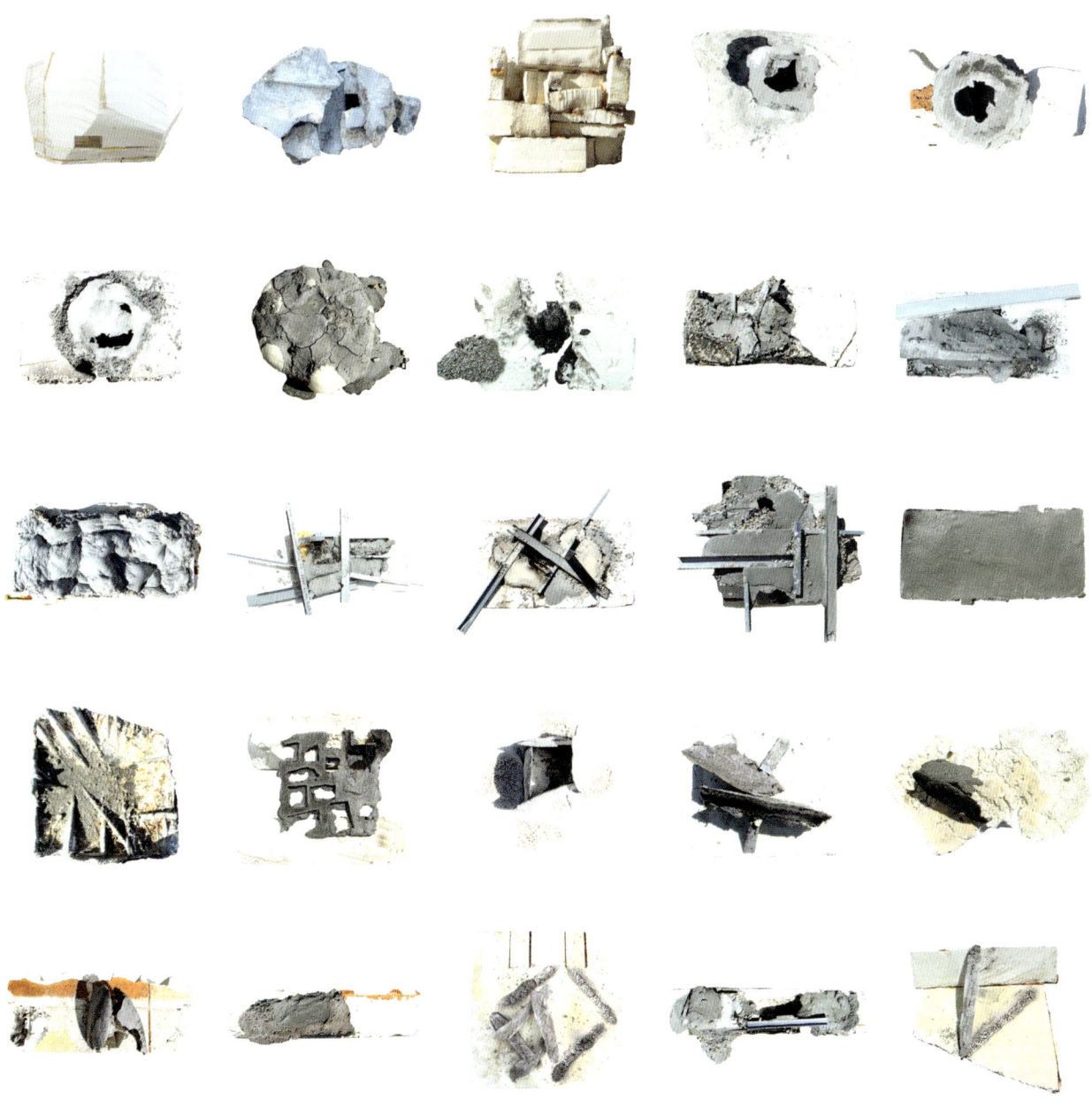

DATE: 2015–2016 (Design); 2016 (Construction) / LOCATION: Fishtail, Montana, USA / STATUS: Built / PRINCIPALS IN CHARGE: Antón García-Abril and Débora Mesa / TEAM: Javier Cuesta, Ricardo Sanz, Borja Soriano, Massimo Loia, Simone Cavallo / STRUCTURAL ENGINEER: Jesús Huerga / COLLABORATORS: Davis and Sons; CMG; Mountain West Steel / CONTRACTOR: OSM / PHOTOS: Ensamble Studio (p. 215-216), Iwan Baan (p. 218-224).

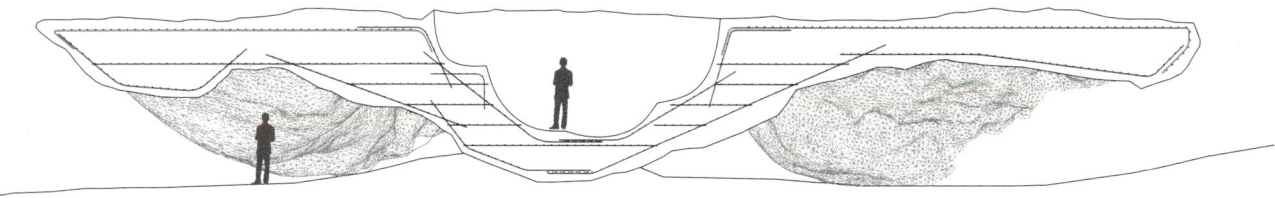

Domo Structure Plan

m 0   1   2   5

ft 0 2   5   10

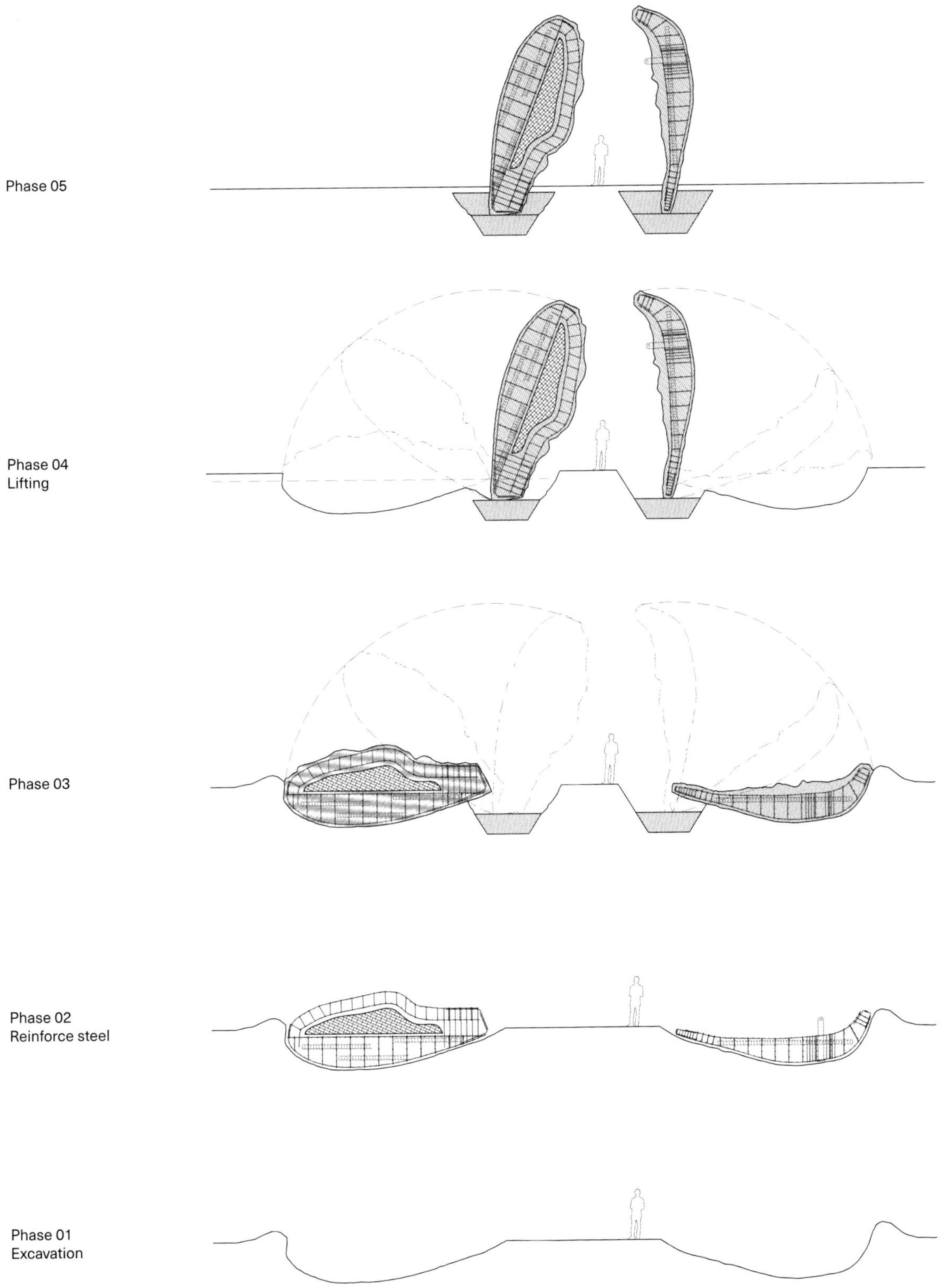

Phase 05
Phase 04
Lifting
Phase 03
Phase 02
Reinforce steel
Phase 01
Excavation

Beartooth Portal Structure Plans

m 0 0.5 1 2
ft 0 1 2 5

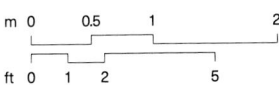

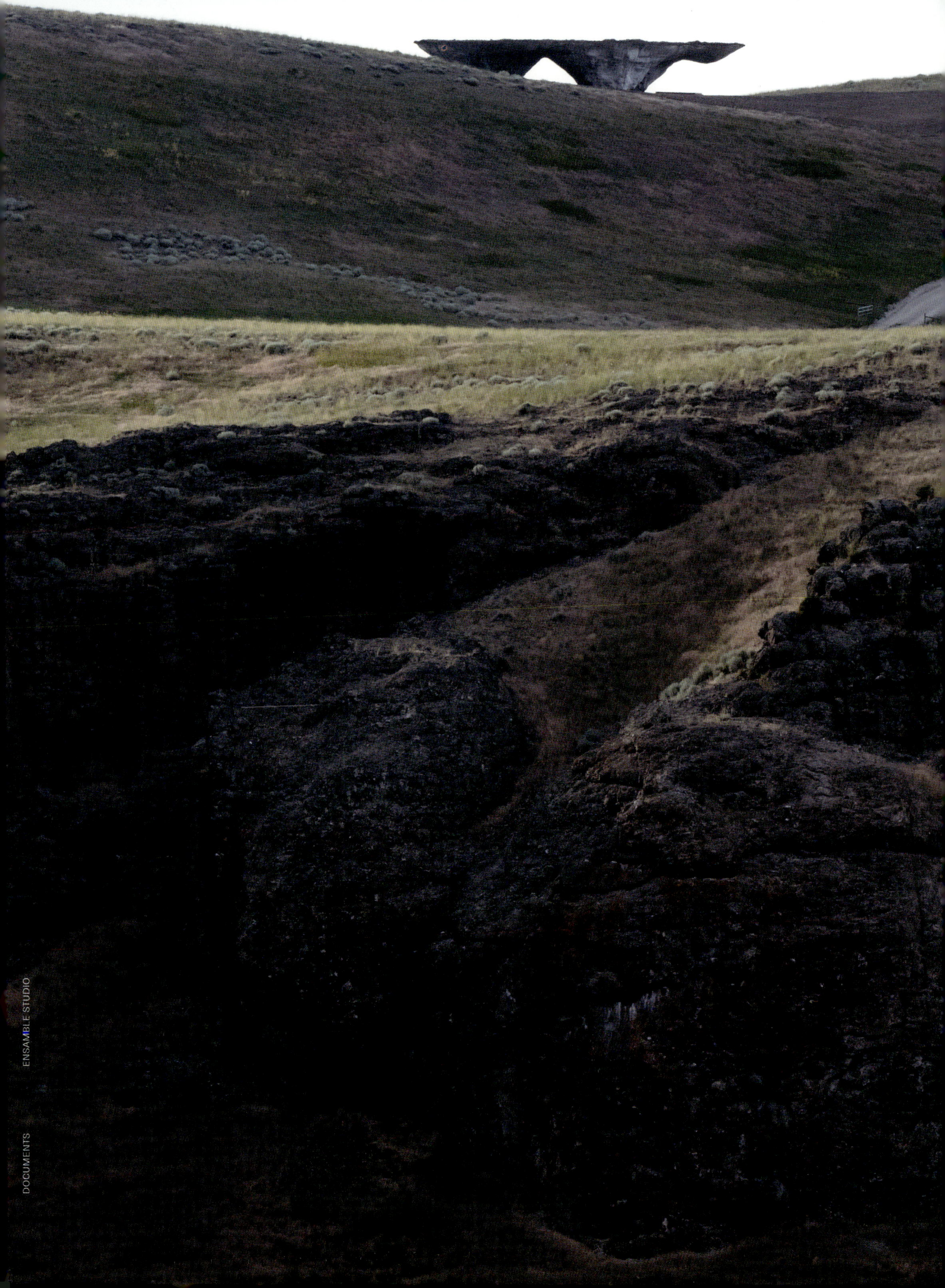